D0837548

Master Tung's Western Chamber Romance

Master Tung's
Western Chamber Romance
(Tung Hsi-hsiang chu-kung-tiao)

董西廂諸宮調

A Chinese *Chantefable*

Translated from the Chinese and with
an Introduction by
LI-LI CH'EN

Emerita Professor of Chinese Language and Literature
Tufts University

COLUMBIA UNIVERSITY PRESS
NEW YORK

Columbia University Press Morningside Edition

Columbia University Press

New York   Chichester, West Sussex

Morningside Edition
Copyright © 1994 Columbia University Press
Copyright © 1976 Cambridge University Press

All rights reserved

Library of Congress Cataloging-in-Publication Data

Tung, Chieh-yüan, dfl. 1189–1208.
[Hsi hsiang chi chu kung tiao. English]
Master Tung's Western chamber romance = Tung Hsi-hsiang chu-kung
tiao : a Chinese chantefable / translated from the Chinese and with
an introduction by Li-li Ch'en.
p. cm.
ISBN 0-231-10119-8 :
I. Ch'en, Li-li.   II. Title.   III. Title: Western chamber romance.
PL2687.T9H813   1994
895.1'142—dc20   94-18056
CIP

Casebound editions of Columbia University Press books are
printed on permanent and durable acid-free paper.

Printed in the United States of America

c 10 9 8 7 6 5 4 3 2 1
p 10 9 8 7 6 5 4 3 2 1

Contents

Acknowledgments

I wish to thank my friends and colleagues in Sinology, among them Patrick Hanan, Victor Mair, and David Roy, who either complained to me about the depletion of the first edition of *Master Tung's Western Chamber Romance* or led the book to its present publisher, whose Assistant Executive Editor, John Michel, guided this second printing with admirable professionalism.

Despite devastating losses—the deaths of my parents and husband—the intervening years between the two editions have been for me a time of growth and fulfillment. Inasmuch as my contentment makes the preparation of the new edition an agreeable task rather than an onerous chore, I wish to thank my dedicated students and supportive colleagues at Tufts, especially Mary Ella Feinleib, Sol Gittleman, Marilyn Glater, Christiane Romero, and Lynda Shaffer, who have not only succored me as a friend but helped the development of the Tufts' Program in Chinese, which I founded and directed for twenty-one years.

Deep gratitude also goes to relatives and friends who have provided warmth and balm over these intervening years: my sisters, brothers-in-law, and my niece Caroline; my French relatives Alfred, Eveline, Françoise, Minou, and Sylvie; my Belgium family Danielle, Yvan, Joëlle and Benoît, Lena, Yusing, Chinnie, Leo, Loring, Ruth, Yaojin, Jim, Renée, Paul-Jean, Aida, C. C. Yenshew, Wu T'ung, the Beckmanns, Jeff and family, Sam and family, the three generations of Hsu's, and my neighbors in Cambridge and Coursegoules: Pozzi, Bob, Lucy, Rick, Annie, Gérard, Alain, Huguette, Jane, Jeannette, Claude, and Michel. Professor (now Dean) Lois Smedick, my Angel Gabriel and literary consultant since our college days, remains a devoted friend despite her dazzling career and deleteriously busy schedule.

To all I say affectionately, "Xiexie!"

For Georges Goy
and my parents:
Ch'en Shu-jen and Ch'en Kuan Yu-Wu

In Memoriam

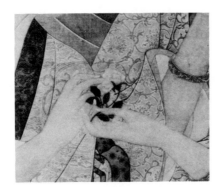

Translator's Introduction

The word '*chantefable*' first appeared in writing in the thirteenth-century French work, *Aucassin et Nicolette*. As the romance concludes, the author, in the persona of the performer, says: '*No cantefable prent fin.*' (Our chantefable comes to an end.) The term is best defined by the work itself: *Aucassin et Nicolette* consists of alternate verses for singing (*canter/chanter*: to sing), and prose passages for narration (*fabler*: to narrate). Thus, *chantefable* is used in literary studies to refer to literature whose outer form is characterized by a mingling of verses intended to be sung and prose intended to be narrated. *Chantefable* literature exists in many cultures beside French, among them, Arabic, Persian, Chinese, Japanese, and Korean, to name just a few. The oldest surviving Chinese texts of this genre, the *pien-wen chantefables*[a], are a group of tenth-century Buddhist hagiographies and historical legends which were found in a temple cave in Tun-huang in 1899. (The monk who found them broke up the collection and sold the choicest pieces to foreigners, so now the texts are scattered all over the world.) In the eleventh, twelfth, and thirteenth centuries, other forms of *chantefable* flourished as well, and one of the most important is *chu-kung-tiao*.

'*Kung-tiao*', a musical term, means 'mode'; and '*chu*', a pluralizing modifier, means 'many'. The form is so named apparently because in it, the verses are set to tunes belonging to various modes. According to twelfth-century memoirs, *chu-kung-tiao* was created by a professional entertainer, K'ung San-ch'uan toward the end of the previous century. K'ung was said to have set fantastic and strange tales to music, and to have sung and narrated his *chantefables* to audiences in the entertainment quarters of the Northern Sung capital, Pien-ching.[b] We do not have the texts of K'ung's *chantefables* (none have survived), and we do not know how *chu-kung-tiao* was introduced to other areas in China. We do know, however, that by the end of the twelfth century, *chu-kung-tiao* was popular both in South and in North China. The popularity lasted for about a hundred years before it began to wane. By the late fourteenth century, *chu-kung-tiao* was so seldom performed that T'ao Tsung-i in his *Ch'o-keng lu* lamented: 'It was not so long ago that Master Tung of the reign of Chin Chang-tsung composed *Hsi-hsiang-chi* (the *Western Chamber Romance*), and yet today only

---

[a] See Li-li Ch'en, '*Pien-wen Chantefable and Aucassin et Nicolette*', *Comparative Literature*, vol. 23, no. 3, 1971.

[b] For this and other historical information on *chu-kung-tiao*, see Li-li Ch'en, 'Some Background Information on the Development of *chu-kung-tiao*', *Harvard Journal of Asiatic Studies*, 1973.

a few people can interpret it.'[c] Even the generic term *'chu-kung-tiao'* seems to have become obsolete by the late sixteenth century. Editors and drama critics could no longer identify *Master Tung's Western Chamber Romance* as a *chu-kung-tiao*. The form remained in obscurity until the second decade of the twentieth century when scholars rediscovered it and published articles on its form.

During the height of its popularity, roughly between 1170 and 1280, *chu-kung-tiao* was one of the performances offered in the entertainment quarters of the South China capital Lin-an. This we learn from four thirteenth-century memoirs which record vividly the myriad activities, the bustle, and the gaiety of that lake city. In the entertainment quarters, in an atmosphere reminiscent of Shakespeare's London or Molière's Pont-Neuf, *chu-kung-tiao* competed for spectators' attention with *tsa-chü* (dramatic sketches); shadow plays; singing, dancing, instrumental music; philosophical and religious compositions; telling of stories, jokes, and riddles; wrestling; manipulation of insects; bear baiting; and no less than five or six types of puppet shows. According to these memoirs, *chu-kung-tiao* performances were accompanied by from one to three wind, string, or percussion instruments, and were given in open-air or mat-shed theatres (*kou-lan*). Literati, the gentry, and affluent young men-about-town as well as merchants, artisans, soldiers and ordinary city dwellers were said to be the spectators.

The surviving *chu-kung-tiao* texts also date from the late twelfth to the late thirteen century. These are: the short *Chang Hsieh chung-yüan chu-kung-tiao* (*The Outstanding Scholar Chang Hsieh*), composed in South China and used as a prologue in a *nan-hsi* (Southern Drama); and three texts from North China, the *Liu chih-yüan chu-kung-tiao* (*A Chu-kung-tiao on Liu Chih-yüan*), the *T'ien-pao i-shih chu-kung-tiao* (*Events of the T'ien-pao Era*), and our text; the *Tung Chieh-yüan Hsi-hsiang-chi* (*Master Tung's Western Chamber Romance*). However, only *The Outstanding Scholar* and the *Western Chamber Romance* survived in their entirety. About one third of the *Liu Chih-yüan* text is known,[d] having been discovered by the Kozlov archaeological expedition at Kharo-khoto in 1907–8. The prose passage of the *Events of the T'ien-pao Era* are completely lost: some fifty suites (*t'ao-shu*) of verses from it are preserved in three formularies and one anthology dating from the fourteenth to the eighteenth centuries.

When one looks at the extant texts, one is impressed by their high literary quality—particularly *Master Tung's Western Chamber Romance,* which is truly exceptional. Although a long work—it has 184 prose passages and 5263 lines of verse (as compared with, say, the 3500 lines of the epic *Beowulf*)—the *chantefable* never falters in interest. Judged by any standard, this *chu-kung-tiao* must

[c] T'ao Tsung-i 陶 宗 儀, *Ch'o-keng lu* 輟 耕 錄 , Shanghai, 1936, p. 405.

[d] The fragments have been translated by M. Doleželova-Velingerová and J. I. Crump: *Ballad of the Hidden Dragon*, Oxford, 1971.

xii

be considered one of the outstanding achievements in Chinese literature. It contains excellent character portrayal; sophisticated narrative techniques; witty manipulation of levels of diction; moving lyrical and nature poetry; a delightful sense of humor; and unabashed treatment of sex, quite unlike the self-conscious, euphemistic approach elsewhere. Moreover, the close-range fight between a group of monks and a troop of rebelling soldiers in the second chapter is unique in Chinese literature. Its use of elaborate and precise details and its modulation of the rhythms of the combat are superb. Surely, the chapter does not pale even in the company of the world's best-known *chansons de geste*.

Little is known of Master Tung. An entry in the *Lu-kuei pu* (A fourteenth-century roster of Yüan lyric writers and playwrights) states that he lived during the reign of the Chin emperor Chang-tsung (1190–1208). The fact that in *Lu-kuei pu* he is referred to by the honorific title *Chieh-yüan* (Master) and is listed with other notables and officials in the category 'Famous Personages of an Earlier Generation Whose Lyrics Have Survived' suggests that he came from an elevated social class. Certainly his *chantefable* reveals an extensive education.

In basic story line, *Master Tung's Western Chamber Romance* is an elaboration of the T'ang *ch'uan-chi* story *Ying-ying chuan* (*The Story of Ying-ying*) by Yüan Chen (779–831).[e] Yet, to juxtapose the two works is to contrast two very different kinds of literature, whose radical unlikeness in outer form is merely the most obvious difference. A comparison of certain aspects of the two works can be meaningful if only for the light it sheds on the deliberate artistic choices of the later writer. *The Story of Ying-ying* is written in the classical language (*wen-yen*); its style is concise, elegant, and evocative. The story focuses on a single plot, the love and failure to marry of a young scholar Chang and his mistress Ying-ying. Only a few scenes carry the plot forward and the fictional arena is purposely contained, peopled by the lovers and a few minor characters who make fleeting appearances. Apart from brief narrator's comments and Ying-ying's self-revelation in her letter, the protagonists' psychological complexity is only expressed implicitly by what they do and fail to do. The two turning points in the plot are Ying-ying's refusal and subsequent consent to be Chang's mistress, and Chang's decision not to marry her after they have been lovers. But something is left unsaid about Ying-ying's change of mind; we are simply given first the scene in which she lectures Chang and then the scene in which she goes to his room. And Chang's stated reason for not marrying Ying-ying is altogether too glib to be convincing. The story fascinates precisely because it invites one to read between the lines, to speculate on possible explanations for seeming inconsistencies and transparent pretexts.

Master Tung's Western Chamber Romance, on the other hand, is written in a mixture of the classical and the colloquial language. The conciseness of the T'ang story gives way to elaborate formal realism. Architecture, interior

---

[e] A new translation of the story appears in J. R. Hightower, 'Yüan Chen and "The Story of Ying-ying" ', *HJAS*, 1973.

decoration, characters' appearances and the like are minutely described. The world of the lovers is part of the world of the temple which in turn is part of the world at large. Incidents tangential to the plot and activities of a host of minor characters add color and excitement to the life lived: the classical restraint of the original story is replaced by a baroque richness. This richness is likewise reflected in the change of the central plot. It is no longer a simple progression from the conception of desire, to the consummation of desire, to separation; instead, the lovers finally marry, but only after a series of obstacles have been overcome. In addition to having a smooth, more readily acceptable ending, the *chantefable* has an air of reasonableness throughout. Always, tensions are created and resolved in highly human terms; the idiosyncrasies of the T'ang characters yield to common, easily comprehensible emotions and psychology. The treatment is explicit: causal relationships between events and reasons underlying decisions are carefully given.

Ying-ying changes her mind and decides to be Chang's mistress because she is moved to pity by his illness. Madam Ts'ui first rejects Chang as a son-in-law because Ying-ying is already betrothed to her cousin Cheng Heng. (The conversation between her and Chang at the banquet suggests that she has another, though unacknowledged objection, that Chang is not yet launched in a career.) When the clandestine affair between Ying-ying and Chang comes to her attention, the face-loving, scandal-fearing lady has no alternative but to put aside whatever obstacle there is and let the lovers marry. That no formal betrothal contract exists between the Ts'ui and Cheng families allows her to do so gracefully. Later, Chang's prolonged stay in the capital, due to another illness, gives Cheng Heng the opportunity to erect a second obstacle. Although his slander, the claim that Chang has recently married the daughter of a prominent official, is unsubstantiated, its efficacy does not in the least tax one's credulity. Madam Ts'ui cannot have had much confidence in Chang's character; after all, did he not seduce Ying-ying under her very nose? Widow of a Prime Minister, she knows the attractiveness of power and high position such as once was hers. Hence, to her, Chang's alleged inconstancy must appear highly possible. Her wounded pride retaliates by quickly giving Ying-ying to Cheng Heng. For the removal of this second obstacle, what can be more convenient than having a friend of Chang as the adjudicating magistrate, the General Tu who has once before proved his loyalty? Tu's elevation to the governorship happens in the most natural way: he was promoted for having subdued the rebels. Furthermore, this *deus ex machina* is given an admirable weapon; marriage between first cousins is forbidden by law (though apparently it was occasionally done in private). Again and again, what were gaps in the narrative of the *Ying-ying chuan* are here filled by rational and carefully arranged chains of events. If *Ying-ying chuan* appeals to one's imagination, *Master Tung's Western Chamber Romance* surely gratifies one's sense of belief.

While all major and semi-major characters come through as individuals, their characterization is nevertheless a mixture of archetypal and individualized beginning both are inexperienced. After a time even the strictly brought-up Ying-ying, not to mention Chang, is described as obsessed with love-making, which in the *chantefable* is always tender and pleasant, uncomplicated by the psychological complexities attendant upon sex acts in, say, the *Chin P'ing Mei.*

Some mores and manners in *Master Tung's Western Chamber Romance* are noteworthy because they reflect so well traditional Chinese values, others because they are at variance with mores and manners depicted in earlier Chinese literary works. Although the sympathetic upper-class characters are on the whole decent enough (viz. Chang's and Tu's rejection of hereditary offices), there are occasional signs of high-handedness, a tendency probably not unusual among the privileged in the stratified society of that era. Governor Tu's promise to execute Cheng Heng, even before the latter has presented his side of the matter, is a flagrant travesty of justice. And it is clear that in Master Tung's world as, surely, in old China, woe betide those who have no influential friends. Loyalty to a friend, and not duty or justice, is often presented as the basis of one's actions, even of actions like quelling insurgent troops or handing down a sentence in court. Another traditional attitude maintained throughout the *chantefable* is the disdain, real or affected, for money. Fa-pen refuses to accept rent from Chang. And Chang is not ashamed of his penury. Only Cheng Heng, the unmannerly boor, brags about the amount of gold and silver he has spent on gifts for Ying-ying. But there is a surprising twist to the traditional class prejudice in the *chantefable*. Key figures belonging to the lower classes are consistently depicted as more astute, more resourceful than their social superiors. All practical solutions to Chang's and Ying-ying's problems are suggested either by Hung-niang or by Fa-ts'ung. Compared with the maid-servant and the monk, the lovers are whimpering, self-indulgent weaklings.

In the man—woman relationship, the *chantefable* is no longer totally male-oriented. In *Ying-ying chuan,* Chang is all-powerful in deciding whether or not he will marry Ying-ying. In the *chantefable,* on the other hand, Chang is the supplicant, and the marriage decision is hardly his alone to make. Though beautiful, Ying-ying is not, as so often in earlier Chinese literature, a *femme fatale*; she does not ruin her lover or wreck a country, and the story is not one of 'folly and consequences'. But this is not to say that the *chu-kung-tiao* is free of misogyny. It is so neither in the fictitious world, nor yet in Master Tung's presentation. By making his Ying-ying a child-woman, Tung flatters the male ego; and in the fictitious world, characters, including women themselves, make sexist remarks: 'Though a woman, [Mother] has the moral integrity of a man.' The characters' denigrating views are reaffirmed by the singer—narrator: 'Ying-ying, though a girl, shows filial piety hard to emulate.'

As has been pointed out, *Master Tung's Western Chamber Romance* consists of alternating verse sections and prose passages. The verse sections can be in any of three forms: a single poem set to one musical tune; a single poem and a coda; and a group of poems set to a suite of succeeding tunes, followed by a coda. The third type of verse sections can be quite long, containing as many as a hundred lines of verse and more. The tunes for each verse section must all belong to the same mode, and one rhyme is used throughout a verse section. With rare exceptions, there are no prose interruptions within the unit of a verse section, and normally, a verse section leads to a prose passage, not to another verse section. In all, fifteen musical modes with 126 different musical tunes,[f] hence, 126 different verse forms[g] are used in *Master Tung's Western Chamber Romance*. This would be comparable to a Western poet using the sonnet, the villanelle, the rondeau and 123 other verse forms in one *chantefable*. In each verse form, the number of stanzas and lines, the number of words per line (excluding *ch'en-tzu*, the 'outrides'), the position of end-rhymes and caesuras, and the inflectional sequence are prescribed. In comparison with earlier *shih* and *tz'u*, certain new prosodic features are noticeable. For instance, rhymes are no longer segregated according to the tones of the characters; as long as they share a rhyming final, level- and oblique-tone characters are used to rhyme with each other. (This is undoubtedly a result of a linguistic change which took place in northern China in the twelfth century. The disappearance of -p, -t, -k, endings in characters of the entering tone had removed the one major incongruity between level- and oblique-tone finals.) The definition of rhyme is also less stringent in *Master Tung's Western Chamber Romance* than in *shih*, *tz'u*, and, surprisingly, than in the *Yüan tsa-chü* as well. Words with similar though not identical finals often belong to the same rhyme group. Altogether, there are fourteen rhyme groups in Master Tung's work, distinguished by the finals $v\eta$, $[y\eta]$; $a\eta$; $e\eta$, en, $[i\eta]$; oen (or on), an, $i\epsilon n$; im, $i\epsilon m$, am; $\int$, l; i, ei; ч, v; ou; a; ϵ; ai; av; o. Whereas in *Yüan tsa-chü*, there are nineteen rhyme groups: $e\eta$, en; oen, an, $i\epsilon n$; im, $i\epsilon m$ and am are kept apart as eight separate rhymes. Rhymes occur very frequently in Master Tung's verses, possibly a result of having relatively fewer rhyme groups, hence more available rhymes within each group. In any event, the end result is that the *chantefable* rhymes have a greater variety of pitches (a function of mixing level and oblique tones) and a greater variety of sounds (a function of mixing similar but not identical finals) than the rhymes of some other genres.

Verse rhythm is likewise more varied in *Master Tung's Western Chamber Romance* than in earlier genres. *Tz'u* rhythm is already more varied than that of *chin-t'i-shih* since *tz'u* verses have lines of unequal lengths. Still, in *tz'u* the line length prescribed by the verse form must be strictly adhered to. For example, the first line of a *tz'u* written to the tune 'Wave Washing Sand' (*Lang t'ao sha*) must always have five characters. In *Master Tung's Western Chamber Romance*, 'outrides' (襯字) may be added to a line, so that even though the prescribed length of the first line of 'Flowers above the Wall'

---

[f] Tunes having the same title and the same verse form but belonging to different modes are counted as one tune. If they are counted separately, the number is 135.

[g] If one includes variant forms, the number is 129.

(*Ch'iang-t'ou hua* in *Pan-she-tiao* mode) is four characters, in actual fact, the six times this verse form is used in Master Tung's work, the six first lines have five, six, five, four, six, four characters each. Clearly, the use of outrides make the actual line lengths highly flexible, which, of course, gives rise to a greater range of rhythmic variations. Furthermore, the *chu-kung-tiao* lines are scanned in more ways. In *shih* and most *tz'u* five- and seven-character lines invariably have a caesura after the second and the fourth characters respectively, creating the rhythms tum tum/tum tum tum and tum tum tum tum/tum tum tum. In the *chantefable*, the caesura in a seven-character line can occur after either the third or the fourth character (3/4 or 4/3), and in a five-character line, after either the second or the third character (2/3, 3/2). This multiplicity of caesura patterns, too, contributes to the greater liveliness of Master Tung's verse rhythm.

In *shih* and *tz'u* verses, each line has its prescribed tonal sequence, and so indeed do the lines in *Master Tung's Western Chamber Romance*. Yet, the use of outrides in the *chantefable* modifies the prescribed sequence in two ways. Outrides may be added in a number of places, at the beginning of the line or immediately following a caesura or a pause. Thus, depending on where the outrides occur, the prescribed sequence is disrupted in different ways. Then, since there is no set tonal pattern for outrides themselves, they can be of any tonal combination, and their admixture alters the total sequence of the line. In tonal patterns as well, Master Tung's verses have greater variation than those of *shih* and *tz'u*.

Parallelism, which had been a prominent prosodic feature in *shih* and *tz'u*, also finds new expression in *Master Tung's Western Chamber Romance*. To be sure, the time-honored parallel couplets with their grammatical, syntactical, and imagistic pairings are still there. But parallel tercets and quatrains too abound, and there are instances where all the lines in a whole stanza or poem are parallel. Close attention has been given to sound effects in the parallel lines. In addition to the subtle use of alliteration, internal rhymes and assonance, there is frequent matching of reduplicated binomes and of identical words and phrases, placed in the beginning or in the middle of the lines. In all, nearly twenty-five percent of *Master Tung's* verses are parallel lines and it seems to me that all of them, but particularly those with special features such as the repetition of identical words and phrases, can facilitate memorization on the part of the singer—narrator as well as enhance comprehension on the part of the audience.[h]

All these prosodic innovations help to make the *chu-kung-tiao* verses marvelously lilting. Yet the technical richness is but secondary to the truly striking achievement of Master Tung as a poet, namely, that in his hands, the verse has become an excellent narrative medium. Despite the difficulty of

[h] Cf. Li-li Ch'en, 'The Relationship between Oral Presentation and the Literary Devices Used in *Liu Chih-yüan* and *Hsi-hsiang Chu-kung-tiao*', *Literature East and West*, vol. 14, no. 4, 1970.

complying with the exigencies of the verse forms, Master Tung manages to attain felicity and vividness in every mood and every situation. Earlier Chinese poetry had mostly consisted of short philosophical, lyrical, or descriptive verses, and the few surviving narrative ballads, notably Han and T'ang *yüeh-fu* are also fairly short. Even in extant *pien-wen chantefables*, the chief narrative medium is still prose. But now, in *Master Tung's Western Chamber Romance*, a total of more than 5200 lines of verse carry the main burden of advancing the very complex story. To be sure, each verse section, whether a single poem or a 'suite' of poems, is the basic unit, but there is impeccable cohesion throughout the *chantefable*. The verses are written largely in the twelfth-century northern vernacular, an early form of modern Mandarin, and although some expressions are now obsolete, the grammar and syntax are identical to those of modern Mandarin. Mixed in with the vernacular are groups of lines in the classical language, with characteristic conciseness and omissions such as of the equative verb and colloquial particles. But the mixture does not jar. It is rather like the refined conversation of highly cultivated people who spice up everyday speech with quotations from the classics or epigrams and adages in *wen-yen*. If the language of the prose passages is 'elevated', the level of diction of the verses is predominantly 'common', with infrequent admixture of the 'base' (viz. the description of Cheng Heng in Chapter 7). And thanks partly to the use of outrides, which often accommodate colloquial particles and expressions, the language of Master Tung's verse is impressively natural and supple.

The prose passages are mostly in *wen-yen*. Dignified and terse, they are as polished as the prose of the *Ying-ying chuan*. A few times, chiefly in the narrator's direct questions, the language is more colloquial and one notices, for example, the equative verb *shih* and the possessive particle *ti*. (It is perhaps interesting to note that in the verse sections direct speech is introduced by *tao* (道), but in the prose passages mostly by *yüeh* (曰); *tao* is used only three times in the prose, all in the narrator's questions.) An economy of treatment prevails in the prose, and generally actions move faster than in the verse sections. But it is misleading to leave the impression that Master Tung's prose passages consist only of *wen-yen* prose, or only of original composition. Many non-*wen-yen* forms and some borrowed passages actually give the whole the appearance of a collage. To begin with, there are extended sections of parallel lines—descriptions or narrator's commentaries; ten *chüeh-chü* and *lü-shih* poems, some of which come from *Ying-ying chuan*; and a sixty-line *ku-shih*, also from *Ying-ying chuan*. Then, there are two *tz'u* poems, a 'zither song' with parallel lines of graduated length, a *Ch'u-ko* (楚歌), and four long passages from *The Ballad of the True Story of Ying-ying* by Li Shen (?–846). Other passages from *Ying-ying chuan*, sometimes with minor modification, are also reproduced with or without acknowledgement. Ying-ying's letter, taken from *Ying-ying chuan*, and Chang's letter to General Tu attract attention with their epistolary form and elaborate language. The long debate between Fa-pen and Chang in Chapter 2 also stands out from the narrative prose. One sees an affinity between it and the sophistry-debates, the *Ch'a-chiu lun* (茶 酒 論) and *Yen-tzu fu* (晏 子 賦), of the tenth-century Tun-huang collection. Possibly such debates were popular with story-tellers of Master Tung's time, either as independent sketches or as parts of longer tales.

Not only is diversity in itself pleasing; to the literate, the inclusion of other literary forms and borrowed pieces in the prose passages must evoke a gratifying sense of recognition, of resonance. The device is of the same fabric as the historical allusion, ubiquitous in *Master Tung's Western Chamber Romance* and in Chinese literature of all ages. One further reason, I suspect, that Master Tung used the other forms in the prose passages is to vary the rhythm. The rhythm of pure *wen-yen* can be monotonous. The emphatic beat of parallel lines of whatever rhythm (5,5; 3,3,4,3,3,4; 8,8; . . .), the 4/3, 2/3 rhythm of seven- and five-character *lü-shih* or *chüeh-chü*, the 2,2,2; 3,3; 4,4; 5,5; . . . rhythm of the 'zither song', and the rhythm of *tz'u*, all provide delightful variations. Certainly I remember that as a child, listening to the story-teller Ch'en Jung-ch'i narrate *Seven Knights and Five Stalwarts* (*Ch'i-hsia wu-i*) in Peking, I always thrilled when the prose broke into the neat rhythm of parallel lines. Ch'en delivered these parallel lines in a heightened tone of voice, quite different from the ordinary tone of voice he used for other parts of the narration.

Yet the most unexpected technical achievement of Master Tung is his sophisticated management of point of view and voices. The only point of view in the *chu-kung-tiao* is that of the omniscient singer—narrator (hereafter often referred to either as the omniscient narrator, or simply, the narrator). Though other voices are used as well as the narrator's, the point of view—how events are interpreted and characters evaluated—is solely that of the narrator. Throughout the *chantefable*, the omniscient singer—narrator is the chess player, the intelligence controlling the game, and the characters are the pawns. Even when they see or speak in their own voices, they merely enact what the central intelligence has willed them to, much like the movements of chessmen. Characters do not add their interpretation of the plot or events to that of the narrator; they are not given the double vision of the participant-cum-onlooker. From the very beginning, the illusion that the singer—narrator *is* the author himself is forcefully created. There is not a Conrad *and* a Marlow; they are one. The two introductory suites are partly devoted to creating this illusion; there, the singer—narrator, speaking in the first person, describes himself and tells the audience how he comes to write the ensuing *chu-kung-tiao*. The author— singer—narrator comes through as an enormously attractive person. A Bohemian with panache and an irrepressible *joie de vivre*, he claims to be an amateur performer but a fine poet. Now he apologizes for his singing and narration, now he praises his own verse with good-humored pride. The authority adduced in the narrative frame is thus the authority of this Bohemian poet who knows the facts and can cite old writings to substantiate his claims.

The three modes of narrative—description, commentary, and presentation—

pointed out by Patrick Hanan as existing in early Chinese vernacular fiction,[i] had already been used by Master Tung in the *Western Chamber Romance*. To a large extent, the characteristics of these modes in the *chantefable* are the same as in the vernacular fiction. The mode of commentary is intimately related to the narrator's control of the story and of audience response. Though it does occur in verse sections, far oftener it is found in the prose passages. In verse sections, the narrator simply interrupts the flow of presentation, steps aside from the action as it were, and comments on the scene. In prose passages, commentaries are expressed in a few set forms, most often a parallel couplet. Sometimes these parallel couplets are aphoristic in nature, with images and details not specifically referable to the scene at hand but to some collective knowledge, public wisdom, or literary traditions tangentially related to the scene. The parallel couplets are often followed by the narrator's queries: 'Who is it?' 'What does he say?', and in answering these questions the narrator resumes the interrupted flow of the story. Or, the narrator's questions may precede instead of follow the parallel couplet. Another form commentary often takes in the prose passages is to begin with 'It is indeed . . .' (真所謂), followed by a proverb, which in turn is followed by the query. Or the commentary may consist of a corroborating poem, of passages from *The Ballad of the True Story of Ying-ying* and a question. Clearly, such interjection reaffirms each time the narrator's authority. He is, after all, the all-knowing author—narrator whose responsibility it is to interpret an action, to predict its future repercussions, to substantiate its authenticity, or to relate it to common human experiences. However a scene may have developed an autonomous life of its own, when the narrator makes his puppeteer presence felt, the scene is once more under his firm control.

Addressing direct questions to the audience is tantamount to inviting them to participate in developing the story, for they are supposed to reply mentally to the queries. Consequently, the audience feels much closer to the events. This device also permits a good performer to establish intimate *rapport* with his listeners. In 1972, I attended Miss Kim So-hee's memorable performance of *P'ansori*, a Korean form of *chantefable*. She, too, addressed questions and commentary to the audience. It was clear that through these questions she managed to establish direct contact with everyone in the audience. They were 'with her' and, through her, with the story the entire evening.

In *Master Tung's Western Chamber Romance*, commentary with questions occurs regularly at suspenseful and humorous moments. Such interruptions create a stasis, and the sense of anticipation and enjoyment is thereby prolonged. Another, perhaps more unusual, way the mode of commentary is put to use is to lend credence to an improbable situation. Twice, dreams are presented as reality in the *chu-kung-tiao*. Without the matter-of-fact interjections of the narrator, who has heretofore established his credibility by repeatedly citing corroborations, the audience would probably dismiss the scenes as impos-

[i] In 'The Early Chinese Short Story: A Critical Theory in Outline', *HJAS*, 1967.

sible. This is not a place to go into the different psychological responses dreams and reality in literature elicit. Suffice it to say that in the *chu-kung-tiao* dream sequences, because of the use of the narrator's commentary, the illusion of reality is successfully maintained, and even bizarre incidents are accepted with a willing suspension of disbelief.

Descriptions in *Master Tung's Western Chamber Romance* stand out and can be considered a mode by virtue of distinct characteristics. In the verse sections, lengthy descriptive passages concentrate exclusively on visual depiction, with close attention to minute details. Since no prosodic difference exists between passages of description and of presentation in the verse sections, transition from one to the other, though noticeable, is not abrupt. In the prose passages, however, the mode of description is conspicuous in form, position, and content. It is always in blocks of parallel lines, placed at the beginning of the prose passage, using classical allusions, elaborate images and stilted conceits. The effect of the mode of description is rather like a cadenza, a parenthetical flourish for the purpose of adornment. In the translation, the parallelism in the mode of description in prose has been maintained and the parallel lines set off by indentation.

The mode of presentation carries the main burden of forwarding the story. In *Master Tung's Western Chamber Romance,* four voices are used: the omniscient narrator's, recounting events and actions, and three voices of the characters: dialogue, interior monologue, and a character's speech addressed directly to the audience. Extensive dialogue occurs both in verse sections and prose passages and each character's speech is successfully individualized, particularly in the verse sections. In fact, Master Tung's skill with the colloquial language is revealed to best advantage in the speeches of Chang, Ying-ying and Hung-niang; the naturalness, the verve and humor of these speeches are unrivaled in Chinese verse literature, vernacular or otherwise. There are moments in the prose passages when dialogue leans heavily toward the dramatic. Character A's speech is immediately followed by character B's which then is followed either by A's again or by character C's, with no intervening narrative whatsoever. If one were to remove the verb 'say' (*yüeh*) after the names of the characters, the passage could well have been from a drama text. The best examples are the later part of the long debate between Fa-pen and Chang in Chapter 2 and dialogue between Chang, Hung-niang, and Madam Ts'ui at the second banquet, when Chang's and Ying-ying's marriage is settled (Chapter 6). Unfortunately, in my translation, to avoid monotony, I have altered the format by sometimes putting the 'character says' after the speech, or sometimes eliminating the phrase altogether, so that in format at least, the drama-like arrangement is lost. But in any event, it is clear that at such moments, characters are allowed to use their own words and act out an imitation of life.

The only instance when a character, in his own persona, addresses the audience directly, occurs at the end of Chapter 7, when Chang recapitulates events of the past year. In his speech (sung in a long suite), he refers to himself as 'I' and to Ying-ying and Madam Ts'ui by name. The recapitulation is clearly intended for a listener and the intended listener cannot be Ying-ying or her mother, the only two characters present with Chang at this scene, since they are referred to in the third person. The monologue must be, therefore, intended as a direct address to the audience. The moment is highly propitious for such a direct address. The audience is at its most sympathetic toward Chang: he is a victim of Cheng Heng's slander and has just recovered from a fainting spell. Now, sitting with Madam Ts'ui and Ying-ying, who does not even reply to his greetings, Chang pours his grievances out to the audience. (Callous indeed would be the spectator unmoved by such a direct appeal.) And I think we have here the prototype for the Yüan *tsa-chü* convention, the convention that in a play, the protagonist (but not other characters), in his own persona, can describe events or express his own feelings in suites of songs.

Two kinds of interior monologue (always in verse sections) exist in *Master Tung's Western Chamber Romance*; the first can be more accurately called 'interior thoughts'. With no break, the narrator's presentation suddenly switches to the inner reflection of a character, and a brief space later, just as suddenly, the presentation resumes. The best way to illustrate Master Tung's dexterity in managing this bi-focal presentation of reality—observable, objective reality portrayed by the narrator momentarily illuminated by flashes of the inner reality of a character's thoughts—is perhaps to call attention to one such instance. Chang visits the Temple of Universal Salvation; the narrator relates his delight and describes the architecture, icons and sculptures (p. 13). Immediately after the narrative presentation 'He noticed the inscription "Erected in the second year of Ch'ui-kung" ', Chang's reaction is presented without filtering through any narrator's mediation, 'If I hadn't seen the temple,/Even a painting wouldn't convince me that such magnificence exists.' The pronoun is changed to 'I' and the audience or reader is in direct touch with Chang's private thoughts. Then once more without any break, the narrator's presentation resumes (p. 13). At times, passages seem to hover between narrator's presentation and characters' thoughts, and an illusion of a simultaneous existence of the two tiers is created. The fact that in Master Tung's verses, as in all Chinese poetry, personal pronouns are not always used contributes to the ambiguity, hence, to the impression of simultaneity.

The second kind of interior monologue is the musings of the *innamorato* and the *innamorata,* expressing love pangs and longing for the beloved. These interior monologues are usually long suites or parts of long suites, often in the form of recapitulation and rumination. The lovers muse to themselves, or from time to time address their thoughts to the beloved. The most striking characteristic of this kind of interior monologue is its rhetorical quality: the words are deployed in patterns referable to literary artistry rather than to psychological truth, at least as we conceive of such truth. It is never a 'stream of consciousness' — the disjointed meanderings of one's mental process expressed in random associations or broken syntax. In fact, the language of these monologues frequently is far more poetic than the spoken discourse of the characters. The inspiration for these monologues is unmistakably tenth- and eleventh-century *tz'u* poems on love and separation.

Elsewhere I have discussed the general influence of *tz'u* poetry on Master Tung's *chu-kung-tiao*.[j] I have pointed out that the mode of expression, thematic elements, and images in the parting scenes and in the musings and recapitulations (frequently expressed in the form of interior monologue) of Master Tung's work are identical with those often used in *tz'u* poems. Some combination of four ingredients is always present: an expression of the lover's sorrow and malaise, references to his or her beloved, his or her reaction to the immediate surroundings, and reaction to nature in general. It is perhaps useful here to examine one particular interior monologue in which *tz'u* influences are more than usually prominent.

The example appears on pp. 189–92. After Chang leaves for the capital, Ying-ying is despondent. One spring night, remembering their earlier happiness, she laments to herself. The suite, four tunes and a coda, has eighty-three lines, and there are three related themes: Ying-ying's reflection on the separation and on her relationship with Chang, a description of her emotional and physical state, and a description of nature and her environment. The very way the separation is conceived adheres to *tz'u* conventions. Though Chang is only away for the Examination, Ying-ying thinks of the separation as if it would last forever (lines 1–3). The distance between them is exaggerated; Chang is placed at the edge of the horizon (34–5). When Ying-ying strains to see Chang, her view is blocked by clouded mountains (49–50) (The device of the 'vain attempt' as well as the imagery are both from *tz'u*.) If she writes him a letter, she fears no one will deliver it (60).[k] Chang seems to her to be a creditor, exacting payment for a wrong she has done him in a previous life (21–30). No matter how stoic they are, their growing sorrow, Ying-ying feels, will eventually overpower them (36–40).

The separation makes Ying-ying distraught with sorrow. Two postures symbolize her forlornness—her leaning on a balustrade and standing alone on deserted steps (4–6). Early in the suite, she merely dreads leaning on the balustrade; toward the middle, she actually tires of it (41). Her suffering is objectified by her physical state; she has become emaciated, her hair is in disarray, the hairpin awry, and she feels listless (16–20). Her reflection in a mirror confirms her haggardness (31–2), and she is ashamed to wear any flowers because of her wilted looks (61–4, 42). Sitting immobile at her dressing-table she cannot control her tears (71–4). Her wretchedness, she is sure, will turn her hair grey before she is old (75–9).

[j] Cf. Li-li Ch'en, 'Outer and Inner Forms of *Chu-kung-tiao,* with Reference to *Pien-wen, Tz'u* and Vernacular Fiction', *HJAS,* 1972.

[k] The adherence to *tz'u* convention here becomes more conspicuous when one notes that later in the chapter Ying-ying has no difficulty finding a servant to deliver her letter and parcel to Chang.

Preoccupied with her misery, Ying-ying examines it from various angles. She compares her thoughts to tangled hemp (13–15). The weight of her sorrow, she thinks, will break a *t'ai-ping* cart pulled by twenty mules (11–12). She knows that her suffering is brought on by herself—by her love, however, and not by a fretful nature (43–6). She finds her loneliness particularly acute at night (51–2). Mentally replying to Hung-niang, she further defines her illness; it is not caused by a hangover or by her grief over the disappearance of spring; rather, it is caused by Chang's absence (80–3).

Natural phenomena are the objective correlatives of her mood. The time is late spring, and all around, there is decay and cruelty. The moss is no longer young and growing but has turned dark green. The wind hurls catkins mercilessly against flapping curtains (7–9). At first the surroundings are only observed; gradually, their effect on her mood is perceived. The moon is as radiant as the year before, but its sameness only makes her realize the more how much she has changed (53–7). The petals are losing their colors but her brows are gaining a new gloom (47–8). In lines 65–70, flowers do not just decompose passively as in an earlier line, they are now seen falling by the thousands, and the force of this desolate shower heightens her melancholy.

It is probably accurate to say that, except for the conceit of comparing a lover to a creditor and Ying-ying's statement that her misery is not caused by a fretful, ungenerous nature, all other motifs are inspired by *tz'u*. Some of these motifs, to be sure, are familiar *topoi* in Chinese lyrics and have appeared in other genres as well, but the stances, the conceits, the imagery, and language through which the motifs are expressed are decidedly those of *tz'u*.

In some instances, one cannot discern the full meaning of the lines without a familiarity with *tz'u* poetry—layers of significance are apt to be lost. These lines are like shorthand symbols, expressing in an abbreviated form well-established *tz'u* conventions; one must first recognize the symbols and then complete the meaning. On the surface, lines five and six, for example, objectify Ying-ying's loneliness. Yet, through frequent use, leaning on a balustrade, standing by deserted steps (as well as standing on a storied pavilion, one might add) are well-known 'waiting' postures in *tz'u*. The person is understood to be gazing out in the hope of espying the return of a lover or a friend. Thus, Ying-ying's fear and dread in these lines are not just caused by her loneliness, they are caused even more by frustration and disappointment. She fully realizes the futility of gazing out and waiting, but her longing compels her to it. Trapped by her obsession, she dreads the renewal of her disappointment each times she gazes out.

In addition to the influences of *tz'u* poetry in general, in this suite of poems, one recognizes also specific imprints of the Sung poetess Li Ch'ing-chao (1084–*c.* 1155), just as in some of Chang's interior monologues one hears echoes of Liu Yung (*fl. c.* 1045) and Ou-yang Hsiu (1007–72). This borrowing, after all, is not surprising, for among Li's poems are some of the most penetrating expressions of longing and grief seen through the eyes of a woman.

Many of Li's *tz'u* are autobiographical, written when she was separated from her husband; the circumstances behind her poems are thus analogues to Ying-ying's at this point in the *chantefable*. In Li's *tz'u* 'Wu-ling Spring',[1] a 'grass-hopper' skiff is said to be too light to support the tremendous weight of her sorrow; in Master Tung's verse, the skiff is changed to a *t'ai-p'ing* cart (line 12). In 'On Remembering the Flute-playing at Phoenix Terrace',[m] Li defines her malaise by eliminating what it is not: 'Not a hangover,/nor autumn grief', Master Tung repeats the two lines, only changing 'autumn' to 'spring' and the two verbs *'kan'* 干 and *'pei'* 悲 to their synonyms *'kuan'* 關 and *'shang'* 傷 (lines 81–2). Line ten in Tung's suite is rooted in three of Li's lines.[n] Standing by itself it is elliptic and the import of the line is unclear. The line could even be taken to mean something positive, quite at variance with the negative decay and destruction expressed in the preceding lines. When the emblematic device is recognized and the verse is complemented by Li's lines, the meaning becomes clear. The dust exudes a fragrant scent because it is mingled with fallen flowers. Instead of contradicting the preceding verses, the line actually reinforces the mood of melancholy, decay and despair.[o]

Such borrowing from *tz'u* conventions and from specific *tz'u* poets will appeal particularly to those already familiar with the genre who can hear the resonance and the echoes. Yet *Master Tung's Western Chamber Romance* can delight anyone who likes 'a good read'. Since the main purpose of this book is to make Master Tung's work available to the English-speaking reader, I should stop talking about it and let it speak for itself.

[1] *'Wu-ling ch'un'*, *Li Ch'ing-chao chi* (Shanghai, 1962), p. 9.

[m] *'Feng-huang t'ai shang i ch'ui hsiao'*, ibid. p. 28.

[n] 'The wind has stopped./The dust is fragrant–/Flowers have all fallen.' *'Wu-ling ch'un'*, ibid. p. 9.

[o] Lines 17, 55–7 and 71 in Tung's suite, because of their use of identical verbs, of similar imagery, posture, and motif, also evoke Li's verses.

Notes on the Translation

The edition used for this translation is *Tung Chieh-yüan Hsi-hsiang-chi* edited by Ling Ching-yen (Peking, 1962). However, since the scansion of the verses in this edition is often arbitrary, I have re-scanned the verse sections according to *Chu-kung-tiao ting-lü* (*Chu-kung-tiao Verse Forms*) by Yeh Ch'ing-ping.[P]

Traduttore traditore: despite the best intentions, much betrayal necessarily occurs. It is impossible to reproduce or even to approximate Chinese literature in English; there are too few linguistic and cultural counterparts. My primary goal, in this translation, has been readability. While trying to be as faithful as possible to the original, I have never aimed at being literal.

I have chosen to render the verse sections in *vers libre*. The language, in keeping with the original, is colloquial. Not all parallelism has been retained, but special features such as reduplicated lines and refrains have been kept. A few times I have altered the order of the lines of a couplet so that the translation would read more smoothly. The tune titles have been translated; one can get the original Chinese titles easily by checking the translation against Ling.

In the prose passages I have made the language more formal, again in keeping with the original. All parallelism in the modes of commentary and description has been reproduced, and these parallel lines are indented. As explained in the Introduction, *shih, tz'u* and other forms of verse are sometimes included in the prose passages. To distinguish them from the *ch'ü* verse of the verse sections, I have used rhyme or assonance in their translation. Specifically, for *lü-shih* I have used the rhyme scheme of abba, cddc, or abab, cdcd; for *chüeh-chü*, -a-a; for *ku-shih*, rhymed couplets; for *tz'u*, internal and end rhymes; for Li Shen's *Ying-ying pen-shih ko* (*The Ballad of the True Story of Ying-ying*), ballad diction and meter. *Faute de mieux*, I have substituted *tra-la* for the *hsi* in the *ch'u-ko*. Needless to say, these prosodic features in no way approximate to those of the original. The intention is merely to suggest that verses found in the prose passages are written in forms other than the *ch'ü* of the verse sections. Another liberty I have taken in the prose passages is to change the format of the dialogues. With no exception, in the original, every quotation is monotonously introduced by 'so-and-so says' (*yüeh*). I have often omitted this introduction or moved it to the end of the quotation, or changed 'says' to 'replies' or 'answers'.

[P] Unpublished Master's thesis (supervisor: Professor Cheng Ch'ien), National Taiwan University, Taipei, 1961.

Chapter 1

(*Hsien-lü-tiao* mode) (Introductory Suite)

Drunk and Wretched, ch'an-ling[1]

> Our emperor, by his example of virtue,
>> has transformed his subjects;
> Happily, we now enjoy peace and leisure.
> Weapons are put away, armor is untouched;
> Livin ʒ at a time like this
> Why houldn't we be merry?
>
> At N dam Ch'in's, at Mlle Hsieh's[2]
> I'm i mous for my gallantry.
> All the smart young blades copy me.
> Never one to create any disturbance,
> I just want a free-floating, romantic life.

Straightening a Golden Cap

> Carrying a jug of wine,
> Wearing a sprig of flowers,
> When I'm drunk, I sing;
> When I feel wild, I dance;
> When I sober up, I stop.
> Every day I loaf—haven't been home lately.
> I do what I please:
> No rules for me.
> Whoever wants to criticize, let him go ahead.

[1] 纏令 , together with 纏達 , are two forms of singing collectively known as *chuan* 賺 , popular in the northern Sung capital Pien-ching in the early twelfth century. A passage in Meng Yüan-lao 孟元老 , *Tung-ching meng-hua lu* defines *ch'an ling* as 'the type of *chuan* with an introductory tune and a coda.' In *Master Tung's Western Chamber Romance* (*Tung Hsi-hsiang chu-kung-tiao,* hereafter referred to as *THH*) twenty-seven of the forty-seven long suites (suites with at least two tunes and a coda) have the label *ch'an-ling*; five more have the simpler label *ch'an.* These labels may be intended to indicate the musical provenance of the suites or to suggest the manner in which the suites are to be performed.

[2] Free translation of *Ch'in-lou, Hsieh-kuan* (Ch'in pavilion, Hsieh mansion), euphemisms for brothels.

Wind Blowing Lotus Leaves

> I don't know how to use a clapper;
> I'm not used to singing and telling stories to an audience.
> Good or bad, off pitch or on, you'll have to put up with me.
> This story is not about knives and cudgels,
> Spears or steeds.

Coda

> Sweet is the tune,
> Pleasing the melody.
> Mixing snow and the moon,
>   the wind and flowers,
> I'll sing you a story of secret love.

(*Pan-she-tiao* mode) (Extra Introductory Suite, Gratis!)

A Whistle Song

> Tai-kao[3] presides over spring.
> When his craftsmen set to work,
> Warm air emerges from the Sun Valley;[4]
> Miles of flowers toss in the eastern wind;
> Willow threads rub together in golden strands.
> In time,
> Peach blossoms turn crimson, apricot pink.
> Water becomes green, mountains verdant.
> And spring riplets rise on misty shores . . .
> But how long can the season's ninety days last?
> Before one expects, turtle doves call for their mates,
> Swallows have hatched their young.
> Fallen petals pile in confusion, driven freely by the wind.
> Catkins, unclaimed, fly about in the air—
> The delicate charm of spring has
> Half entered the pond,
> Half mixed with the dust.
>
> Heaps of fallen coins—elm seeds—cover the ground,
> Yet they can't buy the permanence of spring.

---

[3] The mythical ruler Fu-hsi, said to be in charge of spring. (*Li chi* 禮記 , *Yueh-ling* 月令.)

[4] *Yang-ku*, whence the sun is supposed to rise. Cf. *Shu ching* 書經 , *Yao tien* 堯典 .

2

Summer comes and stays.
In pool-side pavilions visited by the south wind,
Rattan beds, bamboo mats and netting are brought.
When noon approaches,
Caps are removed, hair set loose,
Plums and melons chilled,
And treasured fans flutter their wings of pure white silk.
Ah, how can one pass the interminable summer days?
There is wine to sweep away sorrow, and
Green Slaves[5] to ensure a comfortable nap.
Then, before long, light rain imparts refreshing coolness;
Autumn gale dispels lingering heat;
Unperceived, the lush summer months have slipped away.

Teasing the Child

Dried leaves drop rustling to the ground.
Freezing cicadas respond to each other's whining cries.
Pitter-patter intermittent rain falls on *wu-tung* trees.
Crying *ya-ya*, wild geese return to the south.
A thousand streams reflect a single moon
While soughing wind sifts through riverbank rushes.
When autumn draws to an end,
Forests appear pared,
Every branch withers.

Snowflakes are blown about by the north wind,
        dusk obscures the outline of streams and sky:
The scene is like an ink-wash painting.
Shivering on his donkey, where does Hao-jan[6] go?
To the west suburb of Pa-ling, it seems.

---

[5] *Ch'ing-nu,* cylinders made of polished green bamboo, used as coolers in bed in the summer, rather the reverse of hot-water bottles.
[6] Meng Hao-jan (689–740), a Well-known T'ang poet. The anecdote of Meng shivering on his donkey while viewing blossoms and writing poetry as he rides through the snow to Pa-ling, a suburb of Ch'ang-an, has existed since the ninth century. (cf. T'ang Yen-ch'ien 唐彥謙, fl. 860–888, "I Meng Hao-jan"|憶孟浩然, in Ch'uan T'ang shih 全唐詩, Peking: Chung-hua shu-chu, 1960; vol. 10, ch. 671, p. 7668).
    The anecdote is widely alluded to or used as source material in the Yüan drama.
See Yen Tun-i 嚴敦易, yuan-chu chen-i 元劇斟疑, Peking: chung-hua shu-chü, 1960; vol. 2, 548–53.

Icy air penetrates An-tao's[7] study,
As well as Wen-chün's[8] wine shop.
After nightfall,
A bracing wind rises;
In the dim moonlight slender bamboos stand beside a sparsely
flowering plum.

Peacetime chuan

One season follows another;
Furtively, time carries our years away.
Don't be foolish—
Man's century passes like the morning dew.
Why exert yourself?
Fine days, beautiful nights are to be enjoyed.
Don't let clear wind and bright moon go to waste.
Submit to no constraint.
Rejoice, for in human history
An enlightened reign like ours is hard to come by.

My nature has always been wild.
A wild nature is difficult to control.
What do I think of when I get home?
I'm possessed by the demon of poetry—
I like to set verses to romantic tunes.
My lyrics may not delight as much as those of poets of old,
But among *chu-kung-tiao* songs they will do.
Every poem is graceful, elegant, and neatly turned,
Unlike the works of others.

Songe of Che Tree Branches[9]

Not of Ts'ui T'ao meeting a tigress do I sing.
Nor of Master Cheng encountering a fox-spirit.

---

[7] An-tao, appellation of Tai K'uei 戴逵 (?–396), a recluse-scholar, who figures
in several anecdotes in *Shih-shuo hsin-yü* (pp. 99, 164, 176, and 186, *Shang-wu* ed.,
Shanghai, 1935).
[8] Cho Wen-chün (*c.* 179 – *c.* 117 B.C.), who eloped with the *fu* writer Ssu-ma Hsiang-ju
and was disowned by her wealthy father Cho Wang-sun. When she and Ssu-ma opened a
tavern, her father was shamed into proffering financial aid. Extensively used as stuff-
material in popular literature of the twelfth and thirteenth centuries, the romance of
Wen-chün and Hsiang-ju was first recorded in *Shih chi*, 117; and *Ch'ien Han shu*, 57.

4

Nor the pulling of the silver flask from the well.
Nor the two maidens competing for one man.
Not of the girl whose soul went away.
Nor of Ts'ui Hu, who once begged for a cup of water.
Nor Shuang Chien, the prefect of Yü-chang.
Nor Liu I, who delivered a letter to the dragon king.

Flowers above the Wall

The sights I celebrate
Can still be seen in Ho-chung-fu:[10]
Even the ancient temple stands.
The hero in my tale was a famous Confucian from Hsi-lo.[11]
The heroine, a young lady from Po-ling.[11]

Now as I reflect on their romance,
The wind-welcoming door[12] is unused,
Inscriptions on the wall, though, are intact.

[9] The following eight lines are by no means titles of other *chu-kung-tiao*. They refer
rather to plots well-known at the time, which Master Tung (in the persona of the
singer–narrator) could have chosen as stuff-material for his *chantefable*. Four of these
lines, nos. 1, 2, 5, 8, allude to stories collected in *T'ai-ping kuang-chi*, the repository *par
excellence*, compiled in 977–8 (chüan   no. 433, 452, 358 and 419 respectively). Line
3 alludes to a ballad of Po Chü-i (772–846, *Po Hsiang-shan chi*, I. 52, *Shang-wu* ed.,
Shanghai, 1936) and line 6 to a vignette in Meng Chi's 孟棨 *Pen-shih shih* (preface
dated 886, *Ku-tien wen-hsüeh ch'u-pan-she* ed., Shanghai, 1957, p. 12).
   Existing titles show that certain Sung variety shows (宋 雜 劇), Yüan drama,
Chin *Yüan-pen* (金 院 本), and Southern drama of the late twelfth and early thirteenth
centuries used these plots. (Cf. Chou Mi 周密 *Wu-lin chiu shih*, Ch. 10; Chung Ssu-
ch'eng 鍾嗣成, Chia Chung-ming 賈 仲 名 *Lu-kuei pu* and *Lu-kuei pu hsü pien*; T'ao
Tsung-i 陶 宗 儀 , *Ch'o-keng lu*; and Ch'ien Nan-yang 錢 南 揚 , *Sung-Yüan nan-hsi pai-i
lu*.) Lo Yeh 羅 燁 (Yüan dynasty), in the chapter entitled '*hsiao-shuo k'ai-p'i*' (Exploring
the Art of Story-telling), in *Tsui-weng t'an-lu*, includes 'Ts'ui Chih-t'ao [Ts'ui T'ao] ' and
'Ts'ui Hu Seeking Water', along with 'The Story of Ying-ying' among the repertory of a
master story-teller. Not surprisingly, part of a story-teller's training, as Lo sees it,
consists of studying *T'ai-p'ing kuang-chi* in his youth. (*Ku-tien wen-hsüeh ch'u-pan-she*
ed., Shanghai, 1957, pp. 3 and 4.)
[10] District between Yellow and Fen 汾 rivers in the south-west of Shansi province. At
different periods the area is variously known as Ho-chung-fu and P'u-chou. Both names
are used, however, to refer to the prefectural capital (mod. Yung-chi hsien 永 濟 縣)
and not to the entire district in *THH*.
[11] Hsi-lo, Lo-yang in Honan province; Po-ling, Ting Hsien 定 縣 in Hopei province.
Yüan Chen's *Ying-ying chuan* makes no mention of the native places of Chang and
Ying-ying. Place names are used liberally to create an impression of verisimilitude in
THH.
[12] The door of Ying-ying's chamber, so called because of a poem she wrote to Chang.
See p. 117.

While the moon-waiting veranda[13] remains
The flute-blowing companions[14] have vanished.

Clever audience,
Smart listeners,
    think about this —
Unlike tales full of commotion
A melancholy story is difficult to perform.
Three parts out of ten deal with amorous longing, boudoir grief.
Half concerns passionate love-making.

Coda

Gauche and modest though my efforts be
I here present them to you.
The romantic songs at least
Will please dashing gallants the world over.

[Prose]

This story deals with a young scholar of the T'ang dynasty named Chang Kung, with the appellation Chün-jui, who was a native of Hsi-lo. When he was quite young, his family moved to the capital, Ch'ang-an, where his father served as the Secretary of the Board of Rites. Soon the Secretary died; and because he had been an honest official, within a few years after his death the Chang family became impoverished. Chang Kung was very ambitious. At twenty-two he was still a bachelor.

(*Hsien-lü-tiao* mode)

Flower-Viewing Time[15]

In beauty and grace young Chang of Hsi-lo
Vies with the paragons of old.

---

[13] There are two possible interpretations to this line: the veranda may refer to one on which Chang waits for Ying-ying on a moon-lit night (p. 24), or it may be a substitute for the 'western chamber' of line one of Ying-ying's poem to Chang (p. 117). Both readings are problematical as in the first instance Chang is not waiting for the moon (but for Ying-ying), and in the second a veranda is in no way related to the western chamber. *Tai-yüeh hsi-hsiang,* moon-waiting western chamber, would have been more accurate, but *hsi-hsiang* violates the tonal prescription.

    Since there is no exact counterpart in the West for 迴 廊 , I am forced to render it as 'veranda' throughout the *chu-kung-tiao.* It is actually a covered walkway which often meanders across a garden or a courtyard. Many photographs of the Summer Palace in Peking show the elegant *huei-lang* there.

[14] Metonym for ideal lovers. Chang and Ying-ying are compared to Ch'in Nung-yü 秦 弄 玉 and Hsiao Shih 蕭 史 , expert flutists and model lovers of the Spring and Autumn Era (*fl.* late seventh century B.C.). 'Flute-blowing', *ch'ui-hsiao,* is, of course, a euphemism for fellatio. The possible erotic reading of the line is probably not unintended.

Passionately fond of poetry and calligraphy,
An expert painter and musician,
He's an impeccable prose-writer (and a scrupulous man) as well.
His *shih*,[16] his *fu*[16] are widely sought after,
Whether they scorn the wind, praise the moon,
Portray lute-playing or tea-tasting.

He has passed
Several examinations.
But now the fortune of his family dwindles,
Weary of the capital,
He packs up his zither and books,
To travel and to visit men of unusual discernment.
Six months out of a year,
He roams the remote edges of the world.

Coda

Delighting in solitude.
Free, unbridled,
Wherever his fancy takes him
      there he makes his home
Just like the wild Ssu-ma[17] before his rise to fame.

[Prose]

In the second month of the seventeenth year of Chen-yüan period [801 A.D.]
Chang reached P'u-chou, which is now called Ho-chung-fu. There is a poem
corroborating this,[18] which says:

From the sky a golden torrent tumbles and gushes,
Its silvery wave to the ocean boldly rushes.
Charging great cities, the mighty river turns again and again,
Slowed by Three Gates,[19] it lingers in the Central Plain.

---

[15] The ensuing poem adheres to the verse form of *Cheng-hua-kuan* (*Straightening a Flowered Cap*) and not to that of *Shang-hua shih* (*Flower-Viewing Time*). I suspect a scribal error has substituted the latter for the former.

[16] Literary genres, 'poetry' and rhyme-prose; see Burton Watson, *Chinese Lyricism* (New York, 1971) and *Chinese Rhyme-Prose* (New York, 1971).

[17] Ssu-ma Hsiang-ju, cf. n. 8 above.

[18] The ensuing poem does not at all corroborate the event; it describes instead the grandeur of the Yellow River. Such incongruity in the use of corroboration poems is not infrequent in *THH*.

[19] The Gates of God, Ghost, and Man, hollows in Ti-chu Mountain 砥柱山 , which rises in the middle of the Yellow River near Shan-hsien 陝縣 in Honan province.

Chü-t'ang's[20] grandeur has been exaggerated;
Hsia-k'ou's[21] thunders have been overrated.
Streams and lakes serve it, competing in eagerness,
And the Milky Way attends it with vigilant meekness.

This poem depicts the Yellow River. Where can one get the most impressive view of this river? The best place is Ho-chung-fu.

(*Hsien-lü-tiao* mode)

Flower-Viewing Time

Luxuriant grass lines the road,
Flowers and trees deck the open land,
Spring has come to the Chin Valley.[22]
As Chang approaches P'u-chou
He sees a sight worth sketching.

To the west, the Yellow River; to the east, the Hua mountain.
The city seems to be built in clouds.
Even the lofty fortress of Ju-k'ou[23] is not as high.
The Yellow River rushes by —
From time to time, a surge of wind-tossed waves.

Coda

Eastern wind shakes poplar trees on the banks.
West from the dock stretches the road to Ch'ang-an.
P'u-chou occupies a strategic position on the Yellow River.
A pontoon bridge is secured by inch-thick bamboo cords.

[Prose]

When Chang entered P'u-chou, he was much pleased by the prosperity. He took a room at an inn.

---

[20] One of the three gorges of the Yangtze River, in Szechuan province.
[21] A town on the south bank of the Yangtze, in Hupei province, where the rapids are said to make a deafening din.
[22] Ch'in-ch'uan, modern Shensi province.
[23] I am following the second reading suggested in Ling Ching-yen's note (*Tung Chieh-yüan Hsi-hsiang chi*, p. 26). Ju-k'ou is located near Ching-yüeh hsien 靜 樂 縣 in Shansi.

(*Hsien-lü-tiao* mode)

Drunk and Wretched

> With thoroughfares going in all directions,
> The scene deserved to be painted.
> Roof tiles were half obscured by luminous mist.
> One eave touched another.
> There must have been some seventy thousand families.
>
> Six main avenues, three market places, horses and carriages abounded.
> The inhabitants looked as stylish as people in the capital.
> Before visiting the regional school,
> Chang reined his horse before an inn,
> Where he and his servant would lodge.

[Prose]

He was:

> As elegant as Sung Yü[24]
> As talented as Ts'ao Chih[24]
> As handsome as P'an Yüeh[24]
> As upright as Feng Chih.[24]
> A young scholar with no official position,
> The time for his discovery not yet arrived.

Chang settled in a quiet inn. After a few days he became bored.

(*Huang-chung-tiao* mode)

The Golden Altar Boy

> Chang of Ch'ing-ho,[25]
> Stopping at an inn,

---

[24] These historical personages were considered epitomes of masculine beauty and literary talent. Sung Yü (*c.* third century B.C.), Ts'ao Chih (192–232), and P'an Yüeh (?–300) were writers of *shih, fu,* and *yüeh-fu* ballads. Feng Chih features in a T'ang *ch'uan-ch'i* story by P'ei Hsing 裴 鉶 (*fl. c.* 860; the story is collected in *T'ai-p'ing kuang-chi, chüan* 68), in which he refuses four times the marriage proposal of a goddess on the grounds that proper decorum has not been observed. The story must have been popular during Master Tung's time and in the Yüan dynasty; one version of it is included in Lo Yeh, *op. cit.,* n. 9 above, pp. 68–69. Little else is known of Feng.

[25] A *chün*   . Interestingly, both Ch'ing-ho and Po-ling (where Ying-ying is supposed to have come from, see n. 11 above) had been frequently used as native places for characters in T'ang *ch'uan-ch'i* stories. Cf. Lu Hsün, ed., *T'ang Sung ch'uan-ch'i chi,* Peking, 1956, pp. 148, 30 and 60.

9

Has no companion and
No place to go.
Just as he is becoming desperate, he sees
The inn servant enter his room.

'Tell me',
Chang eagerly asks,
'I have heard
That this district
Has extraordinary sights, unique in the world.
You must know where they are.'

Coda

The servant shouldn't have told him what he did.
With less than ten sentences
He initiated Chang's later suffering.

[Prose]

A few phrases of idle chatter provoked
A trouble-filled romance.

What did the servant say? What did he say? He said: 'A little more than ten miles to the east of P'u-chou there is a temple called Universal Salvation. It was built by the Imperial Treasury during the reign of Empress Wu [A.D. 684–705] who was a devotee of Buddhism. No other temple anywhere is as beautiful. You must go and see it.'

(*Kao-p'ing-tiao* mode)

Magnolia Flowers

The servant said:
'The court took many years to build this temple.
The architecture is truly magnificent.
Even the palaces in heaven, I suspect,
Can't compete with it in splendor.
What would I gain by lying to you?
You won't find another temple like this
In the whole world.'
Chang replied:
'Instead of wandering about idly,
I might as well follow your advice.'

[Prose]

Chang left P'u-chou to pay a visit to the temple. A little over ten miles
outside the city, he reached his destination.

(*Hsien-lü-tiao* mode)

Drunk and Wretched

As Chang rode
In the shadow of the green poplar trees,
His servant pointed east:
'Look over there, what an impressive temple gate.'
Chang gazed

And saw porcelain roof tiles blazing with purple and gold.
'This must be Universal Salvation.'
But from afar he couldn't be sure.
He thought to himself:
'I've been everywhere, and
I've never seen such a splendid temple.'

Coda

Drawing near,
He saw he was right.
Above the gate was a signboard, obviously given by the Court.
On it were inscribed six gold characters each as large as a winnow fan.

[Prose]

Propitious clouds enveloped the sutra chamber.
Auspicious mist covered the bell tower.
The porcelain boss atop the prayer hall touched the sky.
The golden tip of the cinerarium pierced the firmament.
One thousand bamboos rose above the temple wall.
One hundred pine trees encircled the sacred ground.
Poplar leaves flanked the main gate,
Gilt writing adorned the signboard.
Each character was as large as a winnow fan,
Each stroke gracefully drawn by Yen or Liu.[26]

[26] Yen Chen-ch'ing 顏真卿 (709–84) and Liu Kung-ch'üan 柳公權 (778–865),
famous calligraphers of T'ang. The reference to them here is an anachronism since the
temple was supposed to have been built during the reign of Empress Wu (684–705),
whereas Yen and Liu were not born until 709 and 778. Unless, of course, the signboard
Chang sees is a replacement of the original one.

The sign proclaimed: 'Temple of Universal Salvation, Constructed by Imperial Order.' Even from the outside, the young scholar was delighted by the sight. When he entered the temple, the monk in charge of visitors asked a young novice to guide him. At once, Chang felt released from his worldly preoccupations.

(*Shang-tiao* mode)

Yü-pao-tu

>Peerless is the Temple of Universal Salvation.
>It has a three-eaved sutra chamber,
>Seven-tiered pagoda and
>Hundred-foot bell tower.
>In the main hall, canopies are suspended from decorated rafters.
>On the veranda, bamboo screens are held by golden hooks.
>A nimbus[27] hovers over a profusion of porcelain roofs.
>There are one thousand beams, ten thousand arches,
>Broad steps paved with glazed bricks, and
>Richly embellished,
>Deep-set eaves.
>
>Offertory tables are gold inlaid with jade.
>Aromatic incense rises from tripods in animal shapes.
>The central mural,
>The portraits on the side
>Are painted by Master Wu[28] himself.
>*Chin-kang*[29] and *Chieh-ti*,[30] with their sharp features, look brave
>   and fierce.
>While merciful Bodhisattvas fairly move, so alive they seem.
>Looking at them,
>Chang bursts forth: 'It's as good as they say!'
>Repeatedly he nods his head.

---

[27] 瑞烟 commonly thought to be a pink and luminous mist which is supposed to be auspicious in folk tradition.

[28] Wu Tao-hsüan 吳道玄, celebrated painter of T'ang Hsüan-tsung's reign (712–56), particularly well known for his paintings of Buddhist icons and legendary scenes.

[29] 金剛, *Vajra*, 'One who is supreme in preciousness and firmness.' In China, the term designates the guardian spirit of a Buddhist temple.

[30] 揭帝 (possibly an acronymic transliteration of *kata-pūtana*) 'a malodorous and ugly demon'. In popular usage, it refers to the ferocious god who supervises the enforcement of Buddhist laws.

About to inquire when the temple was built,
He notices the inscription: 'Erected in the second year of
      Ch'ui-kung.'[31]

Coda

> 'What the inn servant said was true.
> If I hadn't seen the temple,
> Even a painting wouldn't convince me that such magnificence exists.'

[Prose]

This temple was indeed luxurious; it had
> Walls of red, pepper-scented clay,
> Beams with carvings and jade inlay;
> Sandalwood pillars painted in gold,
> Stone steps trimmed with tortoise shell.
> Pines and junipers intermingled.
> Flower trees and bamboos grew side by side.

Such unusual riches befitted a heaven on earth. Only the imperial treasury
could have paid for it!

(*Shuang-tiao* mode)

Wen-ju-chin

> The elegance of the scenery
> Dispelled all vulgar thoughts.
> Universal Salvation
> Was unsullied by worldly dust and mire.
> Gold and jade glistened.
> Neatly pruned,
> Ingeniously grafted
> Were tall pines, dwarf cedars,
> Rare flowers and exotic plants.
> Bamboos and rockeries
> Clustered around
> A murmuring stream.
> Luminous mists drifted about.
> A pagoda, ten thousand feet high,
> Touched the very clouds and the rainbow in the sky.

[31] 687 A.D.

The novice said: 'Sir, if you want to see the sights,
Let's not just wander about,
Let's begin.'
Turning on the veranda,
He raised a bamboo screen.
They went north to the sutra chamber,
West to the worship hall,
South to the kitchen,
East to the bell tower.
Then, next to a pine arbor,
On the bank of a flower-lined stream,
Partially concealed behind a white-washed wall,
A complex of houses appeared.
The vermillion gate was half-open.
Chang wondered what these houses could be . . .
Suddenly something caught his eye.
He stood transfixed, as if his soul had left him.

Coda

Startled, almost deranged,
He refused to move on.
Rooted in place, he looked frozen and numb.

[Prose]

What did Chang see just then? What did he see? He came face to face with his predestined lover who had come to avenge herself for the wrong he had done her five hundred years before.

An inn servant's advice caused the vexation of this day.
A novice's suggestion induced sorrows of later times.
A passionate romance
Began with this encounter.

(*Hsien-lü-tiao* mode)

Adorning Crimson Lips

An abundance of buildings, high and low, dotted the temple site.
A nimbus floated overhead,
	the warm air was charged with incense.
Chang had visited the worship hall, the front chapel, and some
	other sights.

When passing under dense foliage and blossoms,
He approached a compound graced by weeping willows.
The scented air stirred,
The vermillion gate opened,
A face, a flower, appeared.

Wind Blowing Lotus Leaves

The lady was not plump and not slim.
At first, only her profile was visible.
Her eyebrow, painted in the palace style, resembled a distant ridge.
Utterly charming,
She could have been
A Bodhisattva,
A goddess.

The Inebriated Tartar Woman

Ignoring Chang's stare,
She twisted a blossoming twig between her fingers.
On her alabaster wrist
A gold bracelet gleamed.

Coda

Her vivacious eyes
Were exceedingly alluring.
Chang had never seen such a flawless face.

[Prose]

Fresh from a spring nap, she crushes fragrant pollen between
her fingers.
Leaning against the vermillion gate, she laments the cruelty of
the eastern wind.
Her hair is dressed in a twin chignon;
Her comb is shaped like a phoenix.
Greener than distant hills are her eyebrows;
Brighter than autumn water are her eyes.
Her skin is congealed cream;
Her waist, a fragile willow.
Her fingers, long and slender, are like bamboo shoots;
Her feet, dainty but firm, are like lotus buds.

15

The original T'ang story[32] says: 'Though Chang was already twenty-two, he had never touched a woman. Despite his propriety, he was intensely affected by this young lady.'

(*Chung-lü-tiao* mode)

Hsiang-feng-ho, ch'an-ling

> Turning at the trellis,
> Chang met his future love.
> The moment he saw her
> He was hopelessly smitten.
> Paying no heed to the foolish scholar,
> The beauty withdrew and closed the gate.
> Chang called out:
> 'She has vanished, vanished!'

> Against the evening cloud of her cheeks, cherry lips shone.
> Her hair, parted on the side, was as black as raven's feather.
> Her sensitive face
> Her intelligent, lively, eyes
> Were exquisite and refined.
> Though she feigned haughtiness, she did glance furtively at Chang,
> Who was stricken —
> Stricken with overpowering passion.

Flowers above the Wall

> Unadorned by jewelry or makeup
> Her beauty was dazzling, perfect.
> The simple elegance of her dress,
> The subtle coloring of her face
> Couldn't be captured
> Even by the brush of Chou Fang.[33]

> Resting her hand against her cheek,
> She looked timid and shy.
> Her demeanor
> Suggested that she was unmarried.
> What was her name?
> Chang wished he could ask.

[32] *Ying-ying chüan* by Yüan Chen, on which *THH* is loosely based. See Introduction.
[33] 周昉 (*fl.* second half of the eighth century), court painter of T'ang, famous portraitist.

He had never seen her before.
He had never talked with her.
Yet you wouldn't need a soothsayer to tell you
He'd never get her out of his mind.
Her style, her elegance
Left him helpless with desire.

Coda

She was so lovely
So lovely that
Flowers wilted with shame in her presence.

[Prose]

However brilliant the flowers,
They dared not face the Beauty of Peach Blossom Cave.[34]
When the young lady saw Chang, she retired shyly.

(*Ta-shih-tiao* mode)

Kun Section of [the Elaborate Melody] I-chou

Chang
Was completely dazed.
He thought to himself: 'Who has ever seen such a beauty!
I'm certain she's unique
In the world!'
Wild with excitement,
He became reckless
And did something outrageous.
True, he had been willful before,
But *now* he tried to force the gate
Without knowing who lived within!

Addled,
Impetuous,
Careless,
Unthinking,
He was rash to an extreme —
Yes, young people are often mindless —

---

[34] Cf. the story of Liu Ch'en 劉晨 and Juan Chao 阮肇 in the *T'ai-p'ing kuang-chi* and in the *Tsui-weng t'an-lu*. Certain aspects of the story were probably inspired by T'ao Ch'ien's *Peach Blossom Spring*.

Lifting his robe and
Taking large steps Chang rushed forward
To push open the gate.
Just then someone surprised him from behind.
Alas, what was Chang to do?

Coda

An imposing figure seven and a half feet tall,
Seized Chang with one hand and
Dragged him quickly into a willow grove.

[Prose]

Indeed:
    'Concentrating on the adversary in front
    He left the enemy behind unguarded.'
Who seized Chang? Who was it? It was the monk Fa-ts'ung. Perplexed,
Chang asked for an explanation. The monk said: 'This compound is private,
Sir. Please go elsewhere.' Chang retorted: 'I intend to see all the sights in the
temple. Why can I not go in there?' Fa-ts'ung said: 'Madam Ts'ui, wife of the late
Prime Minister, now lives within.'

(*Hsien-lü-tiao* mode)

Cherishing the Chrysanthemum

Seeing that Chang was annoyed,
Fa-ts'ung soothed him:
'Honestly,
There's nothing worth seeing inside.
I haven't detained you out of perverseness.
Let me explain:
These buildings have no religious significance.

For a while they were dormitories;
Recently they became guest houses.
Prime Minister Ts'ui's family
Resides in them now.'
Chang said: 'What nonsense!'
There must be rare and precious sights.
I'll brave death to get in.

Coda

'Stop your excuses and
Pretended explanations.
You claim the Ts'ui family lives inside.
How is it that just now
Kuan-yin[35] herself appeared before me?'

[Prose]

The monk smiled: 'Sir, you are wrong. It was not Kuan-yin who appeared
before you; it was the daughter of Minister Ts'ui.'

Chang asked: 'With such a beautiful daughter why are the Ts'uis staying
here and not in an inn?'

Fa-ts'ung said: 'Madam Ts'ui is a high-born lady whose father was Minister
Cheng. She maintains strict discipline in her household. Every manservant
and maid has assigned duties. Should a servant be called to the inner court,
he knows better than to raise his eyes and look around. Absolute order and
decorum are insisted upon. Since commercial inns teem with all sorts of
people, Madam Ts'ui prefers to stay here in the temple.'

Chang then inquired: 'When do they plan to leave?'

Fa-ts'ung said: 'That I do not know. But I do know that in a few days
they will hold a service for the late Minister. You see, it is not propitious to
inter the Minister this year, so Madam Ts'ui has had the coffin placed in one
of the pavilions, while she, her young daughter and son, meticulously observe
the mourning rites. When a year has expired, they will travel to the capital
and bury the Minister there. Till then, they must keep their vigil here in the
temple.'

How do I know such things actually happened? They are corroborated by
The Ballad of The True Story of Ying-ying written by the T'ang poet Li Shen.[36]
The Ballad sings:

When shrikes fly slowly and swallows swift,
When willow turns golden and flowers glow,
A pampered damsel called Ying-ying
Reaches the age of seventeen.
Her father has died, her mother's alive;

---

[35] Goddess of Mercy.

[36] 李紳, appellation Kung-ch'ui 公垂 (?–846), a friend of Yüan Chen. The last
paragraph of Yüan's *Ying-ying chuan* in fact mentions that Li wrote *Ying-ying ko* (*The
Ballad of Ying-ying*). The ballad no longer survives in its entirety; in what form it was
extant at Master Tung's time is not known. Tung quotes from it four times, forty-two lines
in all, and judging from the content, these lines represent less than half of the ballad.
Ch'üan T'ang shih 全唐詩 preserves only the first eight lines. (*Ch'üan T'ang shih*,
Shanghai, 1887, 18.41a.)

19

Solitary and aloof this lotus white
Ignores spring, the blossoms' dazzle,
And sequesters herself in a Buddhist temple.

(*Ta-shih-tiao* mode)

Fording a Mountain Stream

Fa-ts'ung repeatedly exhorted Chang:
'Cease your vain imagining, sir,
And listen to me.
Surely I wouldn't lie to you.
The beauty you just saw
Is the daughter of Minister Ts'ui.
She must be sixteen or seventeen.
Her name is Ying-ying.
In no manner did you witness the apparition of Kuan-yin.'

Hearing this
Chang became even more restless.
He seemed, in fact, nearly insane.
He said the same thing, asked the same questions over and over again.
That he was incoherent
Didn't bother him;
He chattered on and on.
Until finally gongs were sounded
To announce the noon-day meal.

[Prose]

As Chang talked with Fa-ts'ung, a novice came to invite Chang to lunch. He
was presented to the abbot Fa-pen. When Fa-pen saw that Chang wore a
scholar's robe and looked unusually refined, he came down from his seat and
returned Chang's salutation with a Buddhist bow.

(*Hsien-lü-tiao* mode)

Lingering in the Perfumed Quilt

Fa-pen quickly left his seat
And adjusted his embroidered vestment.
Chang bowed;
The abbot returned his salute; and

They sat down in the proper places.
When the vegetarian meal was served,
Every dish
Was more delicious than meat or fowl.

Although Chang was hungry
He was too agitated
To eat
Or swallow.
Presently lunch was over and the trays removed.
The abbot ordered tea.
Hot water poured into a silver flask:
On snow-white waves flowers opened and floated.

Coda

The papered windows were translucent.
The abbot's room was furnished with taste.
Having finished their tea
They chatted amiably.

[Prose]

Finding each other congenial, they behaved like old friends. Fa-pen inquired about Chang's background and Chang said: 'I am trained in Confucian scholarship and I intend to take the next metropolitan examination. At present I am traveling in the provinces to seek advice from men of discernment. I chanced to come to your temple and am delighted by the silence here. If it is possible, I would like to rent a room to review my studies.'

(*Pan-she-tiao* mode)

Nocturnal Visit to the Palace

Chang replied thus:
'I'm a poor scholar from Hsi-lo
Taking a study tour in the provinces.
I happened to come to P'u-chou,
Thence to your temple.

The moment I arrived, I felt liberated from petty worries.
May I have a study here?
Of course, I shall pay full rent.
Reverend abbot,
Please grant my request.'

[Prose]

Chang said: 'At the end of each month, I shall pay you 2000 coins as rent. Would you accept this offer, Master?'

(*Ta-shih-tiao* mode)

A Southern Air

> Seeing that the abbot liked him
> Chang urged:
> 'Please allow me
> To stay here for two or three months
> So as to review the poems and books I've studied.'
> Without the abbot's consent
> I wouldn't have this story to tell you today.

[Prose]

Fa-pen replied: 'We Buddhists are not concerned with making money. Besides, there are many spare rooms in the temple. You may eat with us in the refectory; I shall provide you with two meals a day and you will give me three months of good conversation! Why pay rent? That's much too vulgar!'

(*Ta-shih-tiao* mode)

A Southern Air

> 'Sir, you're wrong to offer me rent.
> We Buddhists and Confucians are of one family.
> As things stand, I can't give you
> A place in our dormitory,
> But you're welcome to stay
> In one of the guest apartments.'

[Prose]

Chang replied: 'You are very kind, reverend abbot. Your generous proposal would be acceptable if I were to stay here only a day or two. But since I intend to stay until winter, it would be far too much of a burden to you. So far as I am concerned, if you do not accept rent, I will not stay. I have here fifty ounces of silver, barely enough to defray part of your expenses for tea.'

Fa-pen refused.

22

Chang left the silver and rose to leave. The abbot tried to detain him. Chang paid no attention and stalked off.

The abbot realized then that Chang was a person who valued probity more than money: a person whose friendship he ought to cultivate. He asked the monk in charge of the household affairs to take Chang to an apartment behind the pagoda. The place was quiet and pleasant. Chang ordered his servant to fetch the luggage.

(*Chung-lü-tiao* mode)

Green Peonies

> A small suite with a closed door,
> The apartment was hidden from view.
> The few rooms were
> Furnished with simple, good taste.
> Their austere elegance
> Dispelled all worldly thoughts.
> Translucent paper windows,
> Fine, textured Hsiang mats,[37] and
> Hanging screens made of sparsely woven bamboo splints.
>
> Evening brought a brief shower.
> Swallows twittered and orioles cried.
> By the rockeries,
> Were scattered two or three well-pruned bamboos.
> An excellent place for a recluse.
> Nothing vulgar in these rooms:
> There were a few paper paravents,
> Some ink-wash paintings,
> And one earthen-ware incense burner.

Coda

> What else would keep Chang company?
> An inkwell, a writing brush, sheets of paper.
> A zither on the wall and books on the table.

[Prose]

> When he was free, he could talk with the abbot in the monk's cell.
> When he was bored, he could chant a poem to the moon above the
>   western chamber.

[37] Mats woven of Hsiang - speckled - bamboo splints.

Evening came, the night was as bright as day. Chang walked to the court where Ying-ying lived and chanted a short poem of twenty characters. The poem said:

> A dazzling, luminous, glorious night,
> A flower-shadowed silent spring.
> Why is the lunar goddess
> Invisible in the moon's radiant ring?

He then strolled around the court.

(*Chung-lü-tiao* mode)

Falcon Attacking a Hare

> Cloudless blue sky.
> Perfect moon: a suspended mirror.
> Chang sauntered up
> To Ying-ying's court.
> The temple was quiet,
> Nothing stirred on the verandas.
> Flower shadows criss-crossed, moving confusedly
> In the chilly east wind.
> Inspired by the sight
> Chang chanted softly
> A poem to express his feelings.
>
> He felt lonelier, sadder,
> After the poem.
> The sky glowed with indifferent moonlight;
> The ground was dark with mute flower-shadows.
> His melancholy
> Knew no bounds . . .
> Suddenly a noise
> Attracted his attention.
> A gate was opening;
> A subtle perfume permeated the air;
> He turned and looked: there was Ying-ying.

Coda

> Her beautiful face held every charm.
> Emerging from the gate, she came forward slowly.
> Even the lunar goddess Ch'ang-o was not as attractive.

[Prose]

No clouds drift in the sky,
They have gathered in her bouffant coiffure.
No color decorates the water,
The greenness now adorns her eyebrows.
Weary of restraint, the spring Beauty
Has flown from the lunar palace!
Her beauty is but dimly perceived;
Her low-cut lapels reveal her charm.
Her gauze sleeves flap; her brocade skirt swishes;
Yet she herself makes no sound at all.
She looks like Lady Hsiang,[38]
Leaning against Shun temple's red door.
She resembles the goddess Ch'ang-o
Appearing at the moon's jade gate.

(*Hsien-lü-tiao* mode)

Straightening a Flowered Cap

Charming, oh so charming.
Her colors were exquisite.
Tiny crimson lips.
Curved green eyebrows.
With infinite grace
She crossed over the sill.
Her slender fingers
Plucked a trembling flower.

A low cap became her well.
She smiled with happiness.
Her slim waist — a dancer's —
Could be held in one hand.
Her ample skirt was cut shorter in the front.
A pair of minute bow-shoes[39] on her feet.
What elegance! It was enough to drive one mad!

[38] Either O-huang 娥皇 or Nü-ying 女英 , consorts of the legendary Emperor Shun 舜 . Both are stock symbols of feminine beauty and charm.
[39] 弓鞋 , slippers for bound feet.

Coda

> A tight-fitting jacket
> Set her shapely figure to advantage.
> Again and again, she bowed to the moon.

[Prose]

> What could be on her mind
> As she straightened her dress and bowed to the moon?

The young lady also chanted a poem, using the same rhyme as Chang. The poem said:

> Alone in my secluded chamber,
> I have no way to celebrate spring.
> Will the chanting poet who strolls past
> Take pity and calm my sighing?

Chang was surprised and enchanted.

(*Hsien-lü-tiao* mode)

An Embroidered Belt

> Concealed by the flower shadow
> Chang leans against a low fence.
> The moon shines brilliantly,
> With abandon.
> He fixes his eyes on Ying-ying,
> And studies her carefully.
> Her beauty,
> Reinforced by her chanting,
> Drives him wild.
> She has responded to his poem!
> Her voice is like an oriole's warble.
> Her lips quiver with emotion.
> Little does she expect
> That the person standing under the flowers is deeply moved.
>
> The poem makes him mad with joy.
> He notices with delight that only a stone's throw separates them.
> Tossing caution, prudence to the winds,
> Behaving like a lunatic,
> He lifts his robe
> And rushes to her side.

26

The young lady
Blushes shyly
And trembles with fright.
Yes, Chang of Ch'ing-ho
Is half-crazed,
He doesn't see that someone is coming.
Someone calls out:
'How dare you accost a respectable young lady!'

Coda

Shoulders heaving, panting furiously,
In no time at all, the newcomer is there, standing before Ying-ying.
Alas, a romance, ordained in heaven, is shattered.

[Prose]

This is an excellent example of:
'Lovers rarely have an opportunity to meet.
A romance is always plagued by setbacks.'
Who had come? Who had come? Chang looked. It was Ying-ying's maid
Hung-niang. Ying-ying asked her why she had come.

(*Hsien-lü-tiao* mode)

Flower-Viewing Time

Beautiful Ying-ying was astounded.
She wondered: 'Why is Hung-niang in such a hurry?
I'll bet Mother has sent her here.'
Hung-niang said in a low voice:
'Madam wishes my lady to retire.'

[Prose Insert]

She urged Ying-ying to return with her.

Chang was distraught with anguish.
Perhaps it would have been better
Had he never laid eyes on Ying-ying.
But suffering of this nature can't be avoided;
It's caused by evil karma: he must have wronged her in an
earlier incarnation.

27

Coda

> East wind wrought havoc among the blossoms; fallen petals
>   covered the yard.
> The beauty vanished behind a red gate.
> 'My dear, I suppose I haven't the luck to be your lover.'

[Prose]

Dejected, Chang returned to his rooms. He did not sleep that night.

(*Ta-shih-tiao* mode)

Moon Atop the Plum Tree

> 'A chance encounter
> Made me fall hopelessly in love.
> While clearly it would have been far better
> Not to have met her at all,
> The harm is done: I've seen her.
> Her passionate eyes continue to disturb me.
> I can't sleep.
> Outside, the whippoorwill laments to the moon.
> Wretched bird, he makes me feel worse.
>
> 'How can I explain my sorrow?
> I should probably forget her. But she's so lovely!
> My heart is still frantic with excitement,
> Though my bowels are twisted ninefold with grief.
> If only I could regain the innocuous boredom of last night!
> But this bitter sorrow I know I shall taste again and again.
> I must have shortchanged her in a previous love affair,
> Now I'll pay with my life.'

[Prose]

From this time onward Chang ceased to consider

> Advancement in the world as desirable,
> Wealth and fame as worthwhile,
> Integrity and uprightness as essential virtues,
> Or right and wrong the guide for actions.
> At night he did not sleep,
> During the day he did not eat.

28

His clothes became disorderly,
He himself was in a daze.
That is how much he admired Ying-ying.

(*Ta-shih-tiao* mode)

Jade-Winged Cicada

He remembered Fa-ts'ung
Warn him with an ominous frown:
'The Minister's wife is very stern.
She runs a well-disciplined home.'
So she's not someone he'd dare to offend.
The thought depressed him.
Unable to see Ying-ying
He lost all interest
In his studies.
Absent-minded, distracted, he behaved like a madman.

Water dried in his ink-well.
Dust covered his books.
He devised thousands of schemes to see her.
None was successful.
Though the gate to her court
Remained closed,
He would pass and repass it
Stealthily, on tiptoe.
Words of longing
Filled sheets of embellished stationery
Which no one, alas, dared to deliver.
It was indeed:
'The short distance between the lovers
Is as unbridgeable as an abyss.'

[Prose]

Bamboos should not have been planted outside the guest rooms.
They make such distressing sounds in rain and in wind.

(*Shuang-tiao* mode)

Bean-Leaf Yellow

A cloudy spring day,

Suitable for flower-brewing.
A light rain drizzled.
Gusts rose and fell.
Outside the latticed window,
Next to the peony bush,
The colors were especially bright.
Flowers a deep crimson,
Willow leaves a delicate green.

The nectar-gathering bees
Flew in pairs.
Cunning yellow orioles
Played in twos.
Seeing this Chang was overwhelmed with grief.
'It's spring, but I'm ill.
Within the four seas I have no home!
Singly I drift and roam.

Tuning the Zither and the Lute

'Tears of sorrow
Tears of sorrow
Which wiping can't stop.
How can I describe the misery of illness,
The wretchedness of sleeping alone?
My vigor, my health
Is seriously injured
By this cold, indifferent beauty.

'So much charm
In so young a woman.
She is perfect,
Perfect.
Her beautiful face
Is complemented by a delightful name —
Among birds and insects, the most affectionate
Is the oriole, the *ying-ying.*
Its body is covered with golden silk.
But obviously
I am not fortunate enough
To deserve a love such as she.

Rejoice in the Great Harmony

> 'Fame and wealth no longer attract me.
> I'm thinner every day.
> Languid, I lean on my pillow,
> Feeling sick to my bones.
> I try to send her a *billet-doux*:
> What I write is all muddled.
> I want to fly to her, but I've no wings.
> When can I see you?

Coda

> 'I tell myself to forget her.
> I refuse to admit that I'm haggard —
> The bronze mirror shows me the truth.'

[Prose]

> A hundred devices
> Failed to gain him an interview.
> A thousand contrivances
> Won him not a rendezvous.

(*Cheng-kung* mode)

The Beautiful Lady Yü, ch'an

> 'Just now a passing shower,
>   my zither strings are supple and moist.
> The leafy dragon-incense has burnt to ashes.
> A melancholy moment.
> I dread the approach of evening —
> Then, suddenly, evening is here.
>
> I'm wasted, gaunt; my robe has become loose.
> I fear others' inquisitive questions.
> The door stays closed to my lonely study.
> I raise a pearl blind
> To watch the clouds move.

31

Ying-t'ien-ch'ang

  'Nothing can undo the knot on my brow.
  New sorrow adds to old grief.
  New sorrow has new ways.
  My tears simply will not stop;
  My face is perpetually wet;
  The pain, the anguish refuse to abate;
  And my vitality is sapped.

  'How often have I written her!
  The letters are undelivered.
  I'm despondent with frustration.
  I must have used
  Reams upon reams of paper.
  But no messenger appears, not even in my dreams.
  Once I hurt you,
  Now you hurt me.

The Platform with Gold

  'If I hadn't met her I wouldn't be so unhappy.
  O misery, misery!
  When shall I be well again?
  Is there medicine for this malady?
  I barely touch
  My meals.
  Every hour and minute of the day,
  I keep to my room.

Coda

  'Sight-seeing is boring; strolling is dull.
  I feel dizzy when I sit; I can't sleep well.
  Leaning on my shagreen pillow, I doze away the day.'

[Prose]

Chang was very much troubled after his encounter with Ying-ying. One day as he was on the point of falling asleep, he heard someone open his door. A novice entered to say: 'My master would like to invite you to tea.' Chang rose; apathetically, he went to the abbot's cell.

32

Ying-t'ien-ch'ang

    The room was simple and austere.
    A rattan cushion,
    A meditation bench,
    Desk with sutras,
    And an eartherware incense burner,
    Bamboo shadows moved on the window;
    Landscape paintings decorated the screens.
    An exquisite young tea was brewing in the silver flask.
    Not only did it allay thirst, it removed worries and cares.
    The novice,
    The abbot,
    And Chang
    Were the only ones there.

    Fellow recluses,
    They talked of nothing worldly.
    The revered abbot,
    The acclaimed Confucian
    Exchanged erudite remarks
    In polished language.
    Indeed: 'One evening's good conversation
    Is more valuable than ten years of reading.'

Coda

    Engrossed in their talk, they were surprised to see
    The door open.
    A girl entered and curtsied politely.

[Prose]

    Peach Blossom Cave had long been inaccessible.
    But now the goddess within had ventured out.
Chang looked carefully and recognized the girl as the one who urged
Ying-ying's return the other evening.

(*Pan-she-tiao* mode)

Flowers above the Wall

    Although a serving maid
    She moved with remarkable grace.

So spirited, so attractive.
Her eyebrows were painted in the palace style.
She wore a loosely coiled 'share-joy' chignon.

Her skirt, gathered around her slender waist,
Fell all the way to the ground.
Her beautiful face
Held infinite charm.
She had tiny rosy lips and
Swiftly-moving intelligent eyes.

Her makeup was subtle
And quiet.
Her white clothes
Showed a state of mourning.
She saw Chang, started to speak, but instead, lowered her head.
She looked at the monk, feigned seriousness, yet could not suppress
    a smile.

Coda

After curtsying
She said gently:
'Madam Ts'ui requests a memorial service for tomorrow.'

[Prose]

Fa-pen remarked that he would order the superintendent to make the necessary preparations. Hung-niang started to leave.

Chang stopped her, saying: 'Pardon me for being so bold, but may I ask why I have not seen maid-servants come out of the Ts'ui's residence?'

'Obviously there are reasons unknown to you, sir.'

'May I know what they are?'

'Well, you see, Madam Ts'ui runs a highly disciplined home. Her strictness is well-known in the capital. Just to cite an example, a few nights ago, when the moon was brilliant, our young lady Ying-ying left the court alone for a moment. Her absence was discovered by Madam who immediately asked me to bring her back. When we returned, without the slightest show of motherly affection, Madam stood Ying-ying in front of the dais and scolded her: "You are an attractive girl. You must know when you leave the court on a bright night like this you will be noticed by young monks and guests in the temple. Have you no shame?!" Ying-ying was mortified. She wept and apologized and assured her mother that she would never do it again. Though she had enough courage to utter her promise, she was altogether too frightened to look at her

34

mother. Madam can be extremely forbidding. Now, if the young lady of the house must keep within the court, would we servants dare to venture abroad?'

At this, Hung-niang took her leave.

Chang said to Fa-pen: 'I have here five thousand coins. May I participate in the service tomorrow and have prayers said for my late father?'

'Certainly,' replied the abbot.

(*Chung-lü-tiao* mode)

The Frontier Pass Where Sheep Graze

> 'Just now Hung-niang too says that
> Madam Ts'ui is
> Strict, severe, and
> Relentlessly vigilant.
> So, there *can* be no way to send
> Ying-ying a message.
> Heavens, heavens!
> Only a miracle
> Could bring us together.

> 'I doze lethargically by the window sill.
> My frustration grows and grows.
> I can't extricate myself from this agony.
> I'm helpless, perplexed; there is nothing I can do.
> If I get her it's my good fortune.
> If I lose her it's my fate.
> Evening is approaching again —
> What insufferable misery.

Coda

> 'When I see her tomorrow
> I will look my fill.
> That, at least, will partly compensate for my suffering.'

[Prose]

Chang muttered to himself: 'Tomorrow I shall see you at the service!' Thinking of Ying-ying, he could not sleep.

(*Chung-lü-tiao* mode)

Green Peonies

> Though it's spring, it's still cold,
> Plum trees on the hills are blooming.
> As the night moves on, a sheet of ice forms
> In the jade clepsydra.
> 'Trouble-laden, my mind
> Ruminates on recent events.
> My grief is like unbreakable skeins of silk.
> My sorrow is like tightly-woven fine brocades, and
> The night, slow-moving, is like a year.

> 'Since I saw her
> I haven't touched any books.
> Days are spent
> Expressing my longing on paper.
> I lack strength
> To stop this obsession.
> I appeal to heaven, but heaven . . .
> Heaven is mute.
> Can one chastise heaven?

Coda

> 'Not one day is my mind at ease.
> Not one hour is she out of my thoughts.
> Not one night is she out of my dreams.'

[Prose]

At long last, dawn arrived. Chang saw all was ready for the service.

(*Yüeh-tiao* mode)

The Emperor Pacifying the West

> The moon sets,
> Cocks crow,
> Eastern horizon becomes dimly visible.
> From Fu-sang[40] the sun musters its energy and gradually rises.
> Believers from all walks of life,
> Townsmen and villagers alike,
> Come to the temple for the service,
> They've closed their shops and locked up their stores.

[40] 扶桑, mythical tree in the east from whose branches the sun is said to rise.

Some visit the sutra chambers,
The pagoda,
The Buddha-hall;
Some wait on the veranda.
Others crowd about the dais,
Or admire statues of Hades' kings.
Offerings pile high on the altar.
Golden pennants glitter amid incense and flowers.
The service will deliver the Minister's soul
From hell and damnation.

Fighting Quails

Fa-ts'ung makes a final check,
Then sounds the cymbal and drum.
Monks congregate like clouds
In front of the altar.
There are Fa-wu,
Fa-k'ung,
Hui-ming,
Hui-lang . . .
Solemn,
Stately,
They face icons of heavenly hosts.

Neatly they
Stand in lines.
If they had haloes,
They'd be mistaken for gods themselves.
Fa-pen goes up to the altar;
All watch him with respect.
Everyone bows,
Hands pressed together.
Reverently they pay obeisance to the various gods.

Green Mountain Pass

An elderly lady comes forward, supported by serving maids.
Dressed in deep mourning,
She looks over sixty.
Her hair is white as frost.
She salutes the monks, then
Prostrates herself before the statue of Buddha.
To her left stands a boy attended by a servant,

To her right, a young lady whose every movement is nimble
     and graceful.
The young lady lifts up her veil and
Reveals a face indescribably beautiful.
She wears little makeup:
Her natural beauty is in itself startling.
Her hair is parted on the side,
Her curved eyebrows are trim and long.
No jewelry,
A simple white suit,
But what elegance, what style!

Plum Tree in the Snow

The monks and visitors are taken aback.
They fix their gaze on her.
The chanting stops;
The service founders;
No one remembers to burn incense.

Gentry, farmers, craftsmen and merchants
All press forward to look.
The old, the young,
The handsome, the ugly,
Everyone jostles and stares.

Old monks itch with desire,
Young monks sooth their burning crowns with both hands.
Fa-t'ang is transfixed,
Fa-pao turns berserk, and
Chih-kuang becomes paralyzed.

Coda

The acolyte in charge of incense behaves crazily.
The monk who strikes the chimes misses several beats.
The priest who assists at the service forgets his duty.
No one heeds the abbot.
Pandemonium
Breaks loose.
The presence of Ying-ying
Thoroughly disrupts the ceremony.

[Prose]

For the monks,
Their arduously maintained chastity threatens to come to an end.
For the novices,
Their strenuously observed abstinence will soon be history.
If the rest were so affected, what do you think happened to Chang?

(*Ta-shih-tiao* mode)

A Southern Air

Totally bewitched,
Chang would gladly violate *all eight* commandments.[41]
No longer evincing a suitable reverence for Buddha and
Setting aside the last shred of self-restraint,
He begins to perform
Extravagant and outlandish antics.
What bizarre capers!
Indeed what bizarre capers!

He becomes wilder and wilder.
His neighbours try to calm him, with no success.
The abbot watches from afar.
Chang squirms and twists in his seat.
He ogles Ying-ying and
Makes signs with his eyes.
But the young lady
Completely ignores him.
She completely ignores him.

Coda

'My cruel, my hateful love.
I don't deserve such torture.
My eyes must be paying a debt incurred in our last lives.'

[Prose]

After the evening meal, the service was resumed.

[41] The eight proscriptions of Buddhism, against killing of animals, theft, fornication, lying, drinking, sitting on high and large beds, wearing flowers and fringes, and learning to sing, dance, or play entertainer's music.

(*Pan-she-tiao* mode)

A Whistle Song, ch'an-ling

The evening service
Is attended by the faithful
Alongside the monks.
Incense wafts above jewelled animal-tripods.
To the accompaniment of golden chimes,
The monks bow,
Press together their palms,
And manifest their adherence
To the Buddha.
Madam Ts'ui, despite her age,
Observes assiduously every rite.
Ying-ying, though a girl,
Shows filial piety hard to emulate.
Unceasingly she prays
For the soul
Of her deceased father.

The outrageous young scholar
Again behaves like a lunatic.
He has wholly taken leave of his senses.
Not caring what he does,
He utters pure gibberish.
Undaunted by Madam Ts'ui,
Unabashed by others' sneers,
He jokes flippantly while they pray.
When scriptures are chanted
He sings love-songs out of time and out of key.
Yes, all young scholars are crazy,
But this one has no peer —
He must be the craziest.

A Fast Melody

Why doesn't he leave?
He's driving everyone to distraction.
The monk Chih-shen says with concern:
'Master Chang, please don't get angry—
But wouldn't you prefer sleeping in your room,
To making such a scene here?'

> Chang pays no attention.
> With half-closed eyes he sits idiotically.
> From time to time, he resumes his buffoonery.

[Prose]

Finally sunrise approached. The service ended; the monks asked Madam Ts'ui to burn the written prayer.

(*Shang-tiao* mode)

Calming Agitated Waves

> As the prayer burnt
> Ying-ying was moved to tears:
> A pear-flower awash with rain.
> Madam Ts'ui, too, couldn't control her sobs.
> The sight was too much for Chang.
> He withdrew unnoticed.
>
> After seeing the Ts'ui family off,
> Fa-pen and the monks
> Supervised the servants
> Put vessels and wares away.
> Suddenly from the side door a young monk rushed in.
> Taking giant steps, he ran forward.

Coda

> His open mouth, his bulging eyes, his clay-colored face
> Terrified and petrified the abbot and monks.
> Panting heavily the young monk spoke.

[Prose]

When day broke and the service was over, a young monk rushed in and cried urgently: 'Disaster! Disaster!'

Chapter 2

(*Hsien-lü-tiao* mode)

Trimming the Silver Lamp

Stopping before the steps, the young monk gushed:
'What a fearful sight:
Tumultuous dust seals the sky;
Fluttering banners conceal the sun;
A shower of fine earth rains down from all directions!
Gongs are clashing; drums are rolling;
Lances and swords surge pell-mell
All around our temple!

'One glimpse at the chief bandit
Is enough to freeze you with terror.
He wears a scarlet turban, covered with
Pearls, like rice clinging to the sides of a vat,
Two suits of lion-hide armor,
A pair of green boots
And his mount is a dragon-like
Curly-maned *Ch'ih-t'u.*[42]

Coda

'A yellow birch crossbow arches over his arm,
A mountain-cleaving axe, big as a winnowing fan,
        rests on his shoulder,
He's none other than Flying Tiger Sun, the bridge-guarding general!'

[Prose]

During the T'ang dynasty, troops were stationed in the P'u prefecture.[43] The year of our story, the commander of the garrison, Marshal Hun, died. Because the second-in-command, Ting Wen-ya, did not have firm control of

---

[42] The name of a famous charger owned by Lü Pu (second century A.D.), the Three-Kingdoms warrior.
[43] The text has '*P'u kuan*' (P'u pass). Due to later inconsistencies in the chapter, I am obliged to change the translation to 'P'u prefecture'.

the troops, Flying Tiger Sun, a subordinate general, rebelled with five thousand soldiers. They pillaged and plundered the P'u area.

How do I know this to be true? It is corroborated by *The Ballad of the True Story of Ying-ying.* The *Ballad* says:

> Bridge-side garrison loses its chief,
> Banners and halberds topple in a heap.
> Ere a new head is announced,
> Soldiers mutiny and crowd into town.
> Husbands proffer silk and jade,
> So wives from injury may escape.
> But how can the beauties flee and hide
> When everywhere rebels gallop and riot?
> Mothers cry and wail to heaven.
> Holding daughters they part with ornaments.
> Abandoning rouge to lessen their charm,
> Maidens seem effigies, pale and wan.

(*Cheng-kung* mode)

Master Wen-hsü, ch'an

[The young monk continued]

> 'Reverend elders
> Cease your commotion, and
> Hear me while I explain:
> Marshal Hun Chen
> Recently passed away.
> The bridge-guarding Wen-ya is a profligate.
> He's incompetent;
> His troops mutinied and
> Proceeded to terrorize the countryside.
> City walls and moats, one after the other, are overrun and destroyed.

> 'The insurgents loot and plunder; they
> Seize women and girls.
> None dare oppose them, since
> Rioters don't know right from wrong,
> White from black.
> In the town of P'u, the southern district and the northern ward
>   have been burnt to ashes;
> Booty is carted away;
> Highways and byways
> Are mounds of corpses and seas of blood.

43

Licorice Root

'They wreak a terrible havoc.
Oh, they wreak a terrible havoc.
The rebel-chief's
Crimes are as vast as the sky.
Intrepid, fearless,
He does battle in a heavy coat of mail.
With his military might
He thinks he can overthrow the T'ang.
It will be pure luck if he leaves us alone.
But if not, how can we resist?

Removing the Cotton Garment

'How can we resist?
The thought confounds me.
We're really in a fix. —
Do I hear more troops approach? . . .'

Coda

Within an hour,
Waves of soaring dust have fully eclipsed the sun,
Five thousand bandits throng outside.

[Prose]

The monks had no time to make any preparations. All they could do was to close the temple gate. The bandits beat on the gate with their swords and sent arrows into the temple. One of them shouted: 'We don't want anything else; we just want a meal.' The abbot said to the monks: 'I think we had better open the gate and invite them in. They can stay in the prayerhalls and on the verandas. After giving them a meal, we can soften them up with bribes, so that they will not hurt us. Otherwise, I am afraid they may force their way in, and kill us all. Does my suggestion appeal to you?'

The monk Chih-shen, the superintendent, replied: 'Inviting the bandits in will not harm *us* in any way. But at present we have in the temple Madam Ts'ui's daughter Ying-ying, who is a beautiful girl. If the bandits saw her, they would certainly kidnap her. Minister Ts'ui had many relatives and friends who enjoy imperial favors and occupy important positions. Once Ying-ying is captured, we shall certainly suffer for it. For, although it would be the bandits who had seized her, the fault would be ours for having opened the gate to them. When we are charged with complicity, what can we say in our own defense?'

(*Ta-shih-tiao* mode)

Kun Section of [the Elaborate Melody] I-chou

In the prayer hall
The monks discussed
Whether they should invite the bandits in.
The superintendent said no,
And gave his reasons in detail:
'What shall we do
If the rebels
Should capture Ying-ying?
When the news becomes known
We're sure to share the fate of vanishing waters.'

'What can be done then?' the abbot asked.
'The bandits are at the gate, and
We've no way to fight them.'
From the ranks a monk
Thundered out his angry cry:
'Have no fear, abbot.
You other monks, you three hundred and more,
Jabbering is all you do.
Despite your size, you're helpless babes.
Your chow has been wasted on you, you good-for-nothings.'

Coda

Lifting his frayed Buddhist robe,
Raising his three-foot consecrated sword,
He said: 'Let me put my life on the line and fight
    this horde of thieves.'

[Prose]

Who was this monk? He was none other than Fa-ts'ung. Fa-ts'ung was a descendant of a tribesman from western Shensi. When he was young he took great pleasure in archery, fencing, hunting, and often sneaked into foreign states to steal. He was fierce and courageous. When his parents died, it suddenly became clear to him that the way of the world was frivolous and trivial, so he became a monk in the Temple of Universal Salvation.

'My mind is made up. As long as we are menaced, I will not sit back and watch. For such is not the way of a humane person. If my valiant brothers will help me, we can easily defeat the rebels. In fact, they will dissolve on their own, like a shaken grain-stalk snapping into bits. Actually, only two or three mutineers have a seditious intent; the rest have been tricked into following. While they see the spoils before their eyes they are blind to the dire consequences waiting around the corner. If I can explain to them the gains and the losses, most of them will lose their desire to fight and will disperse.'

(*Hsien-lü-tiao* mode)

An Embroidered Belt

> He didn't know how to read sutras;
> He didn't know how to follow rituals;
> He was neither pure nor chaste
> But was indomitably courageous . . .
> Formerly he had often killed
> Without batting an eye.
> After becoming a monk,
> He left his iron cudgel
> Unsharpened for years.
> His consecrated sword
> Had slain tigers and dragons.
> But once he tired of shedding blood,
> It hung neglected
> On the wall.

> The sword's ram-horn hilt was sealed to the sheath by grime.
> Its icy blade and point had dulled.
> Fa-ts'ung called out: 'Fellow monks,
> Who will follow me?
> Have no fear,
> I guarantee there'll be no risk.'
> To himself he thought:
> 'Today I'll have meat to eat and
> My cudgel will sharpen itself on the thieves.'
> He stood by the veranda
> And counted the gathering monks:
> 'Tough and fierce men
> Who dare to fight.
> You need only shout to cheer me on.
> No danger will befall you.

Coda

'Just open the gate and aid me with war yells,
And I'll mow down the thieves with my sword.
Let them be pastry fillings for our meal!'

[Prose]

A penchant to kill
Has changed into a desire to save;
A former ruffian
Is now a praiseworthy hero.
Fa-ts'ung urged loudly: 'For our religion and for each other, we should do
our utmost. Those who dare help me fight, go to the right of the hall.' In a
short time nearly three hundred monks gathered by the hall, with cudgels
and swords in their hands. They said to Fa-ts'ung: 'We are willing to follow
you and fight to the death.'

(*Shuang-tiao* mode)

Wen-ju-chin

When you looked close you'd see
Fa-ts'ung had a ferocious mien:
Defiant, bold,
Somewhat irregular and somewhat strange.
His bull-like torso was hefty,
His tiger waist supple and long.
He wore a three-foot consecrated sword and
Carried an iron cudgel.
His horse was
An elephant without tusks.
Wearing a tight-fitting cloth corselet, he had
No armor, no helmet.
A full eight feet,
He was spendidly imposing.
A Buddhist Tzu-lu![44]
A tonsured Chin-kang!

His followers, more than two hundred,
Used weapons
Rarely seen.

[44] Confucius' disciple. In *The Analects* the Master says: 'Yu [Tzu-lu] is more inclined to
bravery than I.' (*Yu yeh, hao yung kuo wo.*) See *Shih-san ching,* 8/5/7, Shanghai, 1926.

Some had deep-set eyes;
Some looked savage and fierce.
Some brandished kitchen cleavers,
Rolling pins;
Some banged on temple drums and gongs.
They wore prayer pennants for armor,
Begging-bowls as helmets.
A few novices with disheveled hair
Dashed out of their cells in
Dark-brown clerical gowns.
Giving rein to pent-up valor,
They shouted. 'We too want
To fight on the battleground till the bitter end.'

Coda

Unwilling to follow Tripitaka to search for scriptures,
This lot shouldered brooms and canes to
Trail a homicidal monk!

[Prose]

Before the superintendent could caution prudence, Fa-ts'ung had already led his followers to the gate. Seeing the impressive enemy strength, he knew he could not defeat them easily. At once he dismounted and ascended the belfry to address the rebels in the hope of undermining their morale.

(*Pan-she-tiao* mode)

Spring in the Chin Garden

Closely dotting the vast fields,
Iron halberds pierced the sky,
Embroidered banners reflected the sun,
They formed the backdrop for
A mounted officer
Whose red brocade military cape covered
A suit of oil-glossy, jet-black armor.
Flat-nosed, hare-lipped, with
Thick eyebrows and large eyes,
The general carried on his shoulder a gigantic Ku-ting sword,[45]

[45] A sword wrought in Ku-ting, near P'u-yang hsien in Hopei.

Magnificent as a god,
He had a barrel chest, a bulky torso,
Massive thighs, thick buttocks and waist.

Virile, alert
He playfully prodded with his sword the jewelled stirrup of his mount.
And the warriors in his command? —
It's always difficult to describe
The panache of true heroes —
Some were short, some were tall,
Some thin, some fat.
But all were flawlessly stalwart and brave.
If you counted carefully,
They were less than six thousand,
But certainly five thousand and more.

Flowers above the Wall

In neat formations,
They tightly encircled
The temple's five-mile estate.
A third of them wore black cotton leggings;
Half had yellow-silk wadded jackets.

Their drums rumbled *tung-tung.*
The din of their horns spiraled and whirled.
Their banners danced in the wind, like brilliant tongues of fire.
The combat-urgers made earth-stunning, deafening roars;
The battle-criers uttered sky-lifting yells and shouts.

How could the temple withstand such an onslaught?
Solidly built,
Its walls were like stone ramparts.
The iron-bound gate was impregnable.
An almost impossible feat to get inside
And molest the monks.

Song of Che Tree Branches

Steel axes and swords hacked and hewed.
What cacophony, what confusion.
Politely Fa-ts'ung said to
The rebel general:

'We have no treasures,
Or food or fodder,
How can we offer adequate hospitality
To the immense troops in your command?

The Kun Section of [The Elaborate Melody] God of Longevity

'The court will soon hear of
Your treasonous deeds.
Armies will be dispatched
To quell you.
You're making a grave mistake.
When it's too late, even remorse won't help.
Think over what I say.'

The rebel general
Was outraged by these words.
'You bald-pated criminal, fit to be flogged,
How dare you contravene your lord's will?
We don't mean to
Impose on you monks.
Why should your unchaste lips make such a fuss?

A Fast Melody

'We don't want to take your temple.
We don't want to get your gold.
My men are tired and need a rest.
So why close your gate?
Of all the monks only you behave like a tiger, a leopard, and
Plague your father with tiresome chatter.

Coda

'Your hands should be cut off,
Brains knocked out,
Ears chopped off, and with legs tied,
You ought to be hung upside-down from the lintel till doomsday!'

[Prose]

Fa-ts'ung said: 'Compose yourself, compose yourself. We shall comply with your wishes. Since there are a few thousand of you, I shall be grateful if you

50

would retreat about a hundred paces, so that when the food is ready you can file in slowly, in an orderly way.'

The general said: 'Now that you agree to help us, I would be in the wrong if I didn't cooperate.'

Thereupon he ordered his troops to retreat a hundred paces. In the meantime, Fa-ts'ung came down from the belfry and mounted his horse.

(*Huang-chung-tiao* mode)

The Restless Oriole, ch'an-ling

> When the soldiers heard the order
> They retreated two or three hundred paces.
> Someone removed the cross-bar, the padlock,
>> and threw open the two panels of the temple gate.
> Fa-ts'ung shouted:
> 'Follow me!' and
> With this call
> All the monks plunged through the gate.
> Such a bizarre army was never seen before.

> Rash,
> Fearless,
> They thought nothing of their five thousand foes.
> Fa-ts'ung, holding his cudgel level with the ground,
> Raised his voice and menacingly yelled:
> 'Treasonous rebels!
> Send someone out to fight!
> There's no need for you to sink staves,
>> drive in posts, and make camp.

Ssu-men-tzu

> 'Our country hasn't treated you ill.
> Reckon for yourselves:
> The emperor gives you your uniforms, your food, and your pay.
> You don't know how lucky you are.
> Shame! Disgrace!
> The time is peaceful with no strife.
> Shame! Disgrace!
> You receive your wages without having to work.

> 'At Marshal Hun's death,
> You broke into a lawless mob.

You terrorized the people; you robbed them
    of their wealth and goods.
Now you want to ransack my temple.
Shame! Disgrace!
The food you demand I'll refuse —
Shame! Disgrace! —
I'd rather feed it to my ass.

Willow Leaves

'Why make a racket here?
You'd be better off guarding your mother's tomb.
I know what I say, I don't mean to frighten you,
My sons, it's time to surrender and yield.

Coda

'Wise or unwise,
I'll let you go.
If you don't leave
You'll taste the gall of my sixty-pound cudgel.'

[Prose]

Fa-ts'ung, galloping on his horse, shouted: 'I wish to see the commanding general.' An officer rode forth from the ranks and said to him: 'You are a Buddhist monk, you should be chanting sutras and meditating. Why are you here threatening and menacing us?'

Fa-ts'ung replied: 'You are soldiers and officers; our country pays you to keep peace on the frontier. You and your families receive food rations at the end of every month, and every season you are given new clothes. Not only are you spared the pain of hunger and cold, you are allowed to enjoy the bliss of family life. Now, temporarily deprived of guidance, you forget the great favor our country has conferred upon you, mercilessly you persecute innocent people and leave the whole prefecture in ruins. The court is not far; it will be informed presently; troops will arrive any moment. You yourselves will be reduced to pools of blood on the battlefield and your families will be condemned for complicity. After you are dead and your clans exterminated, what good is the loot? I think it would be wise for you to reflect on this.'

Spurring his horse forward, the rebel officer retorted: 'So, beside refusing us food, you have the impudence to harangue my men!'

Jade-Winged Cicada

> When the officer heard Fa-ts'ung's words,
> Even if he had been a Buddha, he would have been enraged.
> He ground and nearly broke his great wolf-like teeth.
> He scanned his men:
> 'Trusted soldiers
> Do as I bid.
> Help me with just one shout, and
> In one round I'll capture the bald-pated lout.'
> At this the rebels
> Rolled their drums and
> Vigorously waved their multicolored flags.
>
> Their yells penetrated the sky.
> In unison they blew their decorated horns.
> Worried clouds shielded the sun as
> The air of battle reached the firmament.
> The officer growled: 'You, monk,
> Quit your madness and just wait:
> Hold on to your cudgel;
> Sit tight on your saddle;
> Meditate on the Western Paradise.
> In seconds I'll perform the charitable deed
> Of sending you there
> With ten thousand strokes of my sword.'

Coda

> Before you could cover your ears, his horse had dashed ahead.
> A rainbow of dust trailed behind the hoofs.
> The rebel aimed his sword straight at the monk's nose.

[Prose]

A clashing sound was heard. Was the monk dead?

(*Ta-shih-tiao* mode)

Kun Section of [the Elaborate Melody] I-chou, ch'an-ling

> Hell-wind rises.
> The field is packed with lances and armor.

The air of battle darkens the sky.
Soldiers of six divisions yell and shout.
Before the banners, two mounted warriors fight.
The monk Fa-ts'ung,
Deftly defending himself,
Raises his cudgel to his eyebrow.
A clashing sound —
He wards off the slashing Ku-ting sword.

Dragon-like chargers, tiger-like warriors.
The cudgel twirls, the sword strikes,
In ways prescribed by *Martial Arts.* [16]
This combat will separate
The victor from the loser.
After three rounds
The rebel begins to tire.
What does he do?
He adopts a defensive posture and hides behind his sword.
It will be impossible now for him to overcome the monk.

A Red Gauze Garment

Doggedly he fights on,
Desperately he perseveres.
He's like a rabbit facing an eagle,
    a mouse running into a cat.
When finally he manages
A slight advantage
He tries to
Escape to his ranks.
Just then another mounted warrior flies forth,
Holding a spear twelve-feet long,
Dressed with bizarre extravagance that seems to
Add to his brutal ferocity.

The valiant monk
Has mastered the military arts well.
Though the second he fends off the spear the sword is upon him,
He remains confident, relaxed,
Calm, undaunted,
Serene, and cool.
His eyes are sharp, his movements brisk;

---

[46] *Liu-t'ao* 六 韜 (*Six Scabbards*), a pre-T'ang work on military craft.

His steed charges swiftly, his blows are precise and sure.
Circling round him, the two rebels pant and gasp.
They want to quit
But dread their men's jeers.

Coda

Fa-ts'ung's heart pounds violently.
He's furious; his eyes are heptagons, octagons.
The two rebels dare not approach him.

[Prose]

Six arms,
The one holding the cudgel is the strongest.
Three warriors,
The one wearing a helmet withdraws to rest.
The sword-wielder leaves the struggle,
The spear-thruster carries on the fight.

(*Cheng-kung* mode)

Master Wen-hsü

Having recovered his strength,
The sword-wielder puts on his armor again.
No threats are exchanged,
No question asked,
He lunges toward the monk to unhorse him.
The monk dodges and grasps the rebel's belt.
With no pity and
All his strength
He yanks the rebel over to his own horse
And smashes him down across the pommel of his saddle.

A shrill wail —
The rebel is sliding, head-down, through his belt!
Too weary to
Remount his tired horse,
Unable to keep up even the pretence of a hero,
He decides to flee.
Steering clear of
The monk
He sprints south to save his skin.

How to catch him?
How to catch him?
When Fa-ts'ung sees him escape,
His anger flares up.
Feigning to give chase,
He screams and yells thunderously.
Actually he doesn't budge,
His screams alone are terrifying enough.
All the rebels stare with unblinking eyes:
'This bald monk is unbelievably fierce!'

Coda

The monk now noisily taunts:
'You bandits, you criminals, how dare you rebel?
If anyone else is crazy enough to fight, come out this instant.'

[Prose]

Embroidered vanguard banners
Set loose in the wind hundreds of miles of morning clouds.
Rousing military drums
Exploded from the ground a thousand claps of thunderbolts.
One general was so incensed that he took up the challenge. Who was he?
Who was he?

(*Hsien-lü-tiao* mode)

Adorning Crimson Lips

This general
Is famous for his bravery.
Dissatisfied with his rank
He wants to rule the whole country.

Robust, ferocious:
People freeze when he appears.
Fa-ts'ung says to himself:
'I'll bet he always looks
Annoyed and angry.'

The 'hai-hai' Song

> Roly-poly, a portly belly,
> Triangular eyes, enormous nose, thick fleshy lips,
> His forehead is wide, his chin is broad, he has winged eyebrows,
> And a red beard.
> *Hai-hai.*

Wind Blowing Lotus Leaves

> Wearing a military cape with clouds and geese embroidered in gold,
> A pair of green, wolf-skin boots,
> He's superbly fitted out.
> The scarlet turban
> On his head
> Is decorated profusely with pearls.

The Inebriated Tartar Woman

> He wears two suits of armor.
> His courage is unsurpassed —
> Single-handedly he'd take on ten thousand foes.
> He's nicknamed Flying Tiger Sun.

Coda

> Carrying an iron-shafted crossbow,
> A quiver with a hundred pairs of steel arrows,
> He shoulders a mountain-cleaving axe as big as a winnowing fan.

[Prose]

> A moment ago this bandit held sway on the highway;
> Suddenly a challenger entered the chess game.[47]

(*Pan-she-tiao* mode)

A Pock-Marked Old Lady

> Flying Tiger is brave,
> Fa-ts'ung is stalwart.

[47] Similar parallel-line descriptions occur frequently in Chinese stories of Robin Hood type. The lines are inappropriate here as neither Fa-ts'ung nor Flying Tiger Sun is a highwayman. Master Tung seems to have simply borrowed them from the other tradition.

Flying Tiger likes to fight,
Fa-ts'ung refuses to yield.
Flying Tiger's out to sack the temple.
Fa-ts'ung's determined to crush the rebels.
Fa-ts'ung has a plan to subdue the insurgents,
Flying Tiger has a scheme to overthrow the throne.

Fa-ts'ung uses an iron cudgel,
Flying Tiger uses a steel axe.
One smites the monk with his axe,
One attacks the Tiger with his cudgel.
Flying Tiger excels in offensive jabs,
Fa-ts'ung's superb with defensive parries.
Fa-ts'ung has the upper hand,
Flying Tiger tries to escape.

Coda

Fa-ts'ung wins;
Flying Tiger loses.
Fa-ts'ung shouldn't have pursued —
Flying Tiger draws his crossbow.

[Prose]

Fa-ts'ung thought he really had won, but actually Flying Tiger feigned defeat.
Flying Tiger thrust his axe into the saddle, put his boots through the stirrups
and raised his dragon-tendon crossbow. He oiled the release and cranked the
brass gear. Even in the wind his arrows could pierce an aspen tree from a
hundred paces, so how could he possibly miss the seven-foot monk?[48]

(*Cheng-kung* mode)

Master Wen-hsü

The general's flight
Is a ruse.
Fa-ts'ung shouldn't have given chase.
In chasing
He falls into a trap . . . .
Pressing his feet on the stirrups,

[48] Earlier (pp. 18, 47), Fa-ts'ung is said to be seven-and-a-half and eight feet. Such
inconsistency is not infrequent in *THH*.

Flying Tiger rears nimbly.
A clap of thunder —
An arrow leaves the bowstring and
Flies forward like a lightning bolt.

Fa-ts'ung
Sees this
From afar.
Truly a seasoned
Fighter, he's
Completely unruffled.
With quick reflexes,
He pulls at the reins,
Leans forward on his saddle, and
Halts his white-bellied bay.

Coda

Opening wide his murderous eyes,
He lifts his *ta-chiang* whip.[49]
Crash — the whip intercepts and breaks the arrow.

[Prose]

An iron whip was raised: a great python leaped into the air.
A steel arrow was blocked: a meteor plummeted to the ground.
The rebels were petrified. Flying Tiger said to them: 'The monk has no
armor. Although I failed to defeat him at close range you can overpower
him from where you are. If he chases after me again, shoot your arrows at
him in unison; that will certainly finish him off.'
Fa-ts'ung thought: 'The bandits seem to have something up their sleeves.
Moreover, my horse is exhausted and cannot fight on much longer.' He told
his followers: 'Retreat and guard the temple: I shall break through the lines
to carry out a plan I have.'

(*Chung-lü-tiao* mode)

Catching a Snake in a Comical Way

Looking ahead, Fa-ts'ung
Sees a tremendous throng of rebels

[49] 'Beat-the-[opposing] general whip', the term seems to be a coinage expressing the
purported use of this weapon.

Brandish their spears and lances on the field
In a threatening way.
Before the ranks, a general sits on a stallion,
An axe on his shoulder, and
A peevish scowl on his face.

The rebels press forward to
Cut at the passing monk.
But every thrust is cleverly warded off.
Fa-ts'ung is invulnerable.
No one can match his skills.
Flying Tiger despairs at his
Dexterity, his sharp vision,
   his ability to slither away and escape.

Coda

The rebels muse:
'Before we can stretch out our hands,
This damned quick, shaven-headed criminal
Has slipped by.'

[Prose]

The fierce monk:
  Fighting singly,
  Is as brave as Hsiang Yü at Nine-Mile Mount;[50]
  Battling alone,
  Is as bold as Kuan Yü at White-Horse Hill.[51]
He charges into the thick of Flying Tiger's troops without giving a thought
to his life.

(*Hsien-lü-tiao* mode)

I-hu-ch'a

Though the rebels are numerous,
They promptly fall back before the monk.

[50] Hsiang Yü, the Prince of Ch'u (third century B.C.), contended for the throne against Liu Pang and was besieged by his enemies at Chiu-li shan (Nine-Mile Mount), near present-day T'ung-shan hsien in Kiangsu.
[51] Kuan Yü, a (third-century A.D.) general, slew his opponent Yen Liang in a battle at Pai-ma kang (White-Horse Hill, also known as Mao-t'uo kang), near present-day Hua hsien in Honan.

They are like lambs confronting a tiger,
Beasts surprised by a wolf.
Their arrows are useless,
The monk's cudgel is an impenetrable shield.
Sky-rocking wails shoot up in the wake of his horse's hoofs,
Bile and blood splash on the dusty ground.

In half an hour the monk breaks the lines;
His fearlessness is truly magnificent.
Covered with spilt blood —
In emergencies certain things can't be helped —
He looks like the monk of Yao-chou,
After a bout with the fierce Scholar Meng.[52]
Perhaps I shouldn't say this — he's exactly like
A cock[53] having just
Emerged from a cunt.

[Prose]

Unable to defeat the rebels alone, Fa-ts'ung broke out through the enemy lines. The rebels then surrounded the temple and Flying Tiger Sun cried at the gate: 'First I want to give my men some food. Second, I know Madam Ts'ui and her family are here and I want Ying-ying. If you give her to me, we shall withdraw; otherwise, calamity will befall you this instant.' His words were reported to the Ts'uis. Ying-ying was terrified.

(*Ta-shih-tiao* mode)

Jade-Winged Cicada

Braving the lines, whipping his horse,
Fa-ts'ung flees to the south-west.
He hasn't time to worry
That his followers
Aren't protected
By cuirasses or armor.
The rebels shower arrows at them
Without a moment's respite.
Of more than three hundred monks

[52] Apparently this alludes to a story popular at Tung's time. The story is no longer extant.
[53] The Chinese characters are 那 話, a euphenism widely used in later erotic novels such as the *Chin P'ing Mei*, though, as far as I know, not in any surviving literary texts antedating the *THH*.

Seventy or eighty percent are
Killed before they can knock on the temple gate.

A few senior monks[54]
Die serenely from their wounds.
The prior[54] is stricken by a sword;
His blood oozes through his muslin robe.
A number of injured cenobites,[54]
Though at first buoyed up by Buddha,
      are finally trampled to death by the horses.
One slow-moving priest,[54]
Captured by a lieutenant,
Turns ashen
In fright,
Like a figure of wax.
From under the banners Flying Tiger bawled:
      'Drive him hither for interrogation.'

Coda

The rebels think to drag him by the hair, but alas,
      his head has been shaved.
Pulling him by his mendicant robe,
They yank him toward their general's horse.

[Prose]

Flying Tiger asked: 'Why do you refuse me a single meal?'

The monk replied: 'The abbot was willing to invite you, but the super-
intendent argued that you might kidnap the beautiful Ying-ying who is
keeping vigil in our temple over her deceased father, the late Prime Minister
Ts'ui. He said that if this happened, there would be grave consequences as the
Minister had many influential friends.'

Flying Tiger laughed: 'What Fa-ts'ung just said was true, then; there really
is a Ying-ying!'[55] He thought to himself: 'Since Ting Wen-ya likes nothing

[54] My translation of the various types of monks is wholly arbitrary. 'Senior monks' is a
translation of *ts'an-t'ou hsing-che*, monks high in the monastic hierarchy with supervisory
duties. 'Prior' translates *et'on-t'o* (*dhūta*) which, though originally as a verb meant to free
oneself from desires by disciplining one's body and mind, later came to designate an as-
cetic and itinerant monk. 'Cenobites' renders *sung-ching wu-chieh*, those who 'chant
sutras and observe the five proscriptions'. Finally, the original for 'priest' is *ho-shang*,
the general term for Buddhist monks or priests.
[55] This is curious as nowhere has Fa-ts'ung mentioned the existence of Ying-ying. I
suspect that an exchange between Fa-ts'ung and Flying Tiger Sun might have been
inadvertently left out by the copyist who made what was to become the ancestor of all
existing editions of *THH*.

better than wine and women, if I have Ying-ying put on makeup and a
gorgeous dress, and offer her to Ting, I am sure he would be overjoyed. We
can join forces to occupy the entire P'u area, and once this is done, we can
defeat any troops the court may dispatch against us.'

(*Cheng-kung-tiao* mode)

Licorice Root

> Having heard the monk,
> Having heard the monk,
> Flying Tiger strokes his blonde beard[56] and
> Relaxes his peevish frown.
> A few underlings transmit his order
> To the men to quicken their attack.
> He himself shouts at the gate:
> 'Listen, you monks,
> Obey me and I'll withdraw; otherwise,
> You'll have to suffer the consequence.

Removing the Cotton Garment

> 'If you give me Ying-ying, I'll remove my troops.
> If not, I'll destroy you instantly.
> I've wasted enough time
> And enough words with you!

Coda

> 'Even if your temple were wrapped in steel
> And couldn't be broached, I could always
> Block the gate and set it on fire.'

[Prose]

The monks are frightened. Fa-pen takes the injured monks to Madam Ts'ui to
tell her what has happened. When she hears the report, she faints. Alarmed,
Hung-niang and Ying-ying try to revive her. After a long time they succeed.
Ying-ying weeps and says: 'Please do not worry about me, Mother, as you
have Father's coffin to care for. Allow me to give myself up to the rebels.
Though I shall be humiliated, you will be left your remaining years, and the
temple, the monks will likewise be spared. You must not let others be
harmed just so that I may be saved from shame.'

[56] *Huang jan.* Earlier, the beard is red (see p. 57 or Ling, p. 44).

(*Tao-kung* mode)

Chieh-hung

> The sudden report
> Frightened Ying-ying's soul away from her body.
> 'It seems inevitable that
> My family will be torn apart.
> Father has died, and
> While we mourn him, we're besieged by these rebels.
> Alas,
> Brother Huan-lang is still a boy . . .'.
> Just then she heard strident voices
> Clamor for her.
> A thousand knives cut into her heart.
> The widowed mother and her daughter
> Had no place to seek help.

> Ying-ying reflected on the situation:
> 'Only by a miracle
> Could I escape.
> As things stand,
> There's little hope of that.
> If I go with the rebels
> Who'd care for
> My aged mother?
> This worries me even more.
> Though the earth is wide, the sky is high, there's no shelter for me.
> I'm completely at the mercy of a horde of bandits.
> I can worry about neither chastity nor filial piety.
> I must make clear to Mother
> That if she tries to save me
> There'll be three calamities:

Coda

> 'One, her life will be in danger;
> Two, the monks will be killed;
> Three, the magnificent temple will be burned.'

[Prose]

Madam Ts'ui wept: 'It is proper that a mother love her children with all her might, and it is natural that she care for them with the most profound affection. If you give yourself up to the rebels what would be the good of my living on? I am sixty; if I die now I would have had a long life. But you are still young and unmarried. If you die, you would die a spinster, leaving no one behind.' When she had finished, she let go of herself and wailed.

(*Ta-shih-tiao* mode)

Music for Returning to the Capital

> Ying-ying and her mother
> Held on to each other and cried.
> Their loud wailing
> Threw the monks into great confusion.
> 'It's more than likely that
> Mother and I will both be killed this time.
> I'd like to commit suicide,
> But I'm afraid the rebels,
> Frustrated in their desires,
> Would burn the temple in revenge.
> If I give myself up,
> Posterity will learn of my shame;
> Not only will I be
> A laughing-stock for thousands of years to come,
> My father's name will be disgraced as well.

> 'What am I
> To do?
> While Mother and the abbot
> Discuss and ponder,
> Some of the monks
> Are urging reverently —
> With touched palms —
> For my delivery to the thieves.
> It'd be difficult to dissuade them.
> They're so insistent. . . .
> All right, I will die, and
> To appease
> The rebels
> My corpse can be offered
> To their lawless swords.
> They can strike me ten thousand times.
> At least in death
> My reputation will be intact!'

65

Coda

> She lifted her gown and prepared to jump from the steps.
> All became immobile, dazed with alarm —
> Someone laughed and clapped his hands.

[Prose]

> Fa-ts'ung's valor
> Fails to defeat the rebels,
> A weakling's plan
> Succeeds in subduing the bandits.

Ying-ying was about to jump; she was about to jump! Madam Ts'ui and Hung-niang restrained her. Suddenly, peals of laughter were heard; everyone looked around. Who laughed?

(*Huang-chung-kung* mode)

Year of Happiness

> Ying-ying and her mother were beside themselves with anguish;
> Others shared their grief.
> Suddenly someone spoke out claiming that
> He could defeat the rebels.
> All turned and looked.
> A young scholar
> Matchless in beauty
> Emerged from the crowd of monks.

> Over twenty years old,
> Five feet tall,
> Trim eyebrows, lovely eyes,
> Straight nose, strong teeth.
> His lips were red as rouge,
> His face, a luminous moon.
> Compared with him
> P'an An and Sung Yü were ugly ruffians.

Dancers' Exit

> All recognized him to be Chang.
> A monk tugged at his robe and
> Whispered: 'Young gentleman,

66

This is not like chanting poetry in your study!
You should've seen the rows and rows of rebels.

'Are you mad or insane?
How can you make good your boastful claim?
You saw how hard Fa-ts'ung fought
With Flying Tiger on the battleground.
And even he had to flee before he was overcome.

Willow Leaves

'Your muscles and bones are as delicate as a girl's,
How can you wield a sword?
You have no strength in your arms or legs,
How can you ride a horse?

'Your fingers are like bamboo shoots,
How can you let fly an arrow?
You are slight and frail,
How can you support a hauberk?

Coda

'Even holding a brush tires you out,
Yet you claim you can make the troops withdraw.
Tell me, what's your plan?'

[Prose]

Who laughed? Who laughed? Everyone looked around; it was Chang. Chang
said: 'Women have no presence of mind; whenever danger arises, they only
weep. And you monks, you, too, have not been very resourceful. Obviously
you have not come up with a way to deter the rebels; you merely wait to be
slaughtered. But if you follow my suggestion, you can certainly defeat them.'
The abbot Fa-pen knew that Chang was endowed with a rare intelligence,
so that he might well have an unusual plan. He went up to Chang and said:
'Indeed we have no way to escape our predicament. Since you, sir, have an
unusual scheme, please help us.'
    Chang smiled and replied: 'You and your followers are disciples of
Buddha, do you not understand that life is the origin of death and death paves
the way for your next life? Life and death are natural phenomena of human
existence. Even Shakyamuni himself had to die! Moreover, the concept of
retribution is indigenous to Buddhism; it is expounded clearly in your scrip-
tures. If, in your previous incarnation, you did evil to the bandits, it

67

is natural that they should seek revenge now, and there is no escape for you. But if, on the other hand, you never harmed them, then they are not your enemies in this life, and you have no reason to be afraid.'

The abbot said: 'You are quite right, sir. Actually, I only begrudge the destruction of our temple. When they were built, the gate, prayer halls, verandas, bell towers and library cost more than one million [pieces of silver]. A fire would reduce them to a heap of ashes. I wish that, just for the sake of accumulating merits, you would prevent this from happening.'

Chang smiled even more broadly: 'When you preach, reverend abbot, you explicate the *Diamond Sutra.* You seem, however, to be ignorant that even our bones, our flesh, our skin and hair are not out own. Our spirit is our true self; our body is but a temporary abode. When death arrives, our spirit leaves, and the four elements which make up our body disintegrate. Those who are dearest to us, our wives and children, cannot follow us; possessions most precious to us, our gold and pearls, must be left behind. And now you manifest such a proprietary attachment to the prayer halls and bell towers!'

The abbot retorted: 'True, true, we who preach the *Dharma* do not care whether we live or die, and we are actually quite indifferent to the destruction of a temple. But it does pain us to see a daughter forcibly taken away from her mother. It is only for this reason that I am asking for your help.'

Chang then said: 'Madam Ts'ui has never bestowed any kindness upon me, and I was not acquainted with the late Minister. There has never been any communication between the Ts'ui family and me, so why should I save them?'

'If you do not save Ying-ying, and Madam Ts'ui refuses to surrender her, the enraged rebels will no doubt attack us with great force. What will *you* do then?'

'You need not worry about me, I can protect myself. You would do well to devise a way to protect *yourself.*'

The abbot tried another tack: 'You are a Confucian, sir, and you uphold the principle of charity and justice. A charitable person loves humanity and abhors that which threatens it; it thus follows that you would want to remove this present threat. An upholder of justice respects order and detests those who subvert it; so, clearly, you would want to dispel the unruly rabble. Now a young woman and her widowed mother are both at the point of committing suicide, yet you sit here and laugh at them. Is this a charitable person's manifestation of love for humanity? On a different plane, these mutinous soldiers have ruthlessly harried innocent people; you see it but make no attempt to curb them. Is this how an upholder of justice shows his respect for order? In antiquity, Duke Chung of Cheng did not restrain Shu-tuan when Shu-tuan behaved incorrectly as a younger brother;[57] the Marquis of Wei did not save

[57] Shu-tuan attempted to usurp the dukedom from his older brother Duke Chung, who, for a long time, took no action to stop him. See *Tso chuan*, entry for the first year of Duke Yin of Lu (722 B.C.).

the Marquis of Li when the latter was attacked by *Ti* barbarians;[58] they were both censured in the *Spring and Autumn Annals*. Sir, you have a scheme to repel the mutineers but you refuse to disclose it. Judged by the criterion implicit in *Spring and Autumn,* your conduct is greatly amiss. Decide for yourself whether I am right.'

Chang smiled again and said: 'Reverend abbot, your knowledge of Confucian teaching is indeed superficial. The Master once said: "When a gentleman is brave but behaves improperly, confusion will result. When a small man is brave but behaves improperly, banditry will result." Thus, a gentleman shuns actions that are brave but lack propriety. In the present situation, although I am fearless, so long as the parties involved do not ask for it, it would be improper for me to offer help. Furthermore, the Master said: "When propriety is observed, pupils seek their teachers; teachers do not go about looking for pupils." Clearly it is beneath a gentleman to recommend himself.'

(*Pan-she-tiao* mode)

A Pock-Marked Old Lady

> Again and again the abbot tried to persuade Chang:
> 'Sir, you're being perverse.
> Everyone is distressed
> But you; you're in high spirits.'
> Chang laughed with glee:
> 'Reverend teacher, how dense you are!
> Surely you must know, since it's recorded
>   in your Buddhist scriptures and not
> In my Confucian books:
>
> ' "Where there is life, there is death;
> Only when birth desists will extinction cease!
> Death, like life, is part of human existence.
> It needn't be feared. . . ."
> There are more than five thousand rebels outside.
> But even if they were as fierce as the God of Water and the
>   God of Wrath[59]

---

[58] During the Spring and Autumn Era (770–481 B.C.), the state of Wei had hegemony over nine other states of which Li was one; the Marquis of Wei was therefore bound by treaty to render whatever help he could to the Marquis of Li. When *Ti* barbarians invaded the state of Li, not only did the Marquis of Wei refuse to dispatch troops to expel the invaders, but he also treated the Marquis of Li shabbily when the latter fled to Wei. See prefaces to '*Shih-wei*' (式 微) and '*Mao-chiu*' (旄 丘) in the *Book of Songs.*

[59] *T'ien-p'eng* and *Hei-sha,* the God of Water and the God of Wrath in folk tradition.

So long as I'm alive
You'll not be captured.'

Coda

'I don't need to mount a horse,
I don't need an inch of weapon,
I don't need to fight in battles,
One look from me will reduce the five thousand bandits
    to messes of fat and blood.'

[Prose]

When the abbot transmitted Chang's words to Madam Ts'ui, she replied:
'Is that so?'[60] With decorum she introduced herself to Chang and said,
sobbing:

(*Hsiao-shih-tiao* mode)

The Center of the Flower Moves

'The rebels
Demand my daughter Ying-ying, and
Whatever can we do?
We, piteous
Widow and orphan,
Put ourselves in your hands.'
Chang responded with a smile:
'Honorable Madam, pray sit down.
Set your heart at ease.
There's nothing to fear.

'I'm not boasting;
I do have a plan which will
Defeat the rebels immediately.
The troops will withdraw,
The temple will stay intact,
The monks will be spared, and
You, your family and servants — all fifty of you —
Will not be hurt in any way. . . .
But when this is done
You mustn't start treating me like a stranger again.'

[60] This, of course, refers back to the previous prose passage where Chang says that it is
beneath a gentleman to recommend himself.

70

[Prose]

Madam Ts'ui said: 'Of course not, of course not; your apprehension is quite unnecessary. I only hope you will not consider my offer unworthy: once the catastrophe is averted and we are safe, I should like to have you as a son.'[61] (etc., etc.)[62]

Chang told the abbot: 'Send a messenger to inform the rebels that Yingying has agreed to their demand. She is taking leave of her mother and her father's coffin, and making herself presentable. She will be ready in a moment. Ask them to be patient and to please relax their attack somewhat.'

The rebels slackened their harassment.

Chang then said: 'Mutinous troops cannot be swayed with words; insurgent hordes should not be tackled with mere force. They must be subdued by authority.'

The abbot and Madam Ts'ui asked simultaneously: 'Who has authority?'

'I have a friend who was a Confucian scholar in his youth. Later, he distinguished himself in military campaigns and suppressed many rebellions. He has a just heart and an awe-inspiring countenance. When he was made a governor, all the thieves and brigands left his province. When he was appointed to the frontiers, barbarian horsemen ceased to encroach on our land. From these accomplishments one knows that he must be an invincible warrior replete with goodness and virtue, and that he must command devotion from the people and respect from his troops. Though his surname is Tu, and his given name Ch'üeh, people call him 'White-Horse General', since he often rides a white stallion on the battlefield. He is at present the Commanding General of P'u pass. And because of the unwavering loyalty his men have for him, no one has dared to offend him. General Tu and I are intimate friends and I have here a draft of a letter addressed to him. Please read it, Madam.'

In brief the letter said: 'Your humble friend Chang Kung sends this missive to Your Excellency, the Commanding General:

In haste, I shall not embellish my prose; before Your Excellency, I shall come immediately to my entreaty. An unfortunate event has occurred: Marshal Hun of P'u prefecture recently passed away. His brigadier general, Ting Wen-ya, lost control of the troops, so that certain regiments mutinied and proceeded to ravage the countryside. As villages and towns are burnt, moaning and wailing reverberate throughout the entire region. All citizens

---

[61] The term used is 繼子為觀 which may mean to make someone a son by giving him the hand of one's daughter, or to adopt someone as a son to be the brother of one's daughter. The ambiguity, fully intended by Master Tung, makes later events possible.

[62] 云云, 'et cetera', 'and so forth', set in smaller print than the rest of the text, occurs once more in a prose passage in *THH* (Ling, p. 131). In *Liu Chih-yüan chu-kung-tiao* it also appears, likewise in smaller print, in a prose passage (*Wen-wu ch'u-pan-she* ed. Peking, 1958, p. 8b). I think it is meant to indicate to the performing singer−narrator that at this point he may or is expected to add further elaboration.

are threatened with death and torture; they are in desperate straits like a man hung from his heels. Your Excellency is blessed with unusual farsightedness; you are revered by all who know you. You are famous for your protection of the people and for your courage in combat. In face of the present upheaval, I know you will not stay behind in your fortress and allow the rebels to indulge their savagery. Indeed, Your Excellency seems the only one who can stop this menacing anarchy. Please make haste, since undue hesitation may cause widespread chaos. Once you come, you will easily destroy the rebel leaders and the rest will surrender; the people will be saved and peace will be restored. When the court hears of this, an imperial edict will commend you for your meritorious achievement. If, on the contrary, you refuse to dispatch your troops, then surely you will be censured for your cowardice. Presently the insurgents have surrounded the Temple of Universal Salvation, and I have no way to escape. So it is with some urgency that I beseech you to serve your country and to save your unworthy friend. Trapped in the mouth of death I look forward eagerly to your reply. I shall be exceedingly grateful to you for vouchsafing me a second life.

Once again your humble friend Chang Kung salutes Your Excellency, the Commanding General.'

Chapter 3

(*Chung-lü-tiao* mode)

Green Peonies, ch'an-ling

> 'There's no need to be afraid, Madam,
> So please set your mind at ease.
> Though the rebels are large in numbers,
> To me they are nothing.
> I have a good friend,
> Stationed at P'u pass,
> He and I
> Have been on excellent terms
> For a long time.

> 'Descendant of prominent ancestors,
> Scion of a mandarin family,
> He refused to accept his hereditary post and instead
> Made his own mark through the civil examinations.
> He's a great-grandson of Tu Ju-hui[63]
> Whom he surpasses in talent and bravery.
> He uses a hundred-and-eighty-pound bow,
> Studies the stratagem of the Eight Dispositions[64], and
> Reads enough books to fill five wagons.

The Wooden Fish

> 'At first he governed an inland province,
> Bandits and brigands fled from the region.
> Later he was assigned to the frontier,
> Barbarian horses and soldiers dared not look across the border.
> Now he's the commander of P'u pass.
> Among his men

---

[63] A famous Prime Minister of T'ang T'ai-tsung (r. 627–49). The relationship between General Tu and Tu Ju-hui may or may not be fictitious.
[64] Military formation, reputedly devised by Chu-ko Liang.

Are numbered the most valiant
Fighters in the world.
A scholar, a warrior, a strategist,
He handles spears and lances with consummate skill;
    he shoots arrows and pellets with incredible speed.
Even if the rebels were three thousand billion and
As fierce as the God of Water and the God of Wrath,
When they saw him they'd yield.

Falcon Attacking a Hare

'A white, tiger-like stallion
Is his favorite mount.
A broad-blade sword, the mightiest ever wrought,
Is his weapon.
He's a pillar of society,
He removes wrongdoers from the universe,
He manages affairs of the world,
He keeps peace in the country.
Utterly loyal to the Sovereign,
He never hesitates to suppress mutinous uprisings
Or to reclaim dangerous territories and land.

'Even heroes in history
Are not his peers.
He's braver than ten thousand Meng Pen,[65]
Five thousand Lü Pu.[66]
Hsiang Chi of Ch'u,[67]
Kuan Yü of Shu,
Pai Ch'i of Ch'in,[68]
Sun Wu of Yen[69]
Could learn military art and
Craft from him.

[65] Warrior of the Warring States period (480–222 B.C.), said to be able to remove horns from live oxen with his bare hands.
[66] Warrior of the Three Kingdoms Era (*fl. c.* second century A.D.) and owner of the famous charger Ch'ih-t'u (see n. 42). Lü is much celebrated in *Romance of the Three Kingdoms*.
[67] Appellation of Hsiang Yü. See n. 50.
[68] A general of Prince Chao of Ch'in (late fourth century B.C.), who captured over seventy towns for his prince during the War of the States.
[69] The sixth-century B.C. strategist, well-known for his treatise *The Art of War*.

Coda

> 'He's a better writer than Chia[70] and Ma,[71]
> A better strategist than Sun and P'ang,[72]
> A better fighter than Han and P'eng[73].'

[Prose]

Madam Ts'ui said: 'General Tu is indeed a famous warrior of our time, whose reputation inspires awe. Since he is an old friend of yours, when he receives your letter, no doubt he will dispatch troops to quell the rebels. However, the distance between P'u pass and P'u town is several tens of miles, and if we wait for you to write your letter, it will be too late.'

Chang replied: 'When Fa-ts'ung went forth to fight the rebels, I had already given him a copy of the letter to deliver to General Tu.[74] Please, Madam and reverend abbot, go up to the belfry. You will witness the arrival of the troops.'

(*Ta-shih-tiao* mode)

A Southern Air

> 'Madam Ts'ui,
> Believe what I've said.
> Please relax your frown and
> Set your mind at ease.'
> The Minister's widow leans on the balustrade
> And looks out.
> All around the temple
> The rebels are
> Standing quietly.

[70] Chia Yi (201–169 B.C.), statesman and man of letters of Han Wen-ti's reign. Tutor of Princes Ch'ang-sha and Liang-hwai and writer of much-celebrated *fu*, 'Lament for Ch'ü Yüan' and 'The Owl', and the essay 'Discussion of the Faults of Ch'in.'
[71] Ssu-ma Hsiang-ju. See n. 8.
[72] Sun Pin and P'ang Chüan, warriors and strategists of the fourth century B.C. Sun was a descendant of Sun Wu (n. 69 above); he and P'ang Chüan both studied the art of war with Kuei-ku-tzu. Jealous of Sun's superior ability, P'ang had his feet cut off. Later, they served different princes and at the battle of Ma-ling, Sun's archers severely wounded P'ang, causing him to commit suicide.
[73] Han Hsin and P'eng Yüeh, famous generals of Han Kao-tsu (r. 206–195 B.C.).
[74] This comes as a total surprise to the audience and reader. Fa-ts'ung's departure from the temple is minutely described and the circumstances make it impossible for him to see or receive a letter from Chang. Such a manipulated surprise solution is quite the opposite of the other technique, the well-prepared-for solution, often found in Victorian comedies.

But still,
A miasma of violence
Covers the field. . . .
Suddenly, dust shoots up in the air,
A cumulus rolls in from afar,
Five hundred soldiers appear.
Ferocious, fierce, each
A Messenger of Thunder
Descending from the clouds.

Coda

Armor gliding down the sunlit field
    like stars pouring forth from the Milky Way.
Embroidered banners fluttering
    like rainbows folding and unfolding.
Yes, it is White-Horse General who has arrived.

[Prose]

Joy animates Madam Ts'ui's face.
Happiness stirs in the monks' breast.

(*Yüeh-tiao* mode)

Fighting Quails, ch'an-ling

A sudden dusk,
Brought on by the gathering, billowing clouds.
Tumultuous dust tumbles like shoveled earth, sifted chaff.
The soldiers, in a winnow-fan formation,
Gallop up the glacis.
Not quite six hundred,
More than half a thousand,
They're determined
To destroy the bandits instantly.

They deploy themselves in a Straight-Line Formation,
And hold their lances in place.
Their valor, their bravery
Is impeccable.
Few are as old as thirty,
The shortest is six feet.
They've often captured vicious dragons and

Dragged savage tigers by the tail.
Although the rebels are immense in number,
The sight of the soldiers overwhelms them with fear.

Green Mountain Pass

Proud horses neigh in the wind, shaking their jade pendants.
The cavalry flaunts its impressive, frightening strength.
Infantrymen, common soldiers, and underlings
Beat their wolf-skin drums
And golden gongs.
Swords and halberds,
Shields and spears are densely, frighteningly lined up.
All are impatient to defeat the bandits, to rescue Chang
And the others.

A general rides in the front,
Such a distinguished mien
Has never been seen before.
Smiling, with feet in the stirrups,
He sits obliquely on his jewelled saddle,
A water-polished iron whip curls over his wrist.
He is broad-shouldered
And tall of stature.
Clasped under his arm are arrows, across his back is a bow.
His armor is made of wrought copper,
His cape of madder silk.

Plum Tree in the Snow

When he fights, the gods seem to give him counsel.
His sword has shed rivers of blood.
How can an undisciplined mob of rebels mean anything to him,
He is undaunted even by
The God Liu-ting[75] and the God of Wrath!
Laughing with good cheer,
He can't wait to crush the mutinous thieves.
When they see him
They ponder: 'This redoubtable lord is here.
What can we do?'

[75] A god in popular Taoist religion.

> The bridle-tassel of the general's horse
>> glows like a winnow-fan filled with burning charcoal.
> The steel sword on his shoulder is as wide as a door panel.
> He himself is like Chin-kang.
> His stallion is like a camel.
> Flying Tiger trembles and
> His soul leaves him in fright.
> With profound regret, he laments:
> 'Alas, my desire for a meal
> Will certainly cost me my life.'

[Prose]

> The rebels become dispirited.
> Flying Tiger loses courage.

(*Pan-she-tiao* mode)

Flowers above the Wall

> White-Horse General's
> Five hundred armored soldiers
> Deploy themselves on the field.
> One glance sends Flying Tiger's soul fleeing; and
> One war-cry cracks the bandits' skulls.

> The rebels muse:
> 'We're as good as dead,
> All five thousand of us.
> Who'd dare to fight
> Or to resist?'

> The rebels are like sons;
> The soldiers their fathers.
> The soldiers are fierce as dragons;
> The terrified rebels are meek as turtles.
> If the soldiers are five hundred monks;
> The rebels are six thousand neophytes.

Coda

> Setting down their bows and arrows,
> Swords and axes,

> Abandoning their banners and horses,
> The rebels turn to White-Horse General and thunder out a loud salute

[Prose]

General Tu said: 'Rebellious soldiers, when Marshal Hun died, you lost your commanding general; his temporary replacement Ting Wen-ya indulged himself in wine and women, so that you became unruly and engaged in plunder and pillage. I know this does not necessarily mean that you harbor any seditious plans. As your parents, your wives, and children are staying in army camps, your insurrection will lead to their execution. I am here with my troops, and to destroy you is as easy as mowing down grass. But I fear there are among you some who are not treasonous and these I cannot bear to kill.' He added: 'Those who do not mean to rebel, go to the east, set down your arms and sit on your armor. Those who want to rebel, go to the west, and prepare to fight to the death with us.'

When he finished, all went to the east and set aside their weapons. General Tu executed Flying Tiger Sun on the spot and pardoned the rest. Chang and the abbot emerged from the temple to greet Tu. Tu and Chang exchanged salutations befitting sworn brothers and went into the temple hand in hand. There they drank wine on the veranda to celebrate their reunion. Chang congratulated Tu: 'Now that you have rendered a worthy service to the country, demonstrated your loyalty to a friend, and saved the people of P'u, it will only be a matter of days before the court confers great honors upon you. Allow me to congratulate you now.'

(*Hsien-lü-tiao* mode)

Pink is the River

> The monks were delighted
> To have General Tu in the temple.
> 'You've been a loyal friend and
> A benefactor to the temple;
> I shall send a memorial to the court immediately,
> So that your achievement can be inscribed on the Ling-yen pavilion.[76]
> You as well as your descendants will be rewarded and
> Your fame will last forevermore.
> After all, if you hadn't quelled the rebels,
> The people of P'u
> Would never have known peace again.
> My brother,

[76] Erected by T'ang T'ai-tsung (r. 627–49). Portraits of twenty-four meritorious ministers were painted on the walls.

Let me offer this light wine
In token of my thanks.'

White-Horse General
Drained a cup and replied: 'Chün-jui,
Why be so formal?
Let's send the others away and
Have a *tête-à-tête.*'
Three times the wine-jug was passed around;
 the sun started to set.
White-Horse General rose from his seat:
'I'm afraid, my friend,
I must be gone.'
Chang accompanied him beyond the temple gate.
They said farewell
Reluctantly
And drank a parting cup.
'Till next time,
My brother, I take leave of you.'

[Prose]

Shaking their gilt reins, the horses leave Universal Salvation.
Singing a victory song, the soldiers return to P'u pass.
The following day Chang went to see the abbot and said: 'Yesterday when
the rebels surrounded the temple, Madam Ts'ui offered to take me as a son in
exchange for my scheme to repel the rebels. I wonder what is happening to my
marriage?'

(*Kao-p'ing-tiao* mode)

Epithalamium

'Although I am
But a lowly scholar
I managed to be Madam Ts'ui's benefactor.
She herself
Promised,
Promised to have me as a son.
Nine chances out of ten
She'll betroth Ying-ying to me.

'You'd agree that
I can't very well

80

Approach her myself.
Reverend brother, listen to my request,
Being a Buddhist
You should want to help.
I know I shouldn't trouble your Eminence, but
Please be a matchmaker.'

[Prose]

The abbot gladly consented. 'Please wait here, sir. I shall go directly.'
He went to Madam Ts'ui's court and asked to be announced. Madam Ts'ui received him and invited him to sit down. The abbot said how sorry he was over the unpleasant incident of the preceding day; Madam Ts'ui merely thanked him without saying anything more. The abbot then said slowly: 'Mr Chang is a virtuous person. When he offered his plan to expel the rebels, Madam promised to have him as a son. Mr Chang now asks me to inquire for Madam's esteemed intentions.'
Madam Ts'ui said: 'Of course I am not forgetful of Mr Chang's kindness. I shall invite him to a simple meal so we can discuss the matter face to face.'
Pleased, the abbot withdrew to report her words to Chang.

(*Kao-p'ing-tiao* mode)

Magnolia Flowers

The abbot greeted Chang with felicitations.
'Madam Ts'ui eagerly invites you
To discuss the matter face to face.'
Chang speculated: 'Today being an auspicious day for a wedding,
I'll bet they're preparing
A nuptial feast!'

Chang asked: 'Reverend teacher, what are they cooking?
How many dozen bottles of choice wine have they bought?
How much pastry, cake, savory have they made?'
The abbot laughed, 'Don't kid yourself.
I saw them hull a few pints of stale grain and
Boil half an urn of dried-up leeks!'

[Prose]

Chang was overjoyed with the invitation. He tidied his appearance and waited.

(Hsien-lü-tiao mode)

Lingering in the Perfumed Quilt

    A mirror he takes from the toilet case;
    He wipes his face till it shines.
    He carefully brushes his gauze cap,
    To make sure it will enhance his appearance.
    He puts on a full-length pongee robe, and a long vest
    With matching twin-color crepe lapel.
    His slender waist
    Is set to advantage by a crimson sash.

    He chooses a pair of square-throated shoes and
    Spotless knee-socks of a subdued hue.
    Having dressed,
    He can't sit still.
    He scrutinizes himself in the mirror while his heart runs wild abroad.
    Outside, shadows do move, but how sluggishly!
    He curses the sun,
    Why, it's not yet overhead!

Coda

    His heart pounds; he itches with impatience.
    His stomach rumbles thunderously.
    He doesn't dare to blink; with undivided attention,
        he watches for a messenger to appear.

[Prose]

Chang changed his clothes but did not cook. Single-mindedly he waited for someone to send for him. All day no one appeared. He thought to himself: 'Why does Fa-pen play such a trick on me? Madam Ts'ui is also treating me shabbily.'

(Kao-p'ing-tiao mode)

Magnolia Flowers

    'From breakfast I wait until dusk;
    No one comes near me, let alone asks me how I am.
    I have to bear my hunger in secrecy.
    From dawn to evening,
    I haven't touched one grain of rice, one drop of water.
    I'm ready to collapse.

'Sure enough, my hunger has turned to thirst;
My throat is parched;
A fire burns in my bowels. . . .'
Just then the door opens, Fa-pen enters muttering
    congratulatory remarks.
'What has been decided about
Your marriage?'

[Prose]

Chang could not conceal his annoyance. 'I have never treated you badly,
abbot. Why have you played such a trick on me?'
    'How have I played a trick on you?'
    'This morning, after I asked you to inquire about my marriage, you
reported that Madam Ts'ui would invite me to a banquet today. Yet all day
no one sent for me. Well, have you played a trick on me?'
    The abbot exclaimed: 'Ah, it was indeed my fault! Madam Ts'ui said she
would arrange a banquet tomorrow and not today.'
    Chang taunted him: 'You cannot transmit correctly even a brief message
of two sentences. How can you possibly recite the Gandavyūha sutra? You
shaven-headed prick!'
    Chuckling, the abbot went away.
    That night Chang did not sleep a wink. Soon, day broke, and Hung-niang
came as expected. She curtsied to him, saying: 'Madam Ts'ui wishes to invite
you to a meal.'

(*Hsien-lü-tiao* mode)

Flower-Viewing Time

>   Just as Chang's frustration started to mount,
>   The sudden sight of Hung-niang filled him with joy.
>   Greeting her with a bow,
>   Smiling pleasantly, Chang said:
>   'Please sit down, please sit down.'

[Prose Insert]

Hung-niang said: 'Since I am sent around by Madam, I dare not dawdle.

>   'Madam Ts'ui requests your company, sir,
>   And won't take no for an answer—
>   She wishes to express her gratitude.'

Chang said: 'I'll gladly comply with her request. . . .
Aha, I'm bound to see my darling there.

'It isn't your wine, your food or tea which interest me;
It's what your Madam will say,
     she will say one thing, and that alone,
Mark my words, Hung-niang,
She'll ask me to marry your young mistress!'

[Prose]

Hung-niang laughed and went away.

(*Shuang-tiao* mode)

The Charms of Hsi-nu

It was only the crack of dawn,
Chang already busied himself preening.
It didn't occur to him to verify the invitation this time.
As you know,
Young scholars are always hungry—
Such is the unalterable truth—
Chang waited, leaning on the door, all the while swallowing his saliva.

After Hung-niang left,
Only a miracle could keep him at his books.
Fidgeting, pacing back and forth,
He gazed and stared at the sun.
Soon the midday meal was over.
'Damn her!
So that maid Hung-niang also tricks me?'

[Prose]

As he wondered, Hung-niang reappeared. They went together to see Madam
Ts'ui.

(Shuang-tiao mode)

The Charms of Hsi-nu

Upon seeing Hung-niang,
The gods of his five viscera all rejoiced.
Chang didn't bother with polite demurring but
Followed her firmly, step by step.
When they arrived, he bowed to Madam Ts'ui with alacrity.
'Madam must have suffered a terrible fright,
The day before yesterday.'

The Minister's widow
Couldn't have been more solicitous.
'I'm taking a great liberty, sir, in inviting you like this;
My fatherless children and I
Can't really make adequate preparations.
Forgive us — as you know, this is not our home.
I beg your indulgence.'

[Prose]

She asked Chang to take a seat. After tea was served Chang stood up and
said: 'The bandits rather startled Madam the other day; I am glad the dis-
turbance did not bring on any illness.' Madam Ts'ui thanked him and invited
him to sit down again. She ordered wine.

(Hsien-lü-tiao mode)

Flower-Viewing Time

Even wealthy homes are not as impressive
As this elegant guest house.
The decor is sumptuous:
Cascading curtains have embroidered valences,
Dainty windows in the library have fine silk panes.

Low couches are covered with flowered pads,
        a foot and a half thick or more.
Assorted exotic incense burns in jewelled, duck-shaped censers.
The food and drink are excellent.
All the serving maids
Are girls of fourteen or fifteen.

> Gently, a sandalwood clapper beats time
> > to accompany the drinking of a rare wine fit for the immortals.
> Paintings of famous artists adorn the walls.
> Everything is exactly right.
> Not a profusion, only a few sprays of flowers are arranged in a vase.

[Prose]

Chang thought to himself: 'Ying-ying will certainly be mine.'

(*Huang-chung-tiao* mode)

The Golden Altar Boy

> 'No need of betrothal gifts
> Or a go-between,
> The winsome Ying-ying shall be mine!'
> Madam Ts'ui rose, urging him to drink.
> Chang got up quickly;
> Standing beside his seat, he respectfully waited for her to speak.
>
> He had been ninety percent sure
> Of his marriage.
> Alas, he had not foreseen Madam's difficult personality.
> She could put away her smiles and recant without shame —
> Among the faithless, the shifty,
> She could well be the chief.

Coda

> Forgetting his mountain-high, ocean-deep kindness
> She now used her slick tongue to
> Renege on her promise.

[Prose]

What did she say?

Madam Ts'ui told Chang: 'I chose not to follow my deceased husband in death so that I might bring up the children. When the monks were defeated by the rebels, we were on the verge of death. My son and my daughter truly owe their lives to you and I shall never forget your beneficence.'

She then summoned her son Huan-lang to come out and pay his respects to Chang.

(*Ta-shih-tiao* mode)

A Red Gauze Garment

> After a few rounds of wine,
> Chang speculated to himself:
> 'What marvelous luck!
> My winsome darling,
> Bewitching sister,
> Will soon become my wife!'
> Hung-niang filled his gold goblet, and
> Madam Ts'ui urged: 'Please don't stand on ceremony.
> You did us
> A great favor the other day and
> I wouldn't dare treat you like a casual acquaintance.'

> She whispered to Hung-niang:
> 'Bring my son out.'
> Shortly Huan-lang appeared;
> > his tufts of hair, gathered in white ribbons,
> > shone like raven feathers.
> He wore a soft silk gown that was
> Not too long, not too short,
> Not too loose, nor too tight.
> A lustrous satin sash was tied around his waist.
> A pair of low-vamped, square-throated shoes on his feet.
> Although he was just a boy, with a boy's height,
> He carried himself with distinction, and
> Not a trace of commonness marred his deportment.

Coda

> No wonder Madam loved him like a pearl.
> Erect and assured he came forward and,
> Like an adult, bowed to Chang in the proper manner.

[Prose]

Madam Ts'ui, pointing to Chang, says to her son: 'You should pay Mr Chang the homage due an elder brother.' Huan-lang salutes Chang; Chang removes himself from his seat, thus refusing the obeisance. Madam Ts'ui orders a maid to invite Chang to resume his seat and to receive the salute. Chang turns the matter over in his mind: 'Huan-lang is Ying-ying's brother. Am I not to marry Ying-ying? What is the good of becoming their brother?' Annoyance flickers on his face.

Song of the God of Music

> Chang's anger flares up;
> It boils and seethes.
> To relieve his frustration,
> He grumbles and curses to himself.
>
> Deaf to his mood,
> Madam babbles on:
> 'Forgive us our lack of manners. . . .
> Ask my daughter to meet her elder brother.'

[Prose]

Madam Ts'ui orders Hung-niang to fetch Ying-ying. After a long interval Ying-ying sends her regrets, saying that she is ill. Madam Ts'ui angrily has the following words conveyed to her: 'Mr Chang saved your life, otherwise you would have been captured by the rebels. It is the least you can do to express your gratitude with obeisance. You must not keep aloof.'

Another long interval passes. Finally Ying-ying emerges, wearing an ordinary dress and looking downcast. She has no makeup or adornment, but her beauty is dazzling.

(*Huang-chung-kung* mode)

Dancers' Exit

> Exquisitely alluring,
> She moves with delicate grace.
> Her eyes linger on Chang, but she doesn't say a word.
> Is her mother's presence responsible for this reserve?
> A new gloom casts a darker shadow on her knitted brows.
>
> 'Heaven! Heaven! Such unbearable vexation!
> My helping them brings me only disappointment.
> When she's not around, I want to pursue her,
> Yet her presence reduces me to utter paralysis.
> Indeed it is "So much longing when apart,
>   but bashfulness face to face!"

Coda

'No wonder I've lost weight recently.
My face has thinned.
Thinness itself doesn't worry me;
But have I become less attractive?'

[Prose]

Rendering help,
Chang hoped to have the beauty as a bride.
Expressing gratitude,
Madam wants her to be his sister.
Chang was silent. Drunk with longing, he looked at Ying-ying stealthily and
was even more impressed by her exceptional beauty.

(*Nan-lü-kung* mode)

Moon above the Jasper Terrace

'My beloved, why
Does she look
Languid these days?
She seems to have just awakened,
Without having the time to make up.
Her cheeks are bare, but she seems hesitant to put on any powder.
Her hair undone, the chignon pushed to one side.
Her eyebrows are a moth's green antennae,
            frozen in momentary repose;
The luminosity of her eyes holds all the grace of autumn waves.
Unsurpassable, inexhaustible charm!
Rouge, others' adornment,
Could only blemish her pristine beauty.

Heaven may have a lovely Moon Goddess,
            that I do not know.
But here on earth, my love has no peer.
Her crimson lips are two halves of a dainty cherry
Freshly cut and exposed.
Smiling or sulking, her face is equally endearing.
My love has the perfect height, whether she sits or stands.
Her trim waist moves supplely like willow wands in the wind.
Shod in crimson-silk, embroidered slippers,
            her tiny bound feet

Glide forward silently.
And when she bows,
What infinite softness, what grace!'

San-sha

When Madam wasn't watching,
Chang fixed his eyes on Ying-ying.
'She pretends not to notice me. . . .
My darling,
You're making
My eyes blurred, my heart confused.
I feel dizzy, deranged!'

The wine, acting on his melancholy, made Chang flushed.
'I guess I haven't the luck to win my love after all.
Yesterday's hopes are shattered.
I thought then that Ying-ying and I
Would marry.
But now, she's
To call me brother.

Coda

'I've reckoned wrong.
I've quelled the rebels for nothing.
I'm deceived by this treacherous, worldly old crone.'

[Prose]

How do I know this happened? I shall cite *The Ballad of the True Story of Ying-ying* as my corroboration. *The Ballad* says:
Chang is not yet Madam Ts'ui's friend;
He lives in the temple at the other end.
Moved by the mother's pitiful distress,
To White-Horse General a letter he addresses.
Straightway a mandate urgently commands
Officers brave and soldiers to advance.
The mother's court is left in peace,
And Chang is asked to a sumptuous feast.
Time and again does the hostess aver:
'My daughter is your sister, my worthy sir.'
After Ying-ying finished her salutation, she sat beside Madam Ts'ui, a pensive and sad look on her face as though she was overcome by emotion. Chang stared at her, not knowing what to do.

90

(*Shang-tiao* mode)

Yü-pao-tu

> Disturbed, upset,
> Chang remained silent.
> Madam Ts'ui chattered on,
> But however she tried,
> Chang didn't respond.
> Recklessly he drained goblet after goblet of wine.
> His annoyance showed on his face.
> He nibbled the delicacies, but now
> They had become tasteless
> Like so many lumps of clay.
> He thought to himself:
> 'I had such hopes of marrying Ying-ying!
> Who would've expected
> This criminal old hag to stand in the way. . . .

> 'The beautiful face of my love seems sculpted —
> It's ideally suited to the quiet plum-blossom makeup.
> How truly matchless is her flair,
> Her refinement,
> The perfection of her proportions!
> Her intelligent eyes are indescribably alluring.
> But despite my conspicuous attention,
> She doesn't look to my side.
> It's as if we're separated by the whole world
> Rather than these few inches.
> My sighs are in vain;
> They won't drive away Madam and her obstructions.
> Has heaven no pity on my misery?
> Even the thought of relinquishing my love
> Cuts my bowels to bits.

Coda

> 'How mean and cruel is my love's mother.
> It would've been better had she not invited me.
> Now I'm here, the sight of my love is gall to my eyes.'

[Prose]

Chang inquired about Ying-ying's age. Madam Ts'ui said: 'She is already sixteen.' Several times Chang addressed his remarks to Ying-ying, but she made no response. Thus, Chang could only admire her uneasily from afar. Finally, knowing there was no other way to bring up the subject of marriage, Chang pretended to be drunk and recommended himself: 'Although I am impoverished, Madam, both my father and grandfather were officials. Twice they were governors of large provinces, and later in their careers they handled imperial edicts in court. All my brothers now hold important positions; I am the only one who has not yet settled in a post. I began my studies early, when I was six; it has been seventeen years now. At twelve I studied the *Book of Rites,* at fourteen *Spring and Autumn,* at fifteen the *Book of Songs* and the *Book of Documents,* and altogether I have committed to memory more than five hundred thousand lines. At seventeen I read works of the philosophers, including works of the Zen and the Vinaya School of Buddhism. Later by emulating ancient models, I perfected my style of writing ministerial memorials on current affairs. So my efforts at preparing myself to excel in the civil examination as a means to obtain eminent positions cannot be said to lag behind those of others. Unfortunately a few years ago my father passed away. Because of this, I dismissed from my mind all aspirations for achievement and fame; I moved to the site of his tomb to carry out the funeral sacrifices. It was only recently that all the rites were completed. At present, there is an imperial edict announcing an examination for next year, which, of course, will provide an opportunity for men of worth to distinguish themselves. I certainly expect to succeed in this examination. Madam, please do not be offended by my self-recommendation, for even the great Tung-fang Shuo[77] had to submit self-promoting letters when he sought an audience with Emperor Wu-ti. Times indeed have changed, but the urgency of my cause is as great as his, so I have dared to match his impudence. After all, it was only by accident that I had the good fortune of meeting you in this temple. Since I cherish hopes of becoming related to you, if I do not reveal my past, how will Madam know my background? Emboldened by wine I have spoken freely. Forgive me, forgive me.'

Madam Ts'ui replied: 'I believe what you say, sir. But are you not fated never to be an official?'

'If I had taken advantage of my hereditary rights, I would have been an official years ago. That, however, is against my principles. When a man of worth lives in obscurity, it is because he chooses to do so to register his disdain for the world; once he decides to emerge from seclusion, invariably his renown soars to the skies. My opportunity to distinguish myself comes with the forthcoming examination. But Ying-ying, as you say, is already sixteen. May I ask why she is not yet engaged?'

---

[77] Statesman and man of letters of late-second and early-first centuries B.C. According to his biography in *Han shu,* Tung-fang submitted three thousand memorials to recommend himself to the throne. He was particularly famous for his wit.

Song of the God of Music

> Weeping, genuflecting, Chang
> Said: 'Excuse my impertinence,
>   how old is the young lady?'
> Madam Ts'ui answered: 'Sixteen.'
> Chang asked again: 'Why isn't she engaged?'
>
> Indeed, Madam was experienced.
> Instantly she perceived Chang's intentions.
> Deciding on a sly device,
> She dabbed at her tears with her sleeve.

[Prose]

Tears coursed down Madam's face. Slowly she said: 'Your questions, sir, reveal your gracious concern. My daughter Ying-ying is coarse and ugly. Were she to marry you, there would be three happy outcomes: one, we would show however inadequately, our gratitude for your profound kindness; two, I would gain someone on whom I can depend; three, my daughter would have a talented scholar as her husband. Such a turn of events would be most gratifying to me . . . '

Before she could finish, Chang rose to thank her: 'Though I am unworthy, I eagerly accept this marriage.'

Madam Ts'ui hurriedly rose in her turn and continued her speech: 'However, when my late husband was serving in court, my brother, Minister Cheng, insisted on having Ying-ying betrothed to his son, Cheng Heng, who is now nineteen years old. As Minister Cheng is a close relative, my late husband could not refuse him. Just as Ying-ying was to be married, my husband passed away and the wedding was postponed. Had it not been for this promise to Minister Cheng, I would certainly marry Ying-ying to you, to thank you for having saved my life.'

(*Hsien-lü-tiao* mode)

Rendezvous at the Fragrant Ti-hu Mountain

> When Chang heard this,
> He mumbled an excuse and begged to withdraw.
> Madam persuaded him to finish the meal.
> Chang couldn't decline, so
> He sat down once more.
> But even if nectar were served,
>   it couldn't have tempted him to drink again.

Neither would he speak,
He simply dozed over his wine.
His scheme to defeat the rebels had brought him no reward.
Deliberately he turned his drooping head away from his hostess.
His face was entirely flushed;
His body, numb and weary, half collapsed on the table.

[Prose]

Ying-ying saw how Chang revealed his intentions and how he expressed his admiration for herself. Though her heart did not revolve like a millwheel, it nevertheless moved [78]

(*Shuang-tiao* mode)

Moon Rises above the Crab Apple Tree

The solitary, aloof Chang
Now wished he'd had a confidante.
With his eyes he tried to transmit to Ying-ying an amorous message,
But her stern mother was watchful.
Unhappy, frustrated,
He knit his eyebrows in distress.

The lovers loathed to be kept apart.
They were victims of an evil karma. . . .
Then, amid the commotions of the banquet,
Chang wavered and collapsed in a heap.
Ying-ying said: 'Stop pressing wine on him.
My brother is drunk.'

[Prose]

Ying-ying said to her mother: 'Brother seems inebriated.' Chang opened his eyes and looked at Ying-ying. A smile spread over his face.

Madam Ts'ui said: 'I had hoped to finish the banquet, but now it seems Mr Chang is tired of drinking.' She ordered Hung-niang to accompany Chang to his apartment.

Without uttering a word, Chang left. When they reached his room, he took out a gold hairpin and presented it to Hung-niang. Surprised, Hung-niang

---

[78] A modification of *The Book of Songs* line: 'My heart is not a millwheel; it cannot revolve'.

said: 'Madam ordered me to accompany you, sir. Why should you bestow a gift upon me? Ah, I suspect you must be interested in my mistress Ying-ying, and since you have no way to communicate with her, you wish me to be an intermediary! That is why you are giving me this valuable gift!'

Chang conceded: 'Very intelligent indeed! You guessed exactly what is in my mind. You are Ying-ying's trusted maid, through you I can make my innermost feelings known to her. Should my suit succeed, I shall not forget your help.'

Hung-niang laughed and replied: 'From infancy my young mistress has been carefully brought up by her mother. Chastity and obedience have become part of her nature. Even those whom she respects and cherishes dare not offend her ears with anything improper; she can hardly be expected to follow the suggestions of a servant.'

(*Hsien-lü-tiao* mode)

Flower-Viewing Time

> The effect of wine deepened Chang's sorrow.
> 'Every way I turn, I face an impassable wall.
> Alas, all my sufferings are because of her.
> Is she, your young mistress,
> Aware of my feelings?

> 'My grief finds no relief, still
> I'm grateful to you; you, at least, know my mind.
> Let's consider the situation —
> My marriage to Ying-ying
> Depends entirely on your help.

Coda

> 'Don't refuse this humble gift.
> When I'm married, there'll be more.
> Hung-niang,
> I beg you to help.'

[Prose]

Hung-niang said: 'You are drunk, sir.' Leaving the hairpin behind, she ran off indignantly. Chang was greatly disappointed. Soon, it started to rain; with the sound of falling rain his melancholy grew.

(Chung-lü-tiao mode)

Punting a Solitary Boat, ch'an-ling

> Chang abandoned his ambition for fame and achievement.
> He set aside the Five Classics, the Three Histories.
> Because of Ying-ying, he behaved like a frivolous rake.
> *Hi-ho.*
> 'Madam Ts'ui is unfair and cruel.
> She lies despite her venerable age.
> Whatever hope I might have had,
> I know now that I broke the siege in vain.
> *Hi-ho.*
>
> 'All along,
> My beloved remained unapproachable.
> Hateful darling, am I never to share your quilt?
> *Hi-ho.*
> I tell myself to cease this longing, but my
>   restive eyes continue to gaze outside.
> They dart about, as if crazed, and I itch for a surprise.
> I gather a hundred kinds of anguish, a thousand sorts of distress
> On my knitted brows.
> *Hi-ho*

Alliterative and Rhyming Binomes

> 'The candle burns brightly.
> The night is yet young.
> My remorse multiplies and ramifies.
> My pillow is too large for me alone.
> The quilt is cold.
> Unable to sleep, I toss and turn and turn.
> Useless is my sigh,
> Useless is my grief,
> Useless is my effort to curb my longing —
> I long for her still.
> Inside, my sorrow riots and churns.
>
> 'My tears will not stop.
> Compared with last night
> Tonight seems interminable.
> When will the day break?
> Infatuated to the point of idiocy,
> I feel deranged, insane.

How can I bear this agony?
One moment I try to suppress my feelings,
The next my admiration returns in full force.
If I say I've forgotten her,
I'm but a liar;
Her image is etched on my mind.

Welcoming a Visiting Goddess

'Light-colored jade and
Plum-blossom appliqués show my love off best.
Her face inspires worship.
She behaves with rare grace:
Distinguished in every way.
If she wore a celestial robe,
She would be taken for Kuan-yin.

'Only in my dreams
Have I visited her. . . .
In the animal-shaped censer, the incense has burnt out.
A mouse, snuggling against the low couch,
Peeps at the lamp.
One wretched moth
Circles the lamp's flame.

Coda

'Soughing night-rain lacerates the window's paper panes.
Tattered paper, playing penants, snap in the wind.
Such forlornness, such gut-wrenching grief.'

[Prose]

Rain, driven across sparse latticing by damp wind,
Intensifies insomnia's tormenting sting.
The next morning, Hung-niang reappeared. She said to Chang: 'Madame Ts'ui sends you her greetings, sir. She wishes to inquire if you passed a comfortable night. Yesterday the banquet was not properly terminated and for this she begs your forgiveness.'

'The banquet was fine; in fact, such a sumptuous feast honored me excessively. There is, however, one thing which has been troubling me: at the time when the rioting soldiers clamored at the temple gate, Madam Ts'ui promised Ying-ying to me; yet, yesterday at the banquet, she asked her to treat me as a brother. Has she not greatly humiliated me? I have decided to put an end to my dealings with Madam Ts'ui and return west, to Ch'ang-an.

Song of the Goddess in the Cave

> 'In the throes of a crisis,
> She promised me her daughter in marriage.
> Now she breaks her word, heedless of the rules of correct behavior.
> It would have been better
> Had she made no promise initially.
> Well, so be it, if this is how she chooses to behave,
> I'll just avoid her; I'll shun her gate.
>
> 'I'll return
> To the capital.
> Tell your mistress and her daughter that
> They've lied to me.
> Tell them I've no intention of playing the besotted fool and
> Hanging about
> This temple.
> Give them my best wishes; tell them
> I've put my zither in its case and
> My writing in a folder.'

(*Shuang-tiao* mode)

Yü chieh hsing

> Utterly dejected, Chang was leaving
> For the capital.
> He packed up his zither and his sword, and
>   fastened a case of books on his back.
> He said to Hung-niang: 'Take care . . .'.
> Hung-niang looked at him and exclaimed:
> 'Congratulations, Mr Chang;
>
> 'A heaven-sent rescue
> Is right here before my eyes.
> I've been to your study many times
> Yet never have I noticed it before.
> Because of it
> You needn't leave;
> You'll marry your love.'

[Prose]

Hung-niang said: 'It pains me, sir, to see you so distressed. Allow me to say what is on my mind. A person's temperament is revealed by his likes and dislikes; his friends are those who share his likes and his enemies are those who take exception to them. When searching for a friend, a man looks for someone who shares the same interest. I have a scheme here which would bring Ying-ying to your room. Although I am ignorant and lowly placed, I hope you will attend to my advice.'

Chang answered: 'I have racked my brain and still cannot devise a way to meet Ying-ying. Now you have a plan that will bring her to me, would I dare disobey your directions? Indeed, even if you should ask me to throw myself into boiling water and walk through scorching fire, I would only be too glad to do so. Please give me your counsel and relieve my suffering.'

Hung-niang said: 'Ying-ying has studied music; she is particularly fond of the zither and the lute. I notice you have a zither and I suppose you must have played it for some time. If you are good at it, your playing will induce my young mistress to come.'

At this, Chang laughed with glee.

(*Hsien-lü-tiao* mode)

Lingering in the Perfumed Quilt

> That day Chang had been desperate with grief.
> Hung-niang's words made him smile and nod.
> 'Crazy child,
> You're not teasing me, are you?
> How do I know what you've said is not sheer nonsense?'
> Hung-niang reassured him: 'Don't worry, sir.
> Because of the zither
> You'll get your bride.
>
> 'Since antiquity, women have rarely understood music.
> One exception is Wen-chün.
> But ten thousand Wen-chüns
> Can't match one Ying-ying.
> My young mistress is wise, she's charming;
>   there's infinite subtlety in her personality.
> She loves to play the *cheng*[79] and
> Her skill at playing the zither and the lute
> Is truly unrivaled.

[79] A sixteen-string zither, whereas *ch'in,* which I have rendered as 'zither' throughout the *chantefable,* has seven strings.

Coda

'So you have no way to see her,
And you wonder how you can marry her.
No need for a betrothal token,
This seven-string zither will be your matchmaker.'

[Prose]

Hung-niang said: 'If you play two or three airs late at night, when Ying-ying hears you, she will certainly come. I shall follow her, and I shall cough to signal her arrival. Then you should switch from playing ancient melodies to singing and accompanying yourself on the zither. If you can arouse my young mistress with provocative lyrics, your suit will have a good chance of succeeding. Ying-ying herself is also skilled at composing lyrics extemporaneously; she may even respond to your song favorably. Do think over my suggestion, sir. My only worry is that you cannot play the zither well enough. . . .'

Chang said: 'I may not be talented in other ways, but I certainly am an expert musician on the zither!'

Chapter 4

(*Shuang-tiao* mode)

Wen ju chin

> If Ying-ying is as smart as you say,
> She shall be mine!
> As for my ability to play the zither —
> I'm not bragging like a spoiled child —
> Even while a toddler
> I performed on this instrument
> *The Lamenting Crow, The Grieving Crane* and
> *A Phoenix Taking Leave of Its Mate.*[80]
> Later, I spent thousands and
> Worked hard nearly seven years
> To learn from renowned masters.
> Seated by the window of a scented studio,
> Or in a tea pavilion,
> With verdant pines as my audience,
> I conjured up soaring mountains, flowing waters,
> Accumulating snow, and gathering winds.
>
> 'I understand thoroughly the three hundred new odes.
> When I interpret them,
> They sound like the original *feng, fu, ya* and *sung.*[81]
> Now playing an ancient air, now a new tune,
> I have an inexhaustible repertoire.
> I can depict a hero's uprightness,
> Subtle, secret joy,
> Ten thousand types of sadness,
> One thousand kinds of parting grief.
> I win the approval of connoisseurs;
> I move the sensitive.
> And tonight my playing
> May earn me the visit I desire.
> Should the Beauty appear,
> The skill I've labored for all my life
> Will have been put to proper use.

[80] Names of well-known tunes for the zither.
[81] *Feng, ya,* and *sung* are sections of *The Book of Songs. Fu* refers no doubt to Han *fu.*

Coda

> 'I'm not joking, Hung-niang.
> Just listen to this tune,
> Even a man of stone — let alone your sister — would be moved.'

[Prose]

Hung-niang took her leave.

(*Hsien-lü-tiao* mode)

Flower-Viewing Time

> Left alone, Chang was wild with restlessness.
> He waited anxiously for dusk.
> Flower shadows seeped through the silk panes of the window.
> 'When will it be dark
> So I can see my cursed love?'

> He polished his zither with jasper mountings;
>   he cleaned the incense burner.
> 'Heaven forbid I should fall asleep tonight.
> Let me brew a pot of Chien-hsi tea.'[82]
> In quick succession he gulped down cup after cup. . . .
> 'What luck!
> I hear homing crows, cawing in the yard.'

Coda

> Wisps of colored clouds drifted across the blue sky.
> Evening bells tolled;
> As the ringing died,
> A melancholy horn on the garrison tower sounded 'Plum Blossoms.'[83]

[Prose]

That night the sky was cloudless, the moon dazzlingly bright. Chang put his zither across his knees.

---

[82] Tea from Chien-hsi in Fukien, high in theine content.
[83] A tune dating from the T'ang dynasty. It was used as taps in army camps.

(*Chung-lü-tiao* mode)

Courtyard Covered with Frost

In his quiet room a lamp flickered.
Light breeze sifted through the sparse bamboo curtain,
Ambergris incense blazed in the censer.
Holding and stroking his zither,
Chang felt stirred, excited.
Though small, his study had an unworldly charm,
Quite the equal of a forest dotted with springs.
As he tuned the zither,
Lamenting rooks, grieving cranes
Gathered on the seven strings.

The tuning evolved into an ancient air,
Interpreted with orthodox purity.
Classic techniques were used to reveal the most intricate subtleties.
Gradually the music changed to a modern tune,
With a lyric filled with exquisite sentiments.
One tune brought whispering wind passing through pines,
Then lively creeks rippled over rocky hills.
Nothing made a sound in the courtyard.
If Ying-ying was up,
She'd be bound to come and listen.

[Prose]

The words to one of the tunes were as follows: [84]
My zither has
Jade pegs and
Gold stops.
Elegant is its sound,
Subtle its tone:
It is black cranes congregating by a grotto,
Cawing rooks circling round a wood.
My music cleanses ears contaminated by the clamor of contention,

---

[84] The form of the ensuing passage is delightfully neat in the original. The passage contains
seven sets of strictly parallel lines. The first set has three lines of two characters; the
second, third, fourth, fifth, and sixth sets have two lines of three, four, five, six, and
seven characters respectively; the last set has two lines of ten characters. Although I
managed to retain the parallelism, I was unable to reproduce the form in my translation.

And brings harmony to just and moral hearts.
It washes granite cliffs with pine-scented wind,
And splashes distant water against lonely peaks.
Unlike the *cheng*, appealing to one and all,
My music delights but a few connoisseurs.
A traveller's agonizing homesickness is calmed by
       the refined melodies;
A drunkard's muddled dream is chased away by the solemn notes.
Hung-niang said to Ying-ying: 'Mr Chang is playing the zither; the music is
dignified and elegant. Can we go and listen?'
    Ying-ying asked: 'Has Madam retired?'
    Hung niang said: 'Madam has been fast asleep for some time now.'
Secretly Ying-ying left with Hung-niang.

(*Chung-lü-tiao* mode)

Butterfly

Who plays the zither and
Arouses abruptly this inebriated spirit?
In the coolness of the night, the temple yard is empty.
As Ying-ying and Hung-niang walk, young spring's delicate chill
Penetrates through their feather-light gowns
And thin silk stockings.
The night wanes;
The moon, moving, alters the position of flower shadows.

Ying-ying listens attentively
To the lofty, unworldly sound.
Soon she crosses the yard, and finds herself walking on a
      flower-lined path.
She approaches the middle court
On tiptoe.
As she nears Chang's room
She stops, hesitates,
Her heart thumping violently.

Coda

Her tongue pushes against her teeth; she dares not make a sound.
Inclining an ear toward the window,
She hears a pure, glorious wind vibrating on the strings.

[Prose]

Hung-niang coughs by the window. Hearing it, Chang is seized with joy and surprise. He says to himself: 'Ying-ying is here. Let me see what I can do.'

(*Hsien-lü-tiao* mode)

Cherishing the Chrysanthemum

> Chang of Ch'ing-ho
> Is overwhelmed with joy.
> He puts more incense in the censer,
> Kowtows and bows, praying for divine inspiration.
> 'My ten fingers,
> I have never neglected you.
> Now it's your turn to show what you can do for me.
>
> 'All my life I've slept alone,
> So you, my fingers, haven't been idle for a single night.
> But tonight's performance
> Is something altogether different.
> My sorrow
> Must so move Ying-ying that she'll want to marry me.
> Lucky for me, you'd say,
> > but my luck will bring you your respite from toil.

Flower-Viewing Time

> A strand of green smoke coils up languidly from the censer.
> In a vase,
> Pear blossoms glow amid branches of apricot.
> Chang retunes the zither;
> Soon, a masculine and a feminine voice emerge.
>
> With abandon he expresses his feelings.
> He knows, because of the cough, that Ying-ying has come.
> She stands for a long time by the window,
> Drinking in the music;
> Tears roll down her cheeks, dampening her rouge.

Coda

> It's not an ancient melody, nor a popular song,
> Neither *Flowing Water,* nor *Soaring Mountain,*
> Note after note the song reveals his love.

[Prose]

Accompanying himself on the zither, Chang sings:[85]
> There is a lady *tra-la*,
> Whose beauty I cannot forget.
> She vanishes one day *tra-la*,
> Leaving me insane with longing.
> Like a soaring phoenix *tra-la*,
> I fly off in search of her.
> But the haughty Beauty *tra-la*
> Cunningly eludes me.
> Playing on my zither *tra-lu*,
> I call out to the desired one:
> 'When will you, my lady, *tra-la*,
> Vouchsafe to dispel my misery?
> Promise to be my wife *tra-la*,
> And share your life with me.
> If you reject my suit *tra-la*
> I shall perish in agony.'

The words are moving and Chang's sincerity is obvious. Indeed his singing is like the wailing of a crane when it parts from its mate. Not realizing what she does, Ying-ying sobs audibly. Just as puffs of air spread the perfume she wears, her sobbing broadcasts her emotion. Chang hears Ying-ying weep and knows his song has moved her. He pushes aside his zither and rises.

(*Shuang-tiao* mode)

Water-Chestnut Fragrance
> The night is cold.
> Ten fingers, playing,
> Reveal Chang's feelings.
> After the short song,
> The courtyard is filled with devastating spring grief.
> Intensely moved, Ying-ying
> Can't control her tears.
> In an undertone, she murmurs and sighs.
> Chang hears her,
> And pushes aside the zither.

> Burning with impatience, he throws open the door;
> in the moonlight

[85] This song is in the *Ch'u-ko* style with the syllable *hsi* at the end of each half line. *Faute de mieux*, I have substituted 'tra-la' for *hsi*.

106

He sees Ying-ying, alone,
Standing by the window.
He goes to her,
Embraces her passionately and caresses her with great gentleness:
'My cruel, heartless love,
Don't you see your youth matches perfectly my prime?
Why resist? It's written in our karma,
That we'll
Sleep together tonight.'

Coda

The girl trembles with fright.
In a feeble voice she says: 'Master, Master,
Are you so hot with desire that you can't even open your eyes?'

[Prose]

Whom did Chang embrace? Who was it? Chang bowed and looked at the girl carefully.

(*Chung-lü-tiao* mode)

Falcon Attacking a Hare

Addle-headed,
Foolish,
Reckless, rash,
Without making sure who the girl is,
Chang seizes her and begins to make love to her.
How he vows his devotion!
How he confides his hidden thoughts!
Like a rake, a roué,
He gives free rein to his passions.
After cooing 'Ying-ying!'
He looks carefully
And finds the girl to be Hung-niang!

Absolutely stunned!
Stupefied!
He now hears girdle pendants
Tinkle in the moonlight.
A pair of tiny lily-feet

Step hurriedly;
A skirt, gathered around a willowly waist,
Sways widely;
A startled heart thumps violently;
Panting,
A young lady disappears round the veranda.

Coda

Creak, she half opens a red gate,
Her perfume of musk lingers in the air.
It's obviously not in their karma to make love that night;
Chang is heartbroken.

[Prose]

Chang asked Hung-niang: 'What did Ying-ying say just now?'
'Not a word. She only sighed and wept. From what I know of my
mistress, I would say that she was moved. I shall observe her closely tonight
and report back to you tomorrow morning.'
When Hung-niang got back, Ying-ying had already retired for the night.
Candle light illuminates her room;
Sad thoughts disturb her sleep.

(*Chung-lü-tiao* mode)

Green Peonies

The night grew old; the clepsydra dripped quietly.
Ying-ying was distraught with sorrow.
Hugging her quilt, sleepless,
She mused to herself:
'Brother Chün-jui
Is miserable because of me.
In vain he longs for me,
Suffers for me,
Frets for me.

'Just now he called to me with his zither.
Though I'm inexperienced,
I do see that
He's a good match for me.
I'm young,

108

So is he, and moreover,
He's intelligent;
He's handsome;
He's talented.

Falcon Attacking a Hare

'Unfortunately my mother
Is hard to please.
A perfectionist, she's most exacting.
Though a woman
She has the moral integrity of a man.
My father,
As a Prime Minister,
Had managed affairs of the world.
His loyalty and filial piety were unexceptionable.
I've been brought up properly in the ladies' sequestered quarters.
The slightest indiscretion on my part
Will tarnish my late father's good name.

'Mother's principal objection
Is that Brother Chang hasn't yet distinguished himself.
His wooing just now can only
Tease and taunt me.
Of course I admire his superb Ssu-ma talent.
Of course I admire his handsome P'an Yüeh looks:
But I'm not my own mistress;
My marriage is not for me to decide.
Would that I had someone
To transmit to him
All that I feel and think!'

Alliterative and Rhyming Binomes

The night was drawing to an end.
Ying-ying was wide awake.
From the jewelled, animal-shaped censer, coils of incense rose.
Her pillow was cold,
Her quilt chilly, and
A decorated candle flickered forlornly.
'When will this anguish end?
When?'
Closing her eyes with determination,
She tried to sleep.

The night seemed interminable as she repeatedly
    woke from disturbing dreams.

Her face turned away from the candle,
She wept with muffled sobs.
Countless were her tears.
Till, at the end,
The candle burned out,
The incense was reduced to ashes,
Yet her misery increased.
She scolded herself;
She laughed at herself;
She sighed;
She pounded her bed and kicked her feet.
Anxiously she watched for morning, but morning did not come.

Coda

No morning bell: the doltish novice must have over-slept.
Why did the wretched moon drag its feet and
Sluggish roosters refuse to crow?

[Prose]

Ying-ying did not sleep all night; she only dozed off briefly toward morning.
Hung-niang was greatly affected by her mistress's suffering. At the first light
of dawn, she rose to report to Chang what she had seen.

(*Huang-chung-kung* mode)

The Golden Altar Boy, ch'an-ling

Getting up hurriedly,
Filled with worry and concern,
Hung-niang quickly dressed and left her mistress's room.
'If Master Chang is up,
I'll tell him
Everything I saw.'

She rushed toward the gate,
Unlocked it and
Dashed straight to Chang's study.
In the east, morning light glowed,
    but what was Chang doing

That candles still burned in
His room?

Hung-niang moistened the paper window,
Poked a hole, and
Saw Chang sitting up, with a robe thrown around his shoulders.
Was he busy composing?
Writing *shih* or *fu*?
Studying?
She could see that he was breathing quickly,
Mumbling to himself non-stop.
Now he seemed to scold himself;
Now he looked despondent;
Suddenly he wept, and still weeping, he started to sing —

Dancers' Exit

He was behaving just like a lunatic, with
His eyebrows tightly knit.
Tears stole down Hung-niang's cheeks.
'How can Madam, a Minister's widow,
Be so mean, so excessively cruel!

Coda

'Her action is unworthy of a noble lady;
It's that of a crafty shrew —
Causing my young mistress and Master Chang such unhappiness.'

[Prose]

Hung-niang called: 'Open the door.' When Chang saw her, he was pleased and
surprised.

(*Hsien-lü-tiao* mode)

A Splendid Calabash

With her hair ornament Hung-niang knocked at the door.
Chang asked: 'Who is it?'
'It's me, Hung-niang, I'd like to see you.'

111

Hearing this, Chang
Quickly opened the door, and said at once:
'I'll bet your young mistress has sent you here.

'Yesterday, stupidly I missed seeing her.
I let her slip from my grasp.
All night I was tormented by agony. . . .'
Hung-niang said: 'Now,
Let me tell you what seems
To be on my mistress's mind.'

[Prose]

Hung-niang said to Chang: 'Do not worry, sir. From what I can observe, I
believe my young mistress is very much in love with you. Allow me to tell
you how I think she feels.'

(*Chung-lü-tiao* mode)

Lun-t'ai, an Ancient Border Town

'Don't worry, Master,
Let me start from the beginning.
Last night my mistress
Heard your zither-playing and your song.
She listened, spellbound,
Sometimes murmuring to herself,
        sometimes scratching her head, looking perplexed.
Though her hand covered her mouth,
I could hear her sigh,
"A pity that Mother is so stubborn.
I doubt if she'd ever let us marry."
So, evidently, she had
Understood your song!
My young mistress is not cold —
She is distressed by your sorrow, but
You see, she's not free and that's the trouble.
If I were to guess,
I'd say that she'll lose weight on your account from now on.'

Hung-niang's words
Dispelled without a trace Chang's worry.
'Who would have thought that my darling, my love
Could be so susceptible to my suit!

She was moved by my song, you say;
Clearly she can be seduced.
When the time comes,
I'll caress her with utmost tenderness.
We'll make love behind embroidered bed-curtains and
Stay by each other's side for a hundred years.
Yet her response is really no surprise;
  I'm after all a first-class writer,
A genuinely talented man.
Broad-minded,
Generous,
Handsome.
So how can
Your beautiful mistress resist me?

Coda

 'Now that she knows I'm the equal of Hsiang-ju,
 Maybe she'll find a way
 To emulate Wen-chün and elope with me.'

[Prose]

Chang said: 'Since she was moved by my song, it will not be difficult to guide her actions henceforth.' He brought out a brush and an ink-stone and began to compose a poem.

(*Shuang-tiao* mode)

A Visit to the Imperial Capital

 The four treasures[86] of a gentleman's study were all laid out.
 Chang fussed and fussed with the pine-soot ink
 Before he dipped the brush in the rich, thick fluid.
 He smoothed a sheet of embellished stationery,
 And sobbed as he wrote,
 Pouring out his longing to his love.

 No rough draft, he never paused or groped for words.
 After the usual greeting,
 Swiftly he finished a poem.
 His handwriting was as elegant as that of Hsi-chih.[87]

---

[86] Paper, ink-stick, brush, and ink-stone.
[87] Wang Hsi-chih (321–79), famous calligrapher and writer of the Chin dynasty.

He sealed the letter, stained with his tears.
On the envelope he made the emblem of a pair of mandarin ducks.[88]

[Prose]

Chang asked Hung-niang: 'May I trouble you to deliver this letter to Ying-ying?'
  Hung-niang replied: 'My young mistress is well-known for her fastidious
adherence to propriety, and I have never dared place anything even slightly
provocative before her. Now, because you have saved us from the recent
calamity, and because of my young mistress's admiration for you, I am willing
to make an exception and comply with your command.'
  She took Chang's letter and left it on Ying-ying's dressing table. When
Ying-ying got up and began her toilet, she saw the note.

(*Hsien-lü-tiao* mode)

Flower-Viewing Time

> Rain-drenched cherry blossoms, brilliant as blood,
>   dripped from outstretching branches.
> Each coquettish flower, showing off its color,
>   displayed a different hue of red or purple.
> The morning rain had just stopped.
> Ying-ying got up, began her toilet,
> And was about to attend to her makeup.
>
> She spotted the letter and picked it up:
> Decorated paper with a few lines of writing —
> A poem filled with anguished longing.
> She bowed her head,
> Read it again, and sank in deep thought.

Coda

> Suddenly she turned to Hung-niang and screamed:
>   'How dare you do this to me?
> You perfidious, pernicious, crazy, slave.
> You're asking to be killed.'
> She aimed a mirror at Hung-niang's face.

[88] Symbols of conjugal happiness.

114

[Prose]

A mirror was hurled, tassel-ribbons flew in the air.
The polished disk crashed, patterned tiles broke into bits.
Moving quickly, Hung-niang managed to avoid the mirror. She apologized to
Ying-ying: 'Indeed I deserve to be killed; indeed I deserve to be killed.'
Chang's poem read:
As I long for you, my frustration becomes unbearable,
I entrust my feelings to my zither.
When spring reigns, desire is the master;
Does not your flower-heart[89] stir and tingle?
Do not repress what is natural —
Reputation is but so many bubbles.
Why scorn the moon when it dazzles?
Look, yonder blossoms cast dense, concealing shadows.

(*Hsien-lü-tiao* mode)

An Embroidered Belt

Sitting by the window,
In front of a mirror,
Ying-ying picks up the note
With her delicate, slender hand.
She opens it and sees that
It's a lascivious poem.
She has risen in an agitated mood,
Now the provocative language
Distresses her intensely.
She lowers her head,
With darkened expression and knitted brows,
She bawls loudly: 'Brother Chang is as licentious as a pig, a dog!
If Madam were to find this out,
I'd be in a pretty stew!

'You depraved, contemptible slave, you're not to be endured.
I ought to chop off that ass's head of yours!
It can't have been anyone else,
Helping to lead me astray.
The impudence to leave within my reach
A note of this nature!
I'll let you off this time.

[89] A euphemism for the clitoris.

But if you should do it again,
You'll have no one but yourself to blame.
You may wonder why I'm willing
To drop the matter and
Not get to the bottom of it.
Well, it's because Brother Chang once rescued my mother and myself.

Coda

'If you go to his study again for no good reason
And once more try to compromise me,
I'll break your legs and sew up your mouth.'

[Prose]

Ying-ying said: 'Who could have brought the poem here but you? However, since Brother Chang once saved our lives, I shall not disclose this matter to anyone. You must never participate in such a plot again.'

Hung-niang asked Ying-ying to forgive her.

Ying-ying then added: 'At the moment I do not wish to scold Brother Chang to his face.'

She scribbled something on Chang's letter and asked Hung-niang to return it to him, saying: 'This will tell my brother how I feel.'

Hung-niang became quite alarmed; in fear and trembling she hurried to Chang's room. Chang, startled, asked her what had happened.

(*Hsien-lü-tiao* mode)

Adorning Crimson Lips

Chang was surprised to see
A tearful Hung-niang with knitted brows.
He pleaded: 'Sister, sister,
Don't tease me like this.

'Please reassure me that my winsome Ying-ying
Will be my mate, and
That late at night
She'll emulate Wen-chün and
Elope with me.'

Coda

At this, Hung-niang said scornfully: 'Stop this nonsense,
This wild ranting, this shameless raving.

116

> Your winsome Ying-ying is itching to break my legs
> and sew up my mouth.'

[Prose]

Hung-niang said: 'You almost implicated me.'
   'How so?'
   Hung-niang described in detail what Ying-ying had said. Surprised, Chang pondered aloud: 'What should I do now?'
   Hung-niang showed him Ying-ying's reply. After reading it, Chang said with a smile: 'My wish will be fulfilled.'
   Hung-niang asked with astonishment: 'When I left her, my young mistress was very angry. What could she have written to make you so happy?'
   Chang explained to Hung-niang the meaning of Ying-ying's poem, which bore the title: 'The Moon on the Night of the Three Fives', and which read:

> Waiting for the moon in the western chamber,
> I welcome the wind with the door ajar.
> Above the wall, flower shadows move —
> Is it my lover who's approaching across the yard?

'Now, today is the fifteenth, and Ying-ying's poem is entitled "The Moon on the Night of the Three Fives", thus the poem is intended for tonight. Since the night of the fifteenth is noted for its brilliant moon, the first line of the poem reads: "Waiting for the moon in the western chamber". The second line, "I welcome the wind with the door ajar", indicates that she will leave her door open for me. The third line, "Above the wall, flower shadows move", commands me to climb onto a blossoming branch and hoist myself over the wall; and the last line, "Is it my lover who's approaching across the yard", says that I, Chang Chün-jui, have finally come.'
   Hung-niang laughed and said: 'Your interpretation is most ingenious, but it seems to me to be quite forced. It probably reveals more the depth of your infatuation than the true content of the verse.'
   After saying this, she left. The rest of the day Chang did nothing except wait for the night.

(*Huang-chung-kung* mode)

Dancers' Exit

> 'A stone's throw can outdistance the horizon,
>   I'm so remote from my love!
> It's entirely her fault that I feel ill.
> How many hours yet to evening?
> The perverse sun, why doesn't it move?

Torturing me thus!
Its hypocritical, warm face stays absolutely still,
Not caring what turmoil besets my heart.
General Teng[90], won't you move faster?
I've never been remiss in my offerings,
Now I regret the incense, the flowers I've wasted on you.

Coda

'One quarter feels like a summer.
You may be a Bodhisattva, a god,
But if you don't get moving, you'll be beaten by the Sage.'[91]

[Prose]

That evening, immediately after the first watch, when the moon had scarcely
risen, Chang sneaked off to the eastern wall. No one was in sight.

(*Chung-lü-tiao* mode)

Green Peonies

The night descends; the clepsydra drips quietly;
Chang goes to meet Ying-ying.
Stone steps are strewn with fallen petals, and
The eastern wind, rolling up door-curtains,
        is charged with the scent of flowers.
Holding the edge of his robe,
Chang turns quickly round the veranda.
When he reaches the white-washed wall,
He wonders
How he can get across.

Worried that he might be seen
Or heard,
He seizes a slanting apricot branch.
At his touch, startled blossoms fall.
He clambers onto the wall,
His heart pounds —
He's afraid of the moon's brightness,

---

[90] A very curious bit of particularized anthropomorphism. I have not been able to
discover its origin or details of the myth.
[91] Hsi-ho, charioteer of the sun.

118

Madam's sternness, and
The dogs' menacing bark.

Coda

'Clouds, cover up the moon, so my shadow will not be seen;
Watchdogs, don't bark;
Madam, sleep soundly.'

(*Huang-chung-kung* mode)

The Golden Oriole

Chang Chün-jui,
Chang Chün-jui,
Jumping from the eastern side,
Falls, spread-eagled, on the western ground.
A loud voice cries: 'Who's there?'
Chang says: 'It's me, sent here by fate.'
Hung-niang mocks him: 'Only with feet solidly on the ground,
Can a man hope to achieve anything.
And you expect to vault over the dragon gate.[92]
Just look at you, you can't even scale this wall!'

[Prose]

At first Chang wondered who had called. He was relieved to see that it was
Hung-niang. Hung-niang asked him: 'Coming at this hour of the night, are
you not inviting suspicion?'

(*Shuang-tiao* mode)

Tuning the Zither and the Lute

Hung-niang said loudly:
'What cheek,
Coming to others' courtyards
In the middle of the night.
I'll turn you over to the magistrate tomorrow.
He'll judge you, all right.
You think he'd let you go?
You can be sure that he'll lock you up for at least a few nights.'

[92] Lung-men, a narrow gorge in the Yellow River, between Shensi and Shansi. According
to legend, fish which successfully negotiate this dangerous passage instantly metamorphose
into dragons. The geographic name, which literally means 'a dragon gate', is often used as
a metaphor for the taxing civil examinations.

Chang
Urgently replied:
'Listen,
Listen,
There's no need for you to shout.
I've got a letter in my pocket with the lines:
"To welcome the wind, I open my door;
I wait for the moon in the western chamber."
These lines, with their hidden meaning,
Came from your young mistress.
Why be so obtuse, Hung-niang,
And deny me entry?

Coda

'Your mistress intends to bestow her favors on me tonight.
So hurry in and announce that
Her lover is at the door.'

[Prose]

How do I know that there was a poem inviting Chang to a rendezvous?
Its existence is attested by *The Ballad of the True Story of Ying-ying*. The
Ballad sings:
To express his longing and his love,
An ardent letter does Chang draft.
He sends it by the wind of spring,
Which takes and carries it on its wings.
Ying-ying reads it o'er and o'er,
A poem she pennèd as her answer.
Acting with the greatest care,
She asks a bluebird her message to bear.
Couched in the verse's elegant diction,
Are subtle hints for an assignation:
'When, on the fifteenth, the moon does rise,
Will you, my beloved, come to my side?'
Once more Chang explained to Hung-niang the meaning of Ying-ying's poem.
Hung-niang then said: 'Please wait here, sir. I shall announce your arrival to
my young mistress.'
   Shortly, Hung-niang reappeared, running. Without waiting to catch her
breath she cried: 'My mistress is coming; my mistress is coming!'
   Chang was overjoyed, thinking that his wishes would soon be gratified.
Yet, when Ying-ying did appear, she had on a sombre dress, and her
expression was serious and forbidding. With severity she scolded Chang:

120

'By saving our lives, you have rendered us a great favor; thus, my mother entrusted my brother and myself to your protection. But now, why do you deliver to me, with the help of an insubordinate maid, such a lascivious letter? In the beginning, when you rescued me from the rebels, you acted out of a sense of justice, but now you are yourself using corrupting words as a means to achieve the same goal as that of the mutinous mob. The rebels clamored; you resort to a devious scheme: the methods are different but your aims are the same. I had originally wanted to keep to myself the knowledge of your misconduct, but it became clear to me that a chaste woman must not conceal people's licentiousness. I also had thought of acquainting Mother with what you had done, but that would have been repaying good with evil. If I had asked a maid to reprimand you, I could not have been sure she would express fully the extent of my distress. Had I referred you to some moral essay, in the hope that you would discover the appropriate lesson therein, I would have been afraid you might be unwilling to take the trouble to read it.[93] In the end I decided to entice you hither with a base and suggestive poem. Are you not ashamed of your impropriety? Allow me to remind you, Brother, to keep an upright mind and to avoid all that is immoral and incorrect so that I may safeguard my chastity and continue in my womanly virtue.'

(*Pan-she-tiao* mode)

A Whistle Song, ch'an-ling

> That night Ying-ying
> Rebuked Chang
> At length.
> 'You recall, it all started when we were besieged by the rebels.
> My mother was terrified that
> Her loved ones,
> Her servants, maids,
> Would be
> Massacred and
> Killed.

---

[93] There can be an alternative interpretation to this passage, 'Were I to write you an edifying poem, in the hope that you might discern the lesson yourself, I would be afraid that you would blame me for being unmannerly.' The key difference between the two interpretations is created by giving different meanings to the terms '*chang*' and '*chien-nan*' In this alternative interpretation, the implication must be that Ying-ying feels it is less 'unmannerly' to reprimand Chang to his face than to write him an edifying poem. Since it is hardly reasonable for Ying-ying to feel this way, I have preferred the first interpretation.

When you, sir,
Offered a clever scheme,
    my mother was grateful.
Your benefaction was thought to be
    as splendid as the mountain,
    as profound as the sea.
My brother and I were told
To regard you as our brother.
From that day on, we've never failed
To treat you with the utmost respect.

'This morning you sent to me, through my maid,
A provocative poem.
When I read it,
I couldn't be sure that you had really meant to compromise me.
I therefore
Had a message delivered to you,
Suggesting, as a ploy, a secret rendezvous.
Your presence here proves your guilt.
Surely, you must have studied
The teachings of Confucius:
"Of the five virtues, propriety and righteousness
    are the most important. . . ."
"After the age of seven, a brother must not
    share the same mat with a sister. . . ."
Won't you, Brother, be guided
By these precepts?

A Fast Melody

'It's highly reprehensible for you
To leave your study at night
And come stealthily into a widow's home.
Had it been anyone else, we'd have seized him like a thief.
Let my remonstrances be a reminder:
Learn from your mistake and henceforth mend your ways.'

Coda

'I've been frank and
Direct in my criticism — forgive me —
But when you harbor such ignominious designs on your sister,
You forfeit all the respect due you, including the title "Master".'

122

[Prose]

Chang felt utterly miserable, not knowing whether to stay or to leave. Color drained from Hung-niang's face, so bewildered was she by this unexpected turn of events.

(*Pan-she-tiao* mode)

Nocturnal Visit to the Palace

    When Ying-ying finished speaking, she immediately withdrew.
    Chang was mortified.
    To make matters worse, Hung-niang said:
    'Congratulations! Congratulations!
    I see you're to marry my young mistress!

    'I'm an uneducated, ignorant girl,
    So of course I couldn't understand
        the hidden meaning of my mistress's poem.
    I thought that since you, sir,
        have penetrated the secrets of the Classics,
    Your interpretation must have been impeccable.
    Little did I know that it was but a hasty, slapdash resolution
        of a riddle beyond your comprehension!'

[Prose]

Hung-niang cried: 'For shame! For shame!' Her raillery brought a smile to Chang's face. After regaining his composure Chang said slowly:

(*Hsien-lü-tiao* mode)

An Embroidered Belt

    'What's this? What's this?
    You've seen
    How she rages and rants without
    Any regard for the truth.
    It was she who invited me here, and
    Now she reviles me with such harshness,
    Talking about impropriety!

After all, I'm her brother,
Treating me like an absolute nothing!
Judging from her behavior, one can see that
Her heart must be made of clay, of wood.
By insulting me, she manages to vaunt her own chastity.
To whom can I complain
About this undeserved humiliation?

'Hung-niang, sister, you're observant;
You know how I saved her and her mother.
Could you have foreseen that
She'd forget my kindness so soon?
You see how I stand dumb and
Mute in front of her —
Suffering this frightful lashing without the slightest protest.
To my way of thinking, I've been free of guilt.
Yet I dare not argue with that Meng-chiang-nü,[94] using
All those classical terms and phrases.
What a display of dazzling eloquence!
It reduces me to utter silence.
Though silent, I do feel;
I feel my shame intensely.

Coda

'Well, all right, I'll leave . . .
        ah, I see, the gate is locked.
Hung-niang, why don't I sleep with you tonight?'
Hung-niang said: 'Now you're really getting outrageous.
        Away with you this instant!'

[Prose]

Chang blushed at Hung-niang's reproach. He lingered a little longer and
finally left the Ts'ui court with reluctance.

---

[94] One of the most widely celebrated paragons of womanly virtue, Meng-chiang-nü lived
in the third century B.C. Tradition has it that when her husband, Fan Ch'i-liang, was sent
on corvée to build the Great Wall, she walked the long and arduous journey to deliver
winter clothes to him. By the time she reached the site he had already died. Her grief was
so profound and her wailing so moving that the Wall collapsed to expose the buried body
of Fan.

(*Pan-she-tiao* mode)

Su-mu-che

>Dejected, Chang
>Once more clambered over the wall.
>He stumbled listlessly back to his study.
>The lamp on his wall guttered.
>He lay on his bed, unable to sleep.
>He was beset with sadness; the night seemed as long as a year.

>'How can the heart, only an inch in diameter,
>   contain these ten thousand folds of sorrow?
>I must be paying for something I did
>In a previous existence.
>My eyes refuse to close.
>My tears will not dry.
>I weep to the moon, framed in the western window.

Song of Che-Tree Branches

>'Her petal-like lips can be so scathing.
>How can I explain the mystery that
>I had hoped to have her as my wife,
>But she turned out to be a mortal foe, a Wu to my Yüeh?[95]

>'The frown on my brows can't be unlocked;
>The knot on my heart can't be untied.
>Even if I owed her a debt in a previous incarnation,
>You'd think there'd be a limit to how much I must pay!

Flowers above the Wall.

>'I had hoped
>To have a secret affair.
>Now see what happened.
>Did I spoil it by indiscretion?
>Did someone else sabotage it?

>'She finds it convenient to forget
>The rebels' siege.
>It suits her now to boast about her chastity.
>Oh, fickle, cruel lover, you're a pair with
>Your calculating, faithless mother.

[95] Enemy states of long standing during the Spring and Autumn Era (770–480 B.C.).

'The response you wrote to my poem —
Your note —
Was all a sham.
How can I rid myself of this rancor?
Never will I write another love lyric
Or *billet-doux*.

Coda

'I'll stay here
And watch
How heaven punishes her.
No, no, no, there will be no escape for the ingrate.'

[Prose]

Chang forced himself to rise and remove his robe. He lay down again.

(*Huang-chung-kung* mode)

Dancers' Exit

'It's she who's guilty of ungratefulness,
Yet she scorns and chastises me.
Seeing that I'm meek, she becomes doubly arrogant.
Deliberately she works herself into a rage.
What a contrast between her sharp rebuff and
        her mother's eager promise of marriage
        when the rebels surrounded the temple!

'I pretended not to hear
Her pyrotechnics of abuse.
Now back in my room, I face this annoying lamp —
It won't blaze,
And it won't die.
I am suffocating with frustration.'

Coda

Chang dozed, then woke.
Suddenly, toward the end of the second watch,
He heard someone pounding at his door.

126

Chapter 5

[Prose]

Chang opened the door and could hardly contain his joy. Whom did he see? Whom did he see?

> A pillow for one head
> Is shared by two.
> A single-sized quilt
> Covers a pair.

Who was it? Who was it? It was Ying-ying. Astonished, Chang said: 'But only just now you dismissed me most unceremoniously. . . .' Ying-ying replied: 'Ah, that was merely a ruse to protect me from my maid.' Chang put his arm around Ying-ying and led her to bed.

(*Hsien-lü-tiao* mode)

An Embroidered Belt

> Happy,
> Laughing, Chang embraced Ying-ying.
> Then he set her on his lap.
> Tenderly he reproached her: 'Heartless love,
> You really shouldn't have
> Scolded me like that.
> So this time passion stirs in you, and
> You have come to me!
> You're a terrible tease —
> In the note
> Were clear hints that you'd sleep with me.
> Who'd have thought that you didn't mean a word you wrote.
> Why did you
> Toy with me so?'

> Ying-ying
> Apologized humbly.
> Giggling, she charmed Chang with flattering words.
> Her lips lightly touching his ear,
> She confided her distress.
> Her face was as smooth as powder.
> Her musk lipstick emanated a luxurious scent.

Lying under the embroidered quilt,
    the lovers created a sea of red waves.
His arms entwined with hers,
Chang fondled her passionately.
There was still a touch of the old Ying-ying —
She was coy; yet her very shyness
    invited wilder caresses and love.
With a smile she offered her tongue. . . .
Suddenly Chang woke up.
There was no one by his side.

Coda

Tang, tang tolled the temple bell.
Unable to find Ying-ying, Chang knew he had dreamt.
Such intense disappointment!
By the Ch'u terrace, the clouds and rain had
    vanished without a trace.[96]

[Prose]

A distant bell chased away an erotic dream.
The morning horn brought forth boundless grief.

(*Chung-lü-tiao* mode)

Walking on the Sedge

Because of his unfeeling Wen-chün,
An infatuated Hsiang-ju
Abandoned his worldly ambition.
Chang took to writing poetry;
He filled sheet after sheet with *ying-ying, ying-ying, ying-ying.*

Like Shen Yüeh,[97]
Like P'an Yüeh,[97]

[96] 'Clouds and rain', *yün-yü*, is a euphemism for love-making. The euphemism evolved from the *Kao-t'ang fu* by Sung Yü, (*c.* 290 – *c.*223 B.C.), in which the Goddess of Wu says to King Huai of Ch'u, after having made love to him, 'In the morning I shall transform myself into clouds and in the evening into rain, and every morning and every evening I shall appear by the sun terrace.'
[97] Shen Yüeh (441–513 A.D.), man of letters and statesman, helped King Wu of Liang to overthrow the Ch'i Dynasty and was enfeoffed as the Earl of Chien-ch'ang. P'an Yüeh (?–300 A.D.), a Chin Dynasty statesman and poet, famous for his *fu* and elegiac poetry was considered a paragon of male pulchritude in his youth. He and Shen Yüeh became symbols of handsome scholars gallant in popular imagination.

He was consumed by love.
'Do you know, Ying-ying,
I'll love you though I die from the suffering?'

[Prose]

From this time onward Chang was constantly in a daze; walking, he forgot where he meant to go; eating, he did not know whether he had had enough. He seemed totally confused and oblivious of his actions. Gradually he became ill. When the abbot heard about his illness, he paid Chang a visit. Solicitously he said: 'The weather is unusually fine and spring is at its most glorious. What is troubling you that your natural harmony should have been so upset?'
    'Alas, the cause is not for holy ears like yours to hear', Chang replied.

(*Hsien-lü-tiao* mode)

Flower-Viewing Time

Rain-drenched cherry blossoms, brilliant as blood,
        dripped from outstretching branches.
Each coquettish flower, showing off its color,
        displayed a different hue of red or purple.
Willow strands had grown into long, graceful silken threads.
Such beauty
Inspired in Chang verses of the darkest despair.

His handsome face grew haggard.
All the paper in the world
Was not enough on which to express his longing.
Desperately unhappy,
He paid no attention to the flowers.

Coda

'I don't know how I became so ill.
You ask what's troubling me?
Well, it seems that
A Sea Monkey[98] lies in my heart.'

[98] *Hai-hou-erh*, a pun, as the pronunciation is very close to *hao-hai-erh*, 'pretty child', 'darling'.

129

[Prose]

The abbot smiled and said: 'Are you giving up your prospect of fame and a distinguished career on account of a woman?'

'I too know this to be foolish. But it was inevitable that P'an Yüeh was sickly and Sung Yü had frequent spells of melancholy; people as sensitive as we are are easily affected by the sights and the people around us.'

The abbot knew it would be useless to admonish Chang. After urging him not to neglect his medicine, the abbot left.

Chang stopped eating and sleeping. His breathing became feeble and he kept to his bed a great deal. Madam Ts'ui, worried, sent Hung-niang to inquire after him. Gasping for breath, in a faint voice, Chang asked Hung-niang: 'Does Ying-ying know I am ill? Did she send any poem or letter this time?'

Hung-niang said: 'There you go again; there you go again!'

(*Kao-p'ing-tiao* mode)

T'ang-to Song

'Time passes quickly like a shuttle on a loom.
More and more I'm weighted down with sorrow.
It was all your young mistress's doing:
Returning kindness with hostility.
Yes, it was all her doing.
Hi-ho.

'New sadness
Is added to old grief.
Despair wrecks my health.
Madam Ts'ui, cold, unsympathetic, watchful,
Is determined to keep me from my love.
Hi-ho.

The Frontier Pass Where Sheep Graze

'The days are tolerable,
But at night I'm despondent.
Four desolate walls,
One dim, blueish lamp.
I doze with my clothes on,
Or sit, wrapped in a robe.
My shadow alone
Stays by my side.

130

'How did my health deteriorate so!
For days now I've hardly been able to breathe; I'm always drowsy.
My tongue is parched, my lips dry.
Not a drop of saliva in my mouth.
Acupuncture, medicine and treatment
Bring no relief.
When you see your young mistress and Madam Ts'ui
Spare them none of the details.

Coda

'No friend, no relative, sick to my bones,
I'm homeless, all alone.
Will they come and visit me when they have time?'

[Prose]

Hung-niang wept in sympathy and said: 'I shall certainly relay your message,
sir. But I fear my young mistress really does not care for you.' She was about
to leave when Chang stopped her.

(*Nan-lü-tiao* mode)

A Sprig of Flowers

Hung-niang walked toward the door,
Chang called her back and said:
'When you go back
Tell Ying-ying that
She's responsible
For my illness.
In my unwavering devotion to her
I just didn't expect her
To be so ungrateful and mean.

'Very likely
I shall die.
When I become a ghost,
Yama, the King of Death, will ask me: "Why did you die?"
I'll tell him everything,
From beginning to end.
I'll talk on until he's convinced of my grievances.
In two or three days

At most in ten,
He'll take Ying-ying's life too,
　　　to pay for my death.

'But if he demurs,
Or says I have no proof,
I shan't quarrel with him,
I'll simply cite you as a witness.'

[Prose]

Hung-niang said: 'Do not detain me with such foolish talk,' and left.
　　Shortly, she returned, announcing the arrival of Madam Ts'ui and
Ying-ying. Chang did not turn to look at them; he merely opened his eyes.

(*Ta-shih-tiao* mode)

Grateful for the Emperor's Favor

Chang's illness
Lingers on and on.
He looks an unspeakably
Dismal sight.
His flesh is wasting away; his bones are disintegrating.
Only a layer of skin and a network of veins remain.
No relative
Or friend
Is there to look after him.

What is left of his energy
Is used up in sighing.
Even the elixir of immortality can't save him now.
He hears Madam's inquiry,
But for a long while he doesn't utter any sound.
His eyes, filled with emotion
And tears,
Fix themselves on Ying-ying.

[Prose]

Ying-ying, her hand on his bed, says: 'Brother, you are seriously ill. Please tell
me quickly what is troubling you.'

(*Huang-chung-kung* mode)

*The Kun Section of [the Elaborate Melody] Subduing the Yellow Dragon,
ch'an-ling*

'It seems only ten days ago
That I last saw you.
How is it that suddenly you're reduced to a skeleton?
You can't even reply
To our questions.
Your eyes, staring vacantly, are filled with tears.

'What made you
So ill?
I hope you won't hide anything from my mother.
I suspect
Someone has offended you, and
The vexation has brought this dangerous
        thinness to your handsome face.

Alliterative and Rhyming Binomes

'What sorrow
Has diminished the circumference of your Shen Yüeh waist?
Your beautiful P'an Yüeh hair is now unwashed and uncombed.
Your eyes are heavy with fatigue.
Your head droops.
You wheeze; you pant.
The closer one gets,
The more one sees
How gravely
Ill you are.
Now that I think about it,
I might have done something inadvertently
        to have caused all this.

'Where's your pain?
Where?
I won't know unless you speak.
I'll bet you feel congested,
Your chest filled up.
Let's send for a doctor quickly.
Tell me everything;
Be frank, be open.

You're on the verge
Of death,
And I might have just the medicine for you.'

Earth-Scraping Wind

Chang says: 'Thank you for your concern.
But you've come too late.
This wretched illness of mine
Has been most bewildering.
No potion, no brew seems to help,
I throw up the rice I eat, the water I drink.
I've got no headache,
No fever,
But my pulse is weak.
It's totally incomprehensible
Why this sickness is so difficult to cure.

Coda

'Sister, Madam,
I think I'm going to die.
I can't describe my illness —
        my stomach just feels bloated with misery and unhappiness.'

[Prose]

Ying-ying says: 'I have some medicine which I think can alleviate Brother's misery. I shall ask Hung-niang to deliver it presently.'
    With great effort, Chang manages to voice his thanks.
    Madam Ts'ui adds: 'Yes, please do not neglect your medicine; we must let you rest now.'
    Seeing that his visitors are leaving, Chang forces himself up, and throws a robe around his shoulders.

(*Kao-p'ing-tiao* mode)

Magnolia Flowers

When Chang hears their farewells,
He wraps himself in a robe and
Stands to see them off.

To right and left he sways, looking pitiable, ludicrous.
More dead than alive,
He nonetheless smiles ingratiatingly.

'Madam, do feel free to go, but
Leave me Ying-ying.
She'd be much better than any medicine.'
Hearing this, Hung-niang grits her teeth:
'Had I a rope
I'd strangle this clown.'

[Prose]

Madam and Ying-ying left. Chang watched them as they went.

(*Huang-chung-kung* mode)

The Kun Section of [the Elaborate Melody] Subduing the Yellow Dragon

Even Madam Ts'ui,
Her heart hard as stone,
Was moved by Chang's suffering.
As she and Ying-ying walked
Past the window
Suddenly they heard a thump in Chang's study.
The three women rushed back
To the room.
They saw Chang prostrate by his bed,
Stark naked,
Inert,
And no air passing through his nostrils.

Coda

Madam Ts'ui said with regret: 'What a pity that
He died away from home.
Now, his ghost is doomed to everlasting wandering.'

[Prose]

She asked Hung-niang to revive him. A few minutes later Chang showed signs
of life. Madam Ts'ui asked a servant to gallop into P'u town and fetch a
doctor. When the doctor came, Madam told him to feel Chang's pulse.
'Though the patient looks shrivelled and ill, there is actually nothing wrong
with him', reported the doctor.

(*Huang-chung-kung* mode)

The Golden Oriole

> Strange,
> Strange,
> After the doctor examined Chang
> He laughed knowingly, with sardonic glee.
> 'The patient is perfectly healthy;
> There's nothing which needs to be treated.'

[*Prose insert*]

He asked Chang: 'Sir, you are not ill, so why have you become so thin and weak?

> 'Why is it that your flesh seems pared?'
> Chang replied:
> 'My heart is clogged up with a Ying-ying.'
> The doctor said: 'Then let me give you a laxative.'

[Prose]

The doctor produced some medicine. Madam gave him two thousand coins and he withdrew. Madam Ts'ui said to Chang: 'You must take this medicine and stop torturing yourself.'

After Madam and Ying-ying returned to their court, no one else came to visit Chang. Chang mused to himself: 'My hopes will never be realized; I might as well die.' Infirm and weak, he yet made himself straighten his robe and headwrapper. Then he threw a rope across the ridgepole.

(*Hsien-lü-tiao* mode)

The Shih-ts'ui Section of [the Elaborate Melody] Lu-yao

> The evergrowing, unbearable frustration
> Had sent Chang into a state of drunken stupor.
> Even *shih* and *fu* he could no longer write.
> All day he dozed. . . .
> As he drifted to sleep
> He suddenly heard voices and
> Someone opening his door.
> It was his cruel darling and Madam Ts'ui.
>
> 'You teased me
> With empty promises, insincere words.

136

Though blinded by love, I
Finally saw through your trap.
Shattered, I could only sigh and weep.
I remember how, that spring evening,
I saw you for the first time
By the veranda, under a brilliant moon.

A Section of [the Elaborate Melody] Lu-yao

'You stood amidst the flower shadows.
It took me a long time
To see you clearly, to see
Your delicate, slender waist,
Your emerald-colored jacket and skirt.
Was it spring which made you tired?
　　　You leaned on a garden rock.
For a while I thought that I had surprised
Kuei-fei,[99] lingering to the north of Aloes Pavilion.[100]

'Your charm, your beauty was staggering.
I chanted a verse to the moon, to which you replied.
Our admiration was mutual.
This spell was broken
By the arrival of your maid,
Urging you to return,
　　　so you disappeared behind a closed, red gate.
Alas, even then
Your mother managed to disrupt our incipient love.

The 'hai-hai' Song

'You were sequestered in the ladies' quarters;
I lived alone in my study.
I wrote poems for you but couldn't send them.
Stoically, I tried to bear our separation,
Hai-hai.
My brows constantly knotted in a frown.
Hai-hai

---

[99] Consort of T'ang Hsüan-tsung (r. 712–56), celebrated for her beauty.
[100] *Ch'en-hsiang t'ing*, a pavilion in the T'ang imperial garden. This and the preceding two lines contain an allusion to two lines of Li Po's *'Ch'ing-p'ing tiao'* : 'Well-aware of the sorrow pulsating in the spring wind, she leans on the balustrade to the north of the Aloes Pavilion.' Li's poem commemorates a peony-viewing visit Hsüan-tsung and Kuei-fei made to the pavilion.

The Auspicious Lotus Blossom

> 'The few yards between us felt like ten thousand miles!
> Then, one day, the mutinous soldiers came.
> You and your mother were threatened with death.
> No escape was open to you.
> On that occasion,
> It was *I* who took pity on *you*.

The 'hai-hai' Song

> 'My friend, the governor of P'u pass,
> Subdued the rebels and removed the threat.
> And your mother promised you to me.
> Who would have thought the promise would soon be broken,
> *Hai-hai.*
> And even gods, the witnesses, be deceived?
> *Hai-hai.*

The Auspicious Lotus Blossom

> 'Such humiliation, such mistreatment made me ill.
> Had I known the outcome,
>   I'd have preferred not to have met you.
> For days now I haven't been able to eat or drink;
> I've lost all desire to live.
> Now, who takes pity on *me*
> In my extremity?

Coda

> 'A black rope I tie to the ridgepole,
> A true man does not grieve over death.
> I can well be a gallant ghost in the nether world!'

(*Shuang-tiao* mode)

A Visit to the Imperial Capital

> That day Chang with a broken heart
> Rashly decides to end his life.
> He takes the noose in his hand,
> His eyes full of tears.
> But life and death

138

Are important matters;
They're determined by heaven and earth.

Chang's door has stayed closed since Madam's visit.
Neither is any warning signal sent out.
Yet, precisely at this moment, someone rushes forward,
	opens the door,
And dashes to his side.
With her delicate hands —
Skilled at embroidery and zither-playing —
She firmly stops Chang's attempt.

[Prose]

Calamity and good luck fall at random;
Life and death are fixed in advance.
Had the timing of this kind deed
Altered ever so slightly;
A glorious future
Would have been lost irretrievably.

Who checked Chang? Who? It was Hung-niang. Hung-niang said to Chang:
'Sir, you are being extremely foolish. If I had come but a few minutes later,
you would have died. Unbeknown to you, after my young lady visited you,
she was moved to tears. She actually said to me: "I sent the poem to Brother
in a spirit of fun; little did I know that my levity would have such a conse-
quence. As things stand now, I shall not be considered virtuous, if, in trying
to adhere to propriety and preserve my chastity, I should cost my brother his
life." She asked me to bring this medicine to you.'

(*Chung-lü-tiao* mode)

The Ancient Border Town, Lun-t'ai

Hung-niang
Related to Chang all that had happened.
'After visiting you, my young mistress
Was deeply troubled; alone in her chamber
She murmured to herself;
Her tears profusely fell.
For a long time
She sighed, and
Finally, in a low voice, she called me to her,

And said:
"My brother is gravely ill,
A veritable skeleton
On the verge of death.
I know I've brought this about.
But remorse is useless;
I have now resolved to
Give up my scruples and save his life."

'I shared her anxiety, and was
Moved by her words.
She sent me here with some medicine;
When I arrived,
What did I see? You, sir,
Getting ready to hang yourself!
If I had come just a little later,
You would certainly have
Met Yama, the King of Death.
How foolish you are!
Look, the medicine
Is in this envelope.
You're to follow
The prescription.
How aromatic it smells!
I'm sure after you take it for a while,
Your virility, your vitality will be restored and strengthened.'

Coda

Heavenly marvels are sealed in the envelope.
There's no powder
Or pills;
There's a written cure exclusively for love-sickness!

[Prose]

Hung-niang gave Chang an envelope. On it was written: 'A short poem to be
left on the desk of my talented brother. Sealed respectfully by Ying-ying.'
Chang took out an ancient tripod and asked Hung-niang to fill it with
incense. He put the tripod on his writing table and said: 'Since I was once scolded
for my lack of propriety, on this important occasion, I would not dare to
be negligent!' He paid homage to the letter.

140

(*Kao-p'ing-tiao* mode)

Magnolia Flower

> Hurriedly Chang adds incense;
> Promptly he pays homage.
> He bows, reverently touches his palms,
> Then raises his hands to his forehead.
> He takes the letter and passes it through the smoke;
>   he opens the envelope,
> And carefully unfolds the page
> By a sunlit window.

[Prose insert]

What could possibly be the contents?

> After Chang reads the letter, repeatedly he cries, "Bravo! Bravo!"
> His curious illness
> Seems ninety percent cured.
> Hung-niang counsels: 'Take it easy.
> What's in it that
> You react in this most startling manner?'

[Prose]

Chang spread open Ying-ying's letter and read her poem. He could hardly contain his joy and his illness was instantly cured. The poem read:
> Do not let idle anxiety
> Destroy your god-given talent.
> You once saved me from dire extremity;
> Would I be the cause of your torment?
> To show my gratitude, propriety I set aside:
> I send this poem as a matchmaker.
> There will be clouds and rain[101] this eventide.
> Mourn no longer.

In all, there were only eight lines[102] in the poem. Yet their healing power surpassed even that of the greatest of physicians, Pien-ch'üeh of Lu.[103]

---

[101] See n.96 above.
[102] The Chinese text actually has 'forty characters' here. As I was unable to limit my translation to forty words, I changed the term to read 'eight lines'.
[103] Chin Yüeh-jen, who was nicknamed 'Pien-ch'üeh, and who lived in Lu. A famous physician of the Warring States period, he left several treatises on medicine. His biography is included in the *Shih chi.*

Pink is the River

    Chang of Ch'ing-ho
    Can't stop laughing.
    What Hung-niang has delivered isn't a pill,
    Nor is it medicinal powder.
    It's a letter written in an unusually elegant hand.
    He unfolds and refolds it a thousand times.
    Soon he has learned the contents by heart,
    And the paper is turning limp in his hands.
    No trivial chit-chat,
    The letter contains a four-rhyme,
    Eight-line poem.
    An authentic invitation
    For a secret rendezvous,
    Only without the usual *cachet,*
        the vermillion mark of the sender's seal.

[Prose Insert]

Chang ignores Hung-niang's persistent queries about the letter.

    Hung-niang won't give up.
    Finally Chang relents.
        'I don't really think it's right
    To divulge heaven's secrets.
    But still . . . Your young mistress
    Is proposing a tryst with me tonight.
    I guess there's no harm in telling *you* about it.'
    Hung-niang laughs sarcastically:
    'Stuff and nonsense!
    A pack of shameless lies!
    You two are a pair of spineless, worthless idlers.
    Don't you see she's fooling you?
    Again you take whatever she says in good faith.
    How dense can you be! Don't you understand
    She's using the same trick
    She has played on you before?'

[Prose]

Chang says to Hung-niang: 'If you would like to hear her enchanting words, I can sing them for you. But, alas, there is no one to harmonize with me.'

'Would it be all right for me to harmonize?'
'Fine.'

(*Hsien-lü-tiao* mode)

Ho-ch'uan Song, ch'an-ling

> 'I'll spare you your wild guesses
> And interpret
> Ying-ying's poem for you. . . .
> Miracle of miracles, who would've expected
> Your mistress to change her cruel mind!
> So my suffering wasn't in vain after all.
>
> 'Be patient, Hung-niang, and hear me out.
> The joyous event she now proposes
> Is what I've wanted from the beginning.
> You're sure to cry bravo
> When you hear the lines . . .'
> Hung-niang interrupts him: 'Mr Chang, stop babbling
>   and let's have the poem.'

A Taunting Sketch

> 'Don't fret over unimportant slights,
> (*Harmonization :li-li-lo, li-li-lo, li-li-lai-yeh*)
> And damage your heaven-given talent.
> (*Harmonization*)
> You once saved my life.
> (*Harmonization*)
> Yet, I almost caused your death.
> (*Harmonization*)
> To repay your kindness, I resolve to disregard propriety.
> (*Harmonization*)
> So let this poem be our go-between.
> (*Harmonization*)
> Cease your mournful chanting,
> (*Harmonization*)
> Tonight, without fail, the clouds will gather and rain will fall.
> (*Harmonization*)

Coda

> Hung-niang says:
> 'What? This outlandish stuff is what you read in the poem?

143

I have seen crazy lunatics before,
But never in my life have I seen anyone as unhinged as you!'

[Prose]

Chang said to Hung-niang: 'For a while now I have had no appetite. Now I feel slightly hungry. There must be delicious food in your kitchen; may I trouble you to fetch me some? It does not have to be very much.' Hung-niang consented and soon returned with an exquisitely prepared dish. Chang finished it in a trice.

Hung-niang observed: 'An adage says: "He who can eat can take on anything." It must be right, for you seem eager for action.'

(*Chung-lü-tiao* mode)

Green Peonies

That short poem was the magic cure.
It restored the patient to perfect health.
Chang changed his clothes,
Putting on a suit in the latest style.
With great deliberateness
He affected this pose and that,
All the while asking Hung-niang:
'Do I look chic?
Do I look smart?'

Gazing at the mirror,
He smoothed his sideburns time and again,
And he whistled
Nonstop.
Deliriously he fussed and fussed.
In a loud voice he cried, as though in a trance,
'Aha, it's time for the noon-day meal!'
'Hey, the sun has moved behind the eaves!'
'Look, the sun has set!'

Coda

Hung-niang giggled:
'I haven't even moved one step, and
Three meals are over for this impatient young gentleman.'

[Prose]

Chang gave Hung-niang a gold hairpin and told her: 'If you and your young mistress do not come tonight, I shall wait for you in Hades.'

Hung-niang thanked him for the gift and left. Chang descended the steps with her and repeatedly asked her not to forget to come.

(*Hsien-lü-tiao* mode)

A Splendid Calabash

> At the foot of the steps,
> Again Chang urged Hung-niang not to forget:
> 'When my wishes are fulfilled, you'll have other presents.
> How I long for the moment when I can tell that lady
> All the anguish I've suffered
> On her account!
>
> 'Whether I live or die will depend on what happens tonight —
> I'm not exaggerating,
> If I don't mean every word I say, let heaven and earth destroy me.
> You must beg
> Your enchanting mistress
> To come early tonight.'

Coda

> After Chang returned to his study,
> He couldn't sit still.
> He stationed himself by the door and watched for the moon to rise.

[Prose]

That evening,
> The jade edifice of heaven was spotlessly clean;
> The stars of the Milky Way glistened like dew-drops.
> Glorious moonlight covered the ground,
> Quietly heightening a poet's ecstasy;
> Heady flower scent permeated the air,
> Insidiously undermining a Zen monk's calm.
> Everything on earth was utterly silent.
> The Beauty of heaven, would she come?

Chang allowed nothing to interfere with his vigil. The third watch was sounded; yet no news of Ying-ying.

(*Hsien-lü-tiao* mode)

Flower-Viewing Time

His chin upon his hand Chang waited and waited by the door.
Disappointed that no one came,
Willy-nilly, he returned to his study.
'If my love doesn't show up
How can I survive the night?'

The sensitive scholar was once more despondent.
Suddenly he heard the door open,
He rubbed his eyes and saw
Hung-niang curtsying
And clearing her throat:

Coda

'I hope you're not worried, sir; please be patient
And wait a little longer in your study.
My young mistress apologizes for the delay,
She'll come as soon as Madam finishes burning her evening incense.'

[Prose]

Chang bent over his desk and fell asleep. Someone woke him with the remark:
'The Goddess Vega[104] has descended, yet still you slumber on!' To his
delighted surprise, Chang saw Hung-niang arrive with a quilt and a pillow
while exclaiming excitedly: 'My young mistress is here; she is here!'

Chang went out to greet Ying-ying, who was walking very slowly, as if
too shy to advance, a bashful and endearing smile on her face. When Chang
went up to embrace her, she abruptly turned her face away.

(*Ta-shih-tiao* mode)

Jade-Winged Cicada

A beautiful girl,
Superbly stylish, approaches in the moonlight.
Her dress has
A quiet chic.

---

[104] A reference to that version of the Herd Boy and Weaving Maiden legend in which the
Maiden, after having been restored to her original identity (the star Vega), descends to
earth to visit her lover the Herd Boy once a year.

The black clouds of her hair, adorned with a slanting jade pin,
     cascade over her shoulders –
Such breath-taking beauty!
Sheer silk stockings cover her tiny feet.
Stepping daintily –
Moving lightly –
What exquisite grace!
What pristine, unaffected charm!

When she sees Chang
She turns her face away.
Feigning shyness,
She ignores his greetings.
Chang pleads, but
Her arms akimbo, in a posture of cool hauteur,
Ying-ying doesn't look at him.
'You know I wouldn't dare to reproach you.
Yet, fair is fair, I've never
Mistreated you, not even slightly.
My darling, sweetheart,
Don't you think you've tortured me enough?'

[Prose]

Hung-niang brought Ying-ying to his side,
Much to Chang's astonished delight.

(*Ta-shih-tiao* mode)

Song of the Goddess in the Cave

They're both young,
These two passionate romantics.
They suit each other like a pair of fledgling phoenixes.
Chang holds Ying-ying's waist,
Leads her to his room:
'Darling, really,
You needn't put on such airs for me.'

He caresses and cuddles her,
Incredulous that all this isn't an erotic dream.
With the lamplight pouring over them,
     he fondles her fragrant body ecstatically;
Stroking,

Licking, sucking.
Tightly he holds her and kisses her lips.
Ying-ying is passive, quiet.
No time to remove her dress,
Chang reaches for her bosom and
Plays with her breast.

[Prose]

Ying-ying looks shy and debilitated. She lies motionless, limp, as if paralysed; a totally different person from the dignified young lady of a few minutes ago. Soaring with happiness as though airborne, Chang begins to wonder if Ying-ying is in fact a goddess and not a mortal of human birth.

(*Chung-lü-tiao* mode)

Ch'ien-ch'iu Festival

A perfect evening: the air is warm.
The silver lamp burns gloriously.
On this night, a pair of young phoenixes mate for the first time. . . .
He peels off her tight-fitting stockings,
And pierces her pink flower-heart —
    a new experience for him.
Despite his gentleness, she tries to move away.

It hurts;
She knits her brows.
Yet she wants to please him.
In a seductive, trembling voice she groans.
Sweat dampens her powdered face.
Her makeup now ruined, she looks artlessly bewitching.
Her loins soon are tired; lightly she pants.

[Prose]

Outside, undulating moonlight transmits
The clepsydra's dripping and the watchman's drumbeat.
Inside, Chang, holding Ying-ying, delivers
His sweet tongue into her mouth.
They make love all night. Chang feels he is inside the Fairy Palace, above the Milky Way.

148

(Hsien-lü-tiao mode)

Goddess by the River

> At the height of their joy,
> They hear the melancholy toll of the temple bell.
> Hung-niang urges Ying-ying — now smiling like a hibiscus — to rise.
> The clouds and rain disperse, the Goddess of Wu withdraws,
> Sung Yü is again alone on his couch.[105]
> The lovers say good-bye
> With infinite regret.   .
> The Moon Goddess returns to her crystal palace.
> Chang is left with half a window of moonlight
> And the chilly fifth-watch wind.

[Prose]

How do I know this actually happened? I can cite *The Story of Ying-ying* written by Yüan Chen of the T'ang dynasty as corroboration. Here is the passage: 'Hung-niang took Ying-ying away. All night, Ying-ying did not utter a word. When the sky brightened with morning light, Chang got up, wondering to himself: "Was it all a dream? Was it all a dream?" What dispelled his doubts were the smear of Ying-ying's rouge on his arm, her perfume in his clothes, and her tears which still glistened on the couch.'

(Yü-tiao mode)

Dragon in the Turbid River

> Their ecstasy
> Was rudely disrupted by the morning bell.
> When they parted,
> They hurriedly said a reluctant farewell,
> Each looking at the other with silent emotion.
> Soon after the departure of the Nymph of Lo,[106] dawn arrived.
> Clouds evaporated around the Ch'u terrace;
>   the dream-like visit vanished without a trace.
> An irretrievable night,
> Its passing filled the eastern wind
> With a piercing sense of loss.

---

[105] Cf. n. 96 above. There is of course a transference of identity here; Sung Yü, the author, takes the place of King Huai of Ch'u.
[106] The goddess of the river Lo, whose beauty is elaborately depicted by Ts'ao Chih (192–232) in his *Lo-shen fu.*

When Chang rose,
The sun was high in the sky.
'Did Ying-ying
Really come?
Or was it all a dream?'
Yet her rouge-stains on his arm exuded a delicate scent.
Her perspiration, her dampened powder, clung to his skin.
On the sheet
Two or three red spots remained.

[Prose]

Chang took out a brush and some paper. After composing two *tz'u* poems,[107] he wrote a *ku-shih*[108] poem of thirty rhymes which he entitled 'Encountering a Goddess'.

(*Hsien-lü-tiao* mode)

Ch'ao-tien-chi

Chang seals his letter
Stained with tears,
In which he begs Ying-ying to return again that night.
Anxiously he beseeches Hung-niang:[109]
'Please don't refuse to
Deliver this to your charming mistress.

'Even if you have
No pity,
No feeling for me,
You still might recall that I was once
Kind to your mistress.
You're now giving *her* a chance to be kind to me tonight.

[107] Poems written to existing musical tunes. *Tz'u* verse forms have lines of unequal length and prescribed tonal and rhyme patterns. The genre flourished in the tenth and eleventh centuries.
[108] 'Old-style poems' in contradistinction to *chin-t'i* (modern-style) poems. Unlike the latter, *ku-shih* have no set number of lines or rigid tonal, rhyme and parallel-line prescription. Generally, they are longer than *chin-ti-shih*.
[109] Hung-niang's presence is inexplicable here. Lines could be missing from the text, or it could be Master Tung's negligence.

150

'Tell my darling
Not to break her vows, or forget her words.
If she casually casts aside our happiness,
It would mean there's no hope for me.
Help me, Hung-niang,
Impress upon your mistress
Every point I've made.

Coda

'Without ever blinking
    I'll wait for the arrival of evening.
If by the second watch your mistress is not here,
Prick up your ears, you'll hear
The apricot branch shake above your garden wall.'

[Prose]

Hung-niang returned to give Ying-ying Chang's *ku-shih* and *tz'u*. Ying-ying
read them again and again, each time her enjoyment was keener than the last.
The first *tz'u* reads:
    Ssu-ma grieves at the passing of spring.
    Wen-chün lies ill, languorous.
    Rouge fades from lingering, clinging
        last petals.
    Another day.
        The oriole's cry
    Heralds the sun's imperturbable rise.

    Playing on the zither, I check dejection's gnawing.
    A cup of wine cheers.
    How shall I express my longing, my wanting
        of you, my love?
    A many-colored brush
        tries to describe
    The mystery of meeting a goddess one luminous,
        incandescent night.
(The above *tz'u* is written to the tune 'Dreaming under the Southern Branch'.)

The second *tz'u* reads:
    In 'Encountering a Goddess',
    I celebrate
        our love-making.
    When the ink is made
        I hear tinkles of jade.

The newly written characters
　　are colored like a raven's feather.
My impetuous brush tramples and crushes
　　the paper's embossed flowers.

My lines are plucked
From the secret caves
　　of the Creator.
Pao Chao,[110] a first-rate
　　poet, cannot improve my lay.
Nor can Yü Hsin,[111] who wrote water-
　　limpid, graceful, sinuous verse.
Now to you, a second Tao-yün,[112]
　　I send my lay, my verse.[113]

The *ku-shih* poem reads:
　　When as moonlight filters through latticed window,
　　And the sky, firefly florescent, is unblemished by cloud shadows,
　　Far, far away, a haze doth rise,
　　Cloaking shrubs, trees, in the obscurity of night.
　　Coursing wind, majestic dragons, on bamboo branches bloweth,
　　Gentle rustle, phoenixes' singing, from *wu-t'ung* leaves groweth.
　　Diaphanous skirts sway softly in the mists,
　　While tinkling pendants each the other's music assists —
　　The Golden Goddess[114] doth now appear!
　　Her attendants following in the rear.
　　To a secret tryst she presses,
　　In the profound nocturnal stillness.
　　Her slippers glitter with lustrous pearls,
　　An embroidered dragon on her jacket curls.
　　Jeweled phoenixes dance on her hair,
　　Her cape scintillates with rays of the rainbow fair.
　　The very Goddess of Alabaster Pool,[114]

[110] *Fl. c.* 405–66, one of the foremost poets of the Six Dynasties, Pao also served as secretary to Prince Lin-hai of Sung.

[111] 513–81, poet, man of letters, Yü was a favorite of Emperor Chien-wen of Liang. His *Ai Chiang-nan fu* is much admired.

[112] Hsieh Tao-yün, *fl. c.* 376, woman writer, celebrated for her wit and intelligence. Although the bibliography of *Sui shu* lists two volumes of her works, few pieces are extant.

[113] Unlike the preceding *tz'u*, the tune title of this one is not given in *THH*. It is a *Wang Chiang-nan* (Looking to the South).

[114] Chin mu (Hsi-wang mu), deity in popular myth who rules from Alabaster Pool. Said to have troops of minor gods under her command.

Whose peers the Green Jade Palace[115] rule.
Lured by sublunary pleasure,
She descends to visit her mortal lover.
Bashful, she first repulses his caresses.
Emboldened, her own ardor she soon expresses.
A cicada folds its wings: her chignons become unbound,
The lovers' fast-moving feet stir dust from the ground.
Moistened powder trickles down her face,
He carries her to bed, soft with gauze and lace.
In ecstasy they perform the phoenixes' mating dance,
Two cooing kingfishers losing themselves in a trance.
Enchanting coyness adorns her jet-black brows,
Her burning crimson lips intense desire arouse.
Her breath has the scent of precious orchid,
Her skin, the smoothness of jade polished by liquid.
Far too languorous, she neglects to remove her slippers,
With charming playfulness her knees to her breast she gathers.
Like unstrung pearls her perspiration glistens and shines,
In a dark green mass her hair lies disheveled, untwined.
Just as they marvel at their rare felicity,
The fifth watch is sounded with brutal clarity.
Knowing their meeting must soon come to an end,
Their love-making they yet are loath to suspend.
Sorrow clouds their joyous countenances,
Soberly they pledge unwavering constance.
Giving her a ring he seals his fate with hers,
Her present, a charm, binds hearts that cannot be severed.
She reaches for a mirror; her tears make it damp.
Dim, dark insects circle the drying lamp.
Morning light glimmers, faintly, whitish-gray,
The sun slowly rises to rule o'er the day.
The Goddess must return to her fairyland slough,
Like the immortal Wang-ch'iao,[116] who the earthly world eschews.
Lingering perfume of musk recalls her charm,
A smear of exquisite rouge clings to his arm.
A waving blade of grass, her receding figure totters,
Airborne tumbling weed, her skirt flaps and flutters.
Now alone, a bereaved crane, he wails with piercing agony,
His eyes search the horizons for a second epiphany.
Alas, the girth of the seas cannot be shortened;

---

[115] Another abode for high-ranking deities in popular myth.
[116] Crown prince of Emperor Ling of Chou (r. 571–544 B.C.), who followed the Taoist priest Fu-chiu-kung to Mount Sung to engage in occult practices. It is said that at the end he flew away on a white crane and disappeared from view.

The height of the skies cannot be lessened.
The Goddess is beyond reach, drifting like a cloud,
He waits in his tower, in anxious longing shrouded.
Ying-ying marveled at the beauty of the poem. She looked for paper to
write a response. After meditating for a long time she finally set down her
brush, not having written a line, and laughed to herself: 'Ah, I am not as
talented as my lover!'

(*Ta-shih-tiao* mode)

A Southern Air

> Ying-ying reads the entire poem,
> And exclaims with astonished admiration:
> 'Such beautiful verse with such elegant rhymes
> Can only be written with divine help.
> With my meager talent how can I
> Hope to match it?
> I might as well give up,
> I might as well give up.

> 'What an unusual man!
> He's indeed
> A commanding general among *shih* poets,
> A prepotent marshal amidst *sao*[117] writers.
> Let me prepare
> For my meeting with him tonight.
> Yes, he has made me
> Utterly undignified; wild, forward in fact, but
> It's worth it,
> It's worth it.

Coda

> 'Not only is he romantic, handsome,
> He has such splendid talent.
> How could I help falling in love with him?'

[Prose]

The ensuing evening Chang left his door ajar and waited for Ying-ying. It

[117] Long narrative poems with double lines divided midway by the carrier-sound *hsi*. The
most famous *sao* is *Li sao* (On Encountering Sorrow) by Ch'ü Yüan (fourth century B.C.).

seemed to him a long time before she finally appeared:

>The Moon Goddess emerging from her crystal palace;
>The Fairy Princess[118] descending from her alabaster terrace.

(*Cheng-kung* mode)

Liang-chou, ch'an-ling

>Drop by drop, the jade clepsydra drips, the second watch is sounded.
>The moon shines above tree branches —
>A polished brass mirror in an azure sky.
>*Ya!*
>The door creaks, disclosing the Goddess of Wu.

>Ying-ying's shyness returns when she sees Chang and
>As she leans on him, her timidity invites gentle caressing.
>Her chignon is done up like a green conch.
>Her face — a lotus flower — exudes a subtle perfume.
>What incomparable grace!

Ying-t'ien-ch'ang

>She tries to speak; her voice merely trembles; no word comes out.
>After a long silence, she manages to say:
>'Darling,
>Do you know who my ancestors were?
>My family, unlike others',
>Has had an impeccable name.
>I was brought up properly in the ladies' quarters, and
>Never have I strayed from Mother's teachings.
>Then you, Brother, became ill
>On my account.

>'Because of me,
>You were reduced to a skeleton —
>Skin and bones —
>And no medicine, no treatment helped.
>When I could no longer bear to see you suffer,
>I decided secretly to give myself to you.

[118] 'Hsi-wang mu' ('Chin mu'), which earlier I have rendered as 'Golden Goddess' (cf. n. 114 above). I use 'fairy princess' here to avoid repeating 'goddess'.

Had Mother had any intimation of my decision
  — barring a miracle —
She would've prevented me from sleeping with you.
Now, don't you ever cast me aside
For someone else.'

Licorice Root

Hear the story,
Hear the story.
Chang softly replies:
'How can you say such a thing! You've no cause
To frot,
To taunt.
I'm not a P'an Yüeh, a Shen Yüeh.
Would I have deflowered you casually?
Should I ever be false to you, let heaven punish me!
Does this satisfy you, my love?'

Liang-chou in Three Stanzas

Being as yet a novice
In love-making,
Ying-ying is reluctant to undress before Chang.
Chang reaches for her, sits her on his lap,
        and caresses her soothingly for a long time.
His desire blazes:
        passionately his lips explore her face,
        delving, lingering,
Bruising her cheeks.
With profound tenderness he pats her,
Licks her,
        fondles her,
        hugs her,
        cuddles her.
His eyes devour her beauty.
Her charm
Makes him lose all restraint;
        wildly he showers on her deep, scalding kisses.

Coda

Bashful and timid,
Unaccustomed to his ways,
The child fears this, dreads that,
        shies away from something else.

Adorning Crimson Lips, ch'an-ling

> The rain pours, the clouds thicken,
> Ying-ying presses her waist to Chang's.
> Whispering unintelligibly in a trembling voice,
> Unclenching her encircling arms, she begs him to rest a moment.
>
> Her sandalwood-scented mouth slightly open,
> Smiling, she proffers her tongue:
> A whiff of delicate perfume shoots up into the air.
> Yet when he bites on it lightly,
> She coyly scolds him for being cruel.

Wind Blowing Lotus Leaves

> Such fierce passion she inspires!
> Chang feels exhausted, afraid to continue.
> With compassion he strokes her cheeks:
> > their perfect makeup ruined by his kisses.
> Then, for the first time, he sees that her intoxicatingly fragrant,
> Soft, resilient,
> Butter-smooth breasts are white as snow.

The Inebriated Tartar Woman

> They know they'll rediscover this joy again and again;
> They wish every night will be like this one.
> The decorated candle burns brightly on the silver stand.
> Giggling, Ying-ying asks Chang to blow it out.

Coda

> Her head next to his,
> They chat in a low voice.
> The night is quiet; no one is about; their only witnesses
> Are the flower shadows on the darkened window
> > and the moon, illuminating the western tower.

[Prose]

Hung-niang arrives to urge Ying-ying to leave, saying: 'The day is dawning.'

157

Chapter 6

(*Hsien-lü-tiao* mode)

Lingering in the Perfumed Quilt

> Surely no treasure can buy
>> the lovers' clandestine joy of that night!
> Hung-niang alone is worried,
> Worried that Madam
> Should find out.
> Soon after the rain has stopped, the clouds dispersed,
> Hung-niang arrives, urging Ying-ying to leave.
> Heaven-glorious love
> Yields its place to sorrow.
>
> Chang and Ying-ying draw still closer.
> Hung-niang repeats: 'You must get up, my lady.'
> She puts Ying-ying's cap on her head and
> Fastens her jade ornaments to her hair.
> Ying-ying, procrastinating, nestles once more against Chang,
>> her stocking half pulled up on her calf.
> At long last, she whispers: 'I must leave now,
> But I'll be back tonight.'

Coda

> She inches away languidly.
> Before she reaches the study window,
> Suddenly she turns, rushing back to Chang,
> She whispers something more. . . .

[Prose]

From that time onward, Ying-ying went to Chang's apartment every evening, returning to her own in the morning. When this had gone on for almost half a year, Madam Ts'ui began to notice that her daughter's beauty had redoubled: there was a radiance about her. Suspicious, she thought to herself: 'Chang must have seduced her; they must be seeing each other surreptitiously.'

158

Cho-cho-chi

> The Minister's widow mused:
> 'If Ying-ying were innocent,
> Why has she become so vivacious, so gay?
> Her charm is more alluring.
> She's no longer her old, demure self.
>
> 'All her clothes are now too tight.
> Her eyes often look tired; her bosom has enlarged.
> She must have done something drastic;
> I'm sure
> She has a lover.'

[Prose]

Deeply in love with Chang, Ying-ying was completely preoccupied with her love affair. This did not escape Madam Ts'ui. One evening, as usual, Ying-ying went to meet Chang.

(*Ta-shih-tiao* mode)

A Red Gauze Garment

> Chang and Ying-ying
> Saw each other for more than half a year.
> Every night they met without fail.
> Careless,
> Rash,
> They were far too reckless.
> Ying-ying, obsessed with sex,
> Left her chamber again one night.
> Indeed: 'Grief follows on the heels of happiness.'
> Little did she know,
> She'd soon be embroiled in such a catastrophe!
>
> Madam Ts'ui, the worldly-wise widow,
> Had shrewdly guessed where her daughter had gone.
> She took a seat in the central hall, ordered the lamps brightly lit,
> And questioned all the maids,
> Who, shaking with fear,
> Turned in confusion one to the other.
> Madam Ts'ui asked: 'Why has Ying-ying

Left her chamber stealthily in the middle of the night?
Who's her lover?'
None of the maids dared speak.
Long silence.
Their mouths might as well have been so many firmly fastened locks.

Coda

The Minister's widow raised her voice:
'You slaves, how dare you hide things from me?
Bring Hung-niang here for questioning.'

[Prose]

A maid ran to fetch Hung-niang. Hung-niang and Ying-ying returned immediately. When Ying-ying saw Madam sitting in the hall, she shivered with fright. Madam Ts'ui asked Hung-niang: 'Where did you and Ying-ying go so late at night?'

Hung-niang paid Madam Ts'ui her obeisance and replied: 'I dare not hide anything from Madam. Mr Chang was taken ill suddenly; Miss Ying-ying and I went to visit him.'

Madam Ts'ui said: 'Why did you not inform me?'

'Madam had already retired, and since the illness occurred very suddenly, we did not dare disturb Madam in her sleep.'

Angrily Madam Ts'ui rebuked her: 'Even now you dare fabricate such lies? You shall not go unpunished!'

(*Chung-lü-tiao* mode)

The Frontier Pass Where Sheep Graze

Sitting in the hall, Madam asked Hung-niang in a loud voice:
'Why have you left your chamber secretly?
Do you know
What time it is?
Obviously you're leading Ying-ying astray.
You claim that Chang has taken ill.
Do you expect me to believe
Such a patent lie?

'Heaven must've arranged this disclosure.
Everything suggests that Ying-ying has a paramour.
Why don't you admit it?

It seems you'd rather die than own up to the truth.
Making up lies!
Making up stories!
You drive me beyond my endurance,
You evil slave!

'This is not a matter in which you should keep quiet.·
If you continue
To dream up excuses,
I'll have you spread-eagled against the eastern wall,
            and I'll flog you until you confess.'

[Prose]

Slowly Hung-niang said: 'Please, Madam, abate your anger. Allow me to say a word.

(*Hsien-lü-tiao* mode)

Lu-yao Song

'Please, Madam, abate your anger,
And hear what I say.
There's no need to raise your voice
            or chide and scold without ever a pause
Here in this wide-open hall.
Mr Chang is enormously attractive — talented and clever —
My young mistress is romantically inclined, and
Neither of them is married.
When they meet late at night,
Madam, need one ask questions?

'One is a ravishing beauty, the other a gifted scholar.
What's more, they're of comparable age.
For the past half year,
They've slept together every night.
To be sure, they've done something scandalous,
But "spilt water can't be retrieved."
Hadn't you better keep everything quiet, Madam?

If others were to know,
Wouldn't you be disgraced?

Coda

'They love each other intensely, so
Why should you be an impediment?
Don't be.
The proverb says: "A grown-up daughter is hard to keep."'

[Prose]

'That day, when the mutinous soldiers stationed themselves in the precincts
of the temple, Madam and my young mistress both wanted to commit suicide.
Mr Chang never knew the late Minister; had he not admired my young mis-
tress's beauty and wished to marry her, would he have taken the trouble to
scatter the rebels? It is because of him that you and my young mistress are
alive today. After the crisis was over, Madam asked Mr Chang to be a son, but
as a brother to Ying-ying. This contravened Mr Chang's own wishes and he
became ill. When he was on the verge of death, my young mistress said that
repaying a benefactor's kindness was more important than adhering to
propriety and decorum. She waited on Mr Chang, served him medicine and
comforted him. Madam is an intelligent person; when a young woman secretly
visits a bachelor late at night, is it necessary to ask for details? Of course it is
a breach of decorum. Madam blames me, but is Madam herself blameless? It
would seem that Madam has not only failed to govern her household, she has
also failed to repay the kindness of Mr Chang, her benefactor. And should my
young mistress's misconduct become public knowledge, Madam would have
failed to protect her daughter's reputation as well. You would be laughed at
by relatives and ridiculed by strangers. I hope Madam will consider what I
have just said.'
    Madam Ts'ui asked: 'What should I do?'
    Hung-niang replied: 'Mr Chang comes from an illustrious family whose
fame reverberates throughout the whole country. His talent is attested by
his having passed with honors the preliminary examinations; his ability as a
strategist is demonstrated by how quickly he subdued the monstrous rebels.
He revealed his cleverness by having enlisted the help of a great general with-
out bestirring himself. As for his kindness, did he not save the lives of the
entire Ts'ui household? He is, in short, a perfect gentleman. If as a means to
conceal his and my young mistress's peccadillo, Madam allows them to marry,
the lovers' sincere wish will be gratified and my young mistress's reputation
will remain intact. Such a solution is an excellent way both to discharge your
responsibility as the head of a family and to repay the kindness of a bene-
factor.

(Pan-she-tiao mode)

A Pock-Marked Old Lady

> 'Chang comes from a good family,
> Sister[119] has superb ancestors.
> Chang is the son of a Secretary of State,
> Sister is the daughter of a Prime Minister.
> Sister is beautiful,
> Chang is astute.
> Sister possesses the "threefold submissiveness",[120]
> Chang has read ten thousand books.

> 'Sister is educated,
> Chang is erudite.
> Sister will be a perfect wife,
> Chang will be a perfect husband.
> Sister is more gentle than Wen-chün,
> Chang is more gifted than Hsiang-ju.
> Sister's charm can undermine the security of a city,
> Chang's scholarship can vanquish all the savants of the world.

Coda

> 'With Chang's talent,
> With Sister's luck,
> Sister will certainly become a lady of high rank, as
> Chang is bound to ride in a four-horse carriage some day.'

[Prose]

Madam Ts'ui commented: 'What you say is most sagacious, Hung-niang. However, I wonder how Ying-ying *really* feels. Women being what they are, I am afraid they often lose their chastity without actually meaning to.'

She ordered Hung-niang to bring Ying-ying forward, saying: 'I wish to ascertain her true feelings myself.'

Ying-ying came forward timidly; she did not dare to stand erect.[121]

---

[119] Earlier, when speaking to Hung-niang, Chang refers to Ying-ying as 'your sister'; here Hung-niang herself refers to Ying-ying as 'sister'. A well-favored maid often addresses her young mistress thus in vernacular Chinese fiction.

[120] Literally 'threefold dependence'. The verbal-modifier used here to modify *te* (virtue) is *ts'ung* (to follow, to depend on). According to *I li, Sang-fu chuan* 儀禮 喪服傳 a woman is to follow, hence to be submissive to her father before her marriage, to her husband while married, and to her son when widowed.

[121] Standing erect would make her appear defiant.

Spring in the Chin Garden

> While Madam waited for Ying-ying to approach,
> She was silent,
> A pensive look on her face.
> Ying-ying walked slowly.
> As she drew near, she didn't raise her head.
> Her eyebrows were tightly knit,
> Her peach-like face had blushed to a crimson red,
> Her cherry mouth had turned blue,
> Again and again she rubbed her slender hands.
> It was distressing to watch
> Profuse tears
> Inundate the filigree appliqué on her cheek.
>
> Her mother, an elderly lady of sixty and more,
> Said: 'Don't worry, I'll certainly find a way
>   to forgive you, my daughter.
> After all, a mother always has warm affection for her children.
> I'll not utter any more harsh words.
> Let my sympathy, my pity for you heal our enmity.
> Yes, there are things that can't be undone —
> "You can't unhitch a horse after the cart is loaded", and
> "Spilt water can't be retrieved";
>   but where shall we go from here?
> How vexing!
> What must we do
> To avert disgrace?

Coda

> 'You know you've dishonored your father;
> You know you've brought shame to me;
> For a moment I thought I'd simply send you away,
> But motherly love stayed my hand.'

[Prose]

Madam Ts'ui said: 'Things being what they are, we must make a decision. I do not know what your real desire is. If you wish it, I shall marry you to Chang; but if you do not wish it, you must stop seeing him from now on.'

If Ying-ying were to say: 'No, I do not wish it', she would have lied. Yet, how could she possibly say: 'Yes, I do wish it' to her mother? She remained silent.

Madam asked her once more:

(*Shuang-tiao* mode)

Bean-Leaf Yellow

> 'Set your heart at ease, my child.
> Don't worry.
> We'll keep quiet.
> It won't do us any good to let others know.
> I'm afraid, darling,
> You've really done something quite terrible.
> Never mind; now, just be candid and frank.
> We'll discuss what we ought to do, and
> I'm sure we'll find a solution.
>
> 'Tell me
> What's on your mind.
> I'll weigh everything carefully
> Before making a decision.'
> Her daughter
> Continued to be silent.
> Despite herself, modesty kept her words back.
> Her heart pounded violently.

Coda

> Her beautiful, bewitching face was deeply flushed.
> She was too bashful to tell Madam what she really wanted.
> Suddenly she put out the tip of her tongue;
> > she turned around and giggled.

[Prose]

> She wanted to marry her lover, but shyness made her mute.
> She turned her head and smiled, her smile divulged her wish.
> The following morning, when the day had barely dawned, Madam Ts'ui
> ordered Hung-niang to invite Chang for a drink later in the day. Chang,
> afraid that he was to be reprimanded for the debacle of the previous night,
> declined the invitation with the excuse of illness.

(*Hsien-lü-tiao* mode)

Hsiang-ssu-huei

> Ashamed and apprehensive, Chang
> Thought to himself:

'I wonder if there's yet a way
To conceal my wrongdoing.'
Aloud he said: 'Hung-niang, don't embarrass me so.
You ask me to go to the Ts'uis';
Do you think I'm so brazen that I can
Face Madam, your mistress?

'I know I'm guilty,
And I'm scared stiff;
I haven't the courage
To accept today's invitation.'
Hearing this, Hung-niang
Said: 'Chang, you're really dumb.
Let me tell you something:
You think you're being careful,
Actually, you're being foolish, cowardly, and stupid.'

[Prose]

Hung-niang said: 'It will be to your advantage to accept the invitation. Good news awaits you.'

Chang was surprised by this. He asked: 'How so?'

Hung-niang recounted to him the events of the night. Chang thanked her and said: 'I see that you have helped me enormously. How can I show my gratitude?'

'I did not expect any reward, but there is something you must do. Madam Ts'ui is a relative of Cheng Heng; naturally she is partial to his interest. Although she promised to marry Ying-ying to you last night, you must not rely on her words. When you see her today, you can offer her a token of faith. This way, she will not be able to change her mind and renege on her promise before my young mistress completes the required mourning for her late father.'

Chang said: 'An excellent idea! But I have lodged here in the temple since spring, and my purse has become depleted. What shall I do?

(*Hsien-lü-tiao* mode)

Rejoice in the Approaching Spring

'I've even spent part of my traveling money;
I haven't two hundred cash to my name.
I have one white shirt,
But it's a poor one.
At night I keep warm with three strips of cloth;

166

In the day I lean on a brick which does for a pillow.
These are all I have in the world.

'When I want wine,
I draw water from the spring.
When I want music,
I play on the lute.
If you ask for silk there are two or three scrolls on the wall.
If you ask for poems, I can write you a hundred and more.
The only thing you mustn't ask for is money.'

[Prose]

Hung-niang said: 'Sir, your friend Fa-ts'ung has recently been made the
treasurer of the temple. If you go to him, you can probably borrow any sum
you want.'
 Hung-niang's remark, like a flash of lightning, revealed a solution to Chang.
He went to see Fa-ts'ung.

(*Ta-shih-tiao* mode)

Leaping over the Mountain Creek

 Chang bowed and said:
 'Forgive me
 For troubling you, honorable Temple Treasurer.
 Minister Ts'ui's daughter
 Has been promised to me, to be my wife.
 To settle this betrothal,
 You see,
 I need to offer a token of faith.

 'I'm a visitor,
 I've no family, no relations here to help.
 The money I brought
 Is barely enough for me to live on.
 I know I shouldn't borrow from you.
 But I thought you might not mind, as we're like brothers.
 I'll be most grateful
 For any amount you can spare.
 Please, please don't refuse.'

Coda

> Fa-ts'ung responded with a smile:
> 'Indeed we're like brothers.
> You certainly know how to say things that are pleasing to my ears.'

[Prose]

Chang said: 'if there is any money you do not need to use at present, I shall appreciate it if you will lend some to me.'

Fa-ts'ung replied: 'I would not dare to lend you any money from the treasury. However, I have some money of my own, all of which you may borrow. I am only sorry that it is so little; I hope you do not mind.'

He brought out fifty strings of coins and asked: 'When would you like to pay me back?'

Chang mentioned a date, bowed, and took the money.

(*Shuang-tiao* mode)

Water-Chestnut Fragrance

> Such penury!
> The slightest additional expense
> Sent Chang borrowing.
> Fa-ts'ung took pity on him and
> Lent him fifty strings of coins.
> His entire reserve was
> Emptied to the last coin for this indigent scholar.
> It wasn't easy to save up this much alms:
>> here he received thirty coins,
>> there he collected fifty cash,
> Each time he conducted a service he carefully put the reward away.

> Chang
> Stood up, bowed,
> And said ingratiatingly:
> 'If you didn't help me,
> I'm sure I'd never see my beauty again.
> However, take heart, according to a fortune-teller,
> I have excellent luck this year.
> More likely than not I'll pass my final examination.
> When I'm an official,
> I'll give you a year's salary for the loan.'

168

Fa-ts'ung laughed and said: 'Don't exaggerate.
I won't ask for any interest,
But the loan itself I'll need in a few years.'

[Prose]

Chang exchanged the money for a piece of gold and went to Madam Ts'ui's banquet. He fidgeted with anticipation. When wine was served, Madam rose and said: 'It was my misfortune that first my husband passed away and then before my children and I could return home we were besieged by lawless rebels. Had it not been for you, your compassion, my children and I would undoubtedly have been slaughtered. I have no way to repay your kindness, except, perhaps, by arranging one thing. As you know, my late husband had promised Ying-ying to her cousin Cheng Heng, but there has never been any formal contract. So may I express my gratitude by arranging a marriage between you and my daughter?'

(*Ta-shih-tiao* mode)

Jade-Winged Cicada

Madam Ts'ui said to Master Chang:
'Please fill your cup. . . .
You remember
When the rebels surrounded the temple
And threatened to harm my family and myself,
How you, sir,
Devised a clever scheme
To deliver us from imminent danger.
Your kindness saved our lives.
To show my gratitude, I'll now marry my daughter to you.
So, do tell me, sir, if you're willing to marry her.'

[Prose insert]

Madam Ts'ui said: 'If you are willing, please drain your cup.'

Eagerly, Chang
Nodded and said:
'I'm as yet
A poor and unknown student.
I have no exceptional virtues,
I'm careless and not very learned.

The beautiful daughter of a Prime Minister
Is obviously an excellent match for me.
You needn't waste energy persuading me, Madam.'
He drained his cup:
A weighty mountain of worry instantly toppled in his heart.

[Prose]

Chang offers Madam Ts'ui the piece of gold, saying: 'As I am away from home, I have only this as a betrothal present. Please overlook its meagerness and accept it.'

Madam Ts'ui tries to refuse: 'There is no need at all for you to offer a present . . .'.

Hung-niang interrupts with the remark: 'Mr Chang's gift may be slight, but you should accept it, Madam. Etiquette is after all etiquette.'

Madam Ts'ui takes the gold.

Chang then kneels before the steps of the hall and makes his obeisance to Madam. She says to him: 'Ying-ying is still in mourning and cannot be married right away. . . .'

'That will be all right. I intend to take part in the civil service examination this year anyway; we can be married next year.'

Madam continues: 'I am glad you are mindful of your career. You should probably prepare to leave soon.'

Chang says: 'For almost a month now, I have been counting the days to the examination. I shall leave in two or three days.'

To wish him luck, Madam offers Chang a large tumbler of wine. When Chang finishes it, she asks Hung-niang to accompany him back to his apartment.

As Chang and Hung-niang walk, Chang says: 'I certainly did not expect things to turn out so well.'

'Just now when Madam proposed the marriage, Ying-ying's face lit up with joy; then, when she heard that you are to leave for the examination, she looked heartbroken', Hung-niang says.

'Please tell her that fame and accomplishment are highly esteemed in the world; they are ignored only by those without self-respect. I hope to succeed in the examination and receive an official appointment so that I can leave behind my shabby hut like Yüan Hsien's[122] and wear embroidered robes like Mai-ch'en.[123] Once I am launched on my career, I shall come back and fetch

---

[122] A disciple of Confucius, well known for his indigence. His hut had a hole for a window. The line literally says: 'I shall renounce the puncture-window of Yüan Hsien.'
[123] Chu Mai-ch'en, Han statesman of very humble origin, who was later made the prefect of his birth place, Kuei-chi, by Emperor Wu-ti (r. 140–87 B.C.). Tradition has it that on making the appointment Wu-ti said to Chu: 'Not returning to one's birthplace after one has become famous and prosperous is like parading in an embroidered robe at night.'

170

her. A man must not sacrifice a glorious future simply because he is reluctant to bear the grief of separation.'

When Hung-niang relates Chang's words to Ying-ying, Ying-ying makes no comment. She and Chang do not see each other again. The day of his departure, Madam Ts'ui, Ying-ying, and Fa-ts'ung travel with him part of the way to see him off. They bring wine to a wayside arbor ten miles to the west of P'u-chou.

> A cup of wine marks the sorrow of parting
> or the joy of reunion.
> An intersection joins an east-west highway
> and a north-south byway.[124]

(Ta-shih-tiao mode)

Jade-Winged Cicada

> Leaving for the capital, the candidate
> Said farewell by a country road.
> 'At the height of
> Our happiness,
> I must leave Ying-ying to make my name in the world.
> Cruel Fate!
> Vainly I sigh.
> This parting-grief cuts to the quick!
> Desolate autumn landscape
> Intensifies
> My gloom.

> 'The rain pauses.
> The wind chills my bones.
> Cicadas weep
> In yellowing willows.
> When shall I
> See her again?
> The edges of my sleeves
> Are soaked through with tears.
> A frown locks unutterable sorrow in my brows.
> It's lacerating, this severance, this tearing apart.
> I leave with her
> The thousand ways of love.

[124] In order to maintain parallelism, I am taking great liberty with my translation here. The line says in fact: 'These ten miles can take a traveller east, west, north or south.'

Coda

'They say a man's heart is hard as steel.
Yet, look at the maples on the river banks,
They are red with blood wept by grief-stricken men.'

(*Yüeh-tiao mode*)

The Emperor Pacifying the West, ch'an-ling

Ravaged scenery.
Sighing wind,
Driving rain.
Surrounded by such bleakness, the lovers can't bear to part.
Finally the rain stops,
  the wind drops,
   the sun begins to set.
Chang's servant urges him to leave.
Too wretched to sing the Farewell Song,
The lovers approach the road, hand in hand.

Cicadas whine urgently,
Crickets wail.
A horn plays a mournful tune.
Wild geese lament and cry.
The road stretches farther and farther away,
  reaching for the horizon.
'Don't mount yet. . . .
Lady Hsiang's sorrow was said to be unequalled;[125]
But still she could weep.
I can no longer cry, my tears have all been shed.

Fighting Quails

'My love,
There're myriad enticements
In the capital.
The wines are stronger, the flowers more profuse.
Don't you forget me there and
Marry someone else.
Drink moderately.

[125] Lady Hsiang can refer either to O-huang or to Nü-ying, consorts of Emperor Shun
(cf. n. 38). Legend has it that when Shun died in Ts'ang-wu, O-huang and Nü-ying hurried
thither; they wept profusely and their tears permanently stained a species of bamboo
which was henceforth called 'Lady Hsiang bamboo'.

Refrain from excessive pleasures.
Keep these words in mind and
You'll pass the examination with honors.

'I'll wait
For good news,
For the jeweled cap
And embroidered cape.
I'll lock
My apartment
And put my musical instruments away.
No makeup will touch my face.
You, on your part,
Must write frequently.

Plum Tree in the Snow

'Don't be
So upset, so sad.
What must be
Must be.
It's no use to fret.

'I know you well.
What's hidden from others is obvious to me.
Here's some advice for you
Before
You go.

Coda

'Am I tugging on your coat? Sorry.
I want to ask you when you'll return. . . .
Oh yes, you must be careful on the road.
Be circumspect always.
Don't stay up too late, or get up too early.
Avoid cold tea, cold food.
Look after yourself.
Know that every day I'll stand by the gate to wait for you.'

[Prose]

Chang and Ying-ying found it difficult to leave each other. Madam Ts'ui said to them: 'One could accompany a traveller for a thousand miles; still, there must be the moment of parting.'

173

Lingering in the Perfumed Quilt

> By the dusty, well-travelled road,
> A feast was laid out
> For Madam Ts'ui, Ying-ying, Chang,
> And Fa-ts'ung.
> The prospect of fame and glory
> Made the scholar leave.
> Their imminent separation
> Greatly depressed the lovers.
>
> Chang's sleeves were stained with tears;
> Ying-ying's cheeks were wet.
> He sighed incessantly;
> She never relaxed her frown.
> He asked her to take care.
> She wished him godspeed.
> The two of them
> Shared the same grief.

Coda

> His servant, worried that it would soon be dark,
> Untethered his horse from a willow tree.
> And the heartless Madam Ts'ui
> Had her carriage brought around.

[Prose]

Chang took leave of Madam Ts'ui and Fa-ts'ung; both of them wished him a pleasant journey. Madam then seated herself in the carriage. Chang went to say good-bye to Ying-ying.

(*Ta-shih-tiao* mode)

Leaping Over the Mountain Creek

> The banquet ended,
> Chang had no more reason to linger behind.
> The lovers were despondent
> When they saw
> His horse facing west

Her carriage east.
A servant put cups and dishes away, and
Chang said good-bye
To Fa-ts'ung and Madam Ts'ui.

He began to mount, then turning around, he leaned on the saddle
And asked Hung-niang
For another cup of wine.
He looked at Ying-ying silently.
Ying-ying also couldn't speak.
Wretched with misery,
They both felt numb, as though drunk.

Coda

Chang took the cup and sighed.
Before he could say: 'My love, take care',
The wine had been diluted with an equal amount of tears.

[Prose]

Madam Ts'ui called: 'Let him leave, Ying-ying. It is getting dark.' Ying-ying
wept. She gave Chang a *shih* poem, which read:
You have deserted me; I cannot complain,
Since it was I who fell in love with you.
The tenderness you once showed me,
Show it to the love that is new.[126]

(*Huang-chung-kung* mode)

Dancers' Exit

Of all things lovers endure
Parting is the saddest.
Ying-ying is distraught with grief.
Her tears dry, she weeps blood.
Her mind is filled with thoughts she has had no chance to express.

Madam cries: 'It's late, don't detain Chang anymore.'
Hung-niang, her heart hard as steel,
Takes Ying-ying by the elbow and puts her in the carriage.

---

[126] In *Ying-ying chuan*, this poem is given by Ying-ying to Chang after their love affair
is well over and they have each married someone else. Master Tung borrowed it verbatim
from *Ying-ying chuan* and it is of course egregiously inappropriate here.

His hand upon the saddle, preparing to mount,
    Chang vainly stamps his foot one last time.
Lamely he calls: 'Beloved, please take care.'

Coda

The horse starts on its way;
    the carriage returns to the temple.
The horse heads west:
    the carriage moves east.
Hoofs trot,
Taking the lovers farther and farther apart.

(*Hsien-lü-tiao* mode)

Adorning Crimson Lips, ch'an-ling

Just as they are perfectly in love,
    perfectly happy,
    the lovers have to part!
As he rides, Chang feels stabbing pain in his bowels.
He realizes with anguish that the various ways they made love
Are now the stuff of dreams.

He turns to look at P'u-chou — its vague outline
Barely distinguishable from the surrounding hills.
With the west wind,
Come notes of 'Plum Blossoms'
Played from the cold watchtower.

The Auspicious Lotus Blossom

Withered grass borders the road.
An entire forest is aflame with trembling maple leaves.
Once more the habitual traveller sets forth,
Like a tumbleweed.
Ya-ya, migrant wild geese
    fly past masses of opaque evening cloud.

Wind Blowing Lotus Leaves

Chang remembers the pillow, the quilt Ying-ying has always brought,
And regrets that he can't share them that night.
Everything increases his sorrow —

The red maples,
The light rain, and
The soughing west wind.

Coda

The half-curled whip dangles in the air:
    Chang raises his shoulders to keep warm.
His agony is so enormous,
Even the horse seems to buckle under its weight.

[Prose]

Thirty miles to the west of P'u-chou, as evening descended, Chang came upon a beautiful spot.

(*Hsien-lü-tiao* mode)

Flower-Viewing Time

The sinking sun hung from upstretching branches;
    noisy, chattering crows.
A rider's sleeves flutter, urging his horse on.
The road, ever-narrowing, disappears into the horizon.
Deserted river banks.
Tufts of yellow grass covered with glistening frost.

Lonely woods.
Wattled fence speckled with sand.
Bending, an old man fishes with a net.
A slender bridge,
    quietly flowing water
Reflecting a thatched hut and thickets of reed.

Coda

A fisherman's skiff is tied to a hunchbacked willow.
A tavern streamer reaches out from rush eaves.
Thin streaks of smoke
Lock together two or three cottage roofs.

[Prose]

Chang stopped at the village inn.

Willow in Front of the Hall, ch'an-ling

> Darkness envelops the hushed, melancholy landscape.
> Chang stops for the night at the village inn.
> The night moves slowly, and he can't sleep.
> Sighing,
> He tosses and turns.
>
> Burying his face in the pillow, he gives vent to his grief.
> He weeps uncontrollably, as though demented.
> His sobs mingle with the splashing of oar strokes,
> With the river's gurgling moan, and
> The cicadas' worried hum.

The Barbarian Shield

> 'To be separated from you
> When we're so happy together!
> What has brought this about,
> My bad luck, or your evil karma?
> When I return to you,
> We'll have such tales to tell of
> Our anguish,
> Our misery.
>
> 'Since I'm suffering,
> You must be suffering too.
> Alas,
> This separation
> Will last
> At least half a year.
> Tonight is only the first night.

Wild Hemp Stalks

> 'The rain is falling on plantain leaves;
> Crickets chirp anxiously, without a moment's pause.
> What a vile insect,
> Abetting thus sorrow's sting.
> The later it gets the more frantically they wail.

'My bowels are tied in a thousand knots.
Afflicted with so much sorrow
        only a man of steel could remain stoic and calm.
Dried tears make my cheeks burn with pain.
My eyes are damp again; wiping, I see
I have been weeping blood.

Coda

'What intolerable agony!
The lamp gutters: I might as well put it out.
So, the rain has stopped –
Faint glimmers of moonlight on the window.'

[Prose]

The west wind disturbs a traveler's sleep
A crescent moon spies on a drunkard's stupor.

(*Nan-lü-tiao* mode)

Ying-t'ien-ch'ang

Chang weeps
Quietly, and
Wishes the night would hasten its course.
Events of the day gnaw at him;
He's too disturbed
To sleep.
Languidly he opens the door, and
With a robe around his shoulders
        he paces back and forth in the moonlight,
Gazing at the sky.

Diaphanous clouds veil the moon.
A light-grey sky fuses with light-grey waves.
Dying willows; bent, broken reeds.
In the distance, the hazy contours of a fishing platform.
The desolate scene produces a new surge of sorrow in him.
Suddenly, he hears someone whisper in the willow grove:
'Do please hurry, my lady.'

Coda

> To his astonishment,
> Chang sees two beautiful women—on the south bank, to the east of
> > bridge—
> Approach in the moonlight.

[Prose]

> Her slippers pinch, her stockings are too tight;
> > one lady walks slowly, with difficulty.
> Her breasts heave, her voice trembles;
> > she complains feebly of her fatigue.
> Are they human or ghosts?
> Harbingers of joy or evil?

Before Chang has time to get his sword, they are by his side. In a rude and
menacing tone of voice, Chang asks: 'Who are you that you dare to frighten
me like this?' In the shadow of the willow, cast by the moon, he scrutinizes
them, etc.[127]

(*Shuang-tiao* mode)

Rejoicing in the Great Harmony

> 'If you're human, say so.
> If you're ghosts, get you gone this instant.'
> As he wonders if he has time to fetch his sword,
> The two women come closer
> And closer.

> Chang turns and looks at them again.
> He's dumbfounded, speechless;
> His annoyance turns to joy.
> He bows and says:
> 'So it's you, sisters,
> It's you.'

[Prose]

When he scrutinizes the two women, he sees that they are Ying-ying and
Hung-niang. Surprised, Chang asks them: 'How did you get here?'

Ying-ying says: 'The wine Mother had drunk earlier made her sleep
with unusual soundness tonight. Left to ourselves, I asked Hung-niang
when she thought you would come back to me, and she suggested that we

[127] See n. 62.

180

come and see you, since you could not have traveled very far. I liked the suggestion, so secretly we crossed the river and here we are.'

Chang takes Ying-ying's hand and they return to his room. Before they can get undressed, however, they hear dogs bark at their door. Chang pokes a hole in the paper window and looks out. The sky is red with torch flames and a din of strident voices fills the air. One man cries: 'The women who stole across the river must be inside!'

(*Shang-tiao* mode)

Calming Wind-Blown Waves

> The road to happiness has many obstacles.
> Hardly has Ying-ying removed her cap
> And loosened her skirt
> When she hears dogs bark.
> The wind brings forth a wave of clamoring noises.
> What's happening?
> Chang
> Turns ashen
> With fear.
>
> Torch flames illuminate the windows.
> Hostile, menacing voices
> Call on them to open their door.
> Chang sees
> Five thousand armed men
> Led by a big, strapping fellow,
> Who carries a sword ornamented with wild-goose feathers.
> The man says to the others: 'Search the room!'

Coda

> A boot kicks open the flimsy, wooden door.
> Chang goes forward to stop the intruders. . . .
> He wakes from his dream.

[Prose]

> Why do magpies make so much noise,
> Driving away an incipient amatory dream?

Chang sits up to wait for the day to dawn. His servant has already begun packing.

181

Drunk and Wretched, ch'an-ling

> Chang regretted
> The disappearance of his dream.
> 'How noisy these magpies are!
> Waking me from my dream.
> Heaven shouldn't have made them such glib chatterboxes.'
>
> Vexed by this new disappointment,
> Chang wept as the moon set.
> The quilt, saturated
> With tears,
> Was fit to be wrung.

Wind Blowing Lotus Leaves

> His servant came and urged gently by his pillow:
> 'Master, please get up; the day has dawned.'
> As they finished packing up the beddings, the books, and the lute,
> They heard a horn play reveille in the distance.
> Bells rang, and
> Cocks crowed.

The Inebriated Tartar Woman

> Despite his misery, his reluctance to leave,
> Chang took the reins.
> He knew he was going farther and farther away
> And wondered when he would see his love again.

Coda

> Close at hand, rose the majestic Hua mountain.
> Far away, flowed the sinuous Ch'in river.
> Countless bridges would be crossed.
> Mounted on his lean horse, once again Chang set out for Ch'ang-an.

[Prose]

> A cracking whip quickened the pace of the gaunt horse.
> Piercing sorrow fashioned the lines of a new poem.
> On the way to Ch'ang-an,
> Chang endured the traveller's hardships.
> In the temple of P'u-chiu,
> Ying-ying suffered ineffable misery.

After Chang's departure, Ying-ying wasted away with grief. One day, feeling unusually restless, she visited Chang's study. The altered look of the room intensely depressed her.

(*Huang-chung-kung* mode)

The Golden Altar Boy, ch'an-ling

> Chang's absence
> Upset Ying-ying profoundly.
> Listless, she'd spend hours watching the incense curl and coil.
> Often she dozed, but her naps didn't assuage her gloom.
> Her skirt might be askew; she didn't bother to straighten it.
> Her chignon, carelessly dressed, hung crookedly to one side.

> 'I'm losing weight
> Because of him
> What *am* I to do with this devastating anguish?
> I know he'll eventually return to me.
> Yet the present loneliness
> Is impossible to bear.

Alliterative and Rhyming Binomes

> 'In his study, the inkwell is dry.
> Piles of paper have turned yellow.
> The room looks forsaken, forlorn.
> Cold ashes fill
> The bronze tripod and
> Jeweled censers.
> Books are left
> Scattered about.
> Elegant, powder-white stationery
> Is grey with dust.
> Everywhere one sees signs of neglect.

Earth-Scraping Wind

> 'Cruel, faithless love,
> How could you leave me!
> Who's to paint my eyebrows now?[128]

---

[128] Allusion to Chang Ch'ang 張敞 (first century B.C.), who liked to paint the eyebrows of his wife. Such behavior was considered unbecoming to a high official. Questioned by the emperor, Chang replied: 'I hear that in the privacy of the boudoir, there are conjugal intimacies far surpassing that of a husband painting his wife's eyebrows. . . .'

My eyes are sore with weeping.
My lute is covered with dust –
I haven't touched the plectrum since you left.
Even if I could write a new poem,
A new lyric,
Who would hear them? Who would respond?
Waning autumn further abets my grief.
What should I do, my love?

Straightening a Golden Cap

'Outside, crickets
Make a deafening din.
Such tiny creatures, yet
They never
Rest.
Surely they must be the world's
Most annoying insects!
Will they not give me
One moment's peace?

Sai-erh Song

'Sorrow,
Sorrow,
How can I suppress my sorrow?
I stamp my feet, rub my ears,
But I feel worse.
Do I see a wild goose?[129]
Do I see a wild goose?

Willow Leaves

'Bamboo curtains flap in the morning breeze;
Whirling round and round, leaves fall.
Time flies quickly like shuttles on a loom.
My frustration blazes.

The Magical Staff

'My poor eyes.
My poor eyes
Must have shed ten thousand tears.

[129] Traditional carrier of messages.

Unrestrainable:
The moment I wipe them dry,
They're wet again.
I have more tears than heaven has rain.

Ssu-men-tzu

'Pernicious melancholia.
Can I be cured? When?
I'm skin and bones,
          a skeleton in ill-fitting clothes.
I feel totally alone,
I curse him.
I fret.
Can he have found another love?
I curse him.
I fret.
What adventure is he seeking now?

Coda

'Where's my mirror? I mustn't look too unkempt.
My cheeks are raw.
How I've changed!'

[Prose]

Ying-ying had heard nothing from Chang since his departure in the fall. Now bleak winter was upon her. During the day she could manage a certain equanimity, but at night she was tortured by loneliness.

(*Chung-lü-tiao* mode)

Hsiang-feng-ho, ch'an-ling

Her sorrow knew no bounds, and
She never stopped weeping.
At times she felt insane
With unbearable grief.
One night, sitting by a lamp,
She attempted some sewing
To divert herself from
Her agony.

Her delicate hands
Picked out a thread to put through the needle.
But instead of holding up the eye,
She held up the sharp end.
Next, she cut out a shirt —
The material she mutilated turned out to be
The skirt she wore.

Pomegranate Flowers

Gazing at Hung-niang,
She cried: 'Chang, oh, Chang.'
A long time passed before she realized her mistake.
She wasn't only ill,
She was possessed by evil spirits as well.

'Alas, alack,
When can I put a stop to my grief?
I think of him a thousand, nay, ten thousand times a day.
It's in my karma;
I'm fated to have Sorrow as my companion.'

She felt drowsy
And craved a nap,
Hoping secretly that
She'd see her love in her dream.
But her churning sorrow
Stubbornly kept her awake.

Coda

'I must be paying a debt
Incurred in my last incarnation.
Master Chang, what a merciless creditor you are!'

[Prose]

The following year, Chang took the Palace Examination and passed it with the third highest grade.

Chapter 7

(*Cheng-kung* mode)

Liang-chou, ch'an-ling

> Chang enters the moon and effortlessly breaks off a cassia branch.[130]
> He doesn't need to exert himself, to strain for the limb.
> It's still early when he finishes the examination;
>   the sun has barely started to set.
> He likes the *fu* he has written.
> Pleased with himself, he strokes his beard,
>   a contented smile on his face.
>
> Chia I and Ssu-ma Hsiang-ju couldn't have done better.
> Chang wins high honors.
> The path to the blue clouds is opened to him.
> He's no longer tied to the humdrum, the commonplace.
> He'll pace around the Phoenix Pond[131] in a blaze of glory.

Licorice Root

> Admirable success!
> What admirable success!
> A resounding thunderclap —
> A fish metamorphoses into a dragon.[132]
> The scholar kneels on the scarlet palace steps,
> To show his obeisance, his gratitude to the Emperor.
> Gratified, euphoric,
> Chang thoroughly enjoys the imperial banquet.
> After the feast, flushed with wine,
>   he gallops on a proud horse in the east wind,
> His whip running over rush flowers.

---

[130] Breaking off a cassia branch in the moon is a metaphor for succeeding in the Palace Examination.
[131] Metonym for the Imperial Secretariat.
[132] Having succeeded in the Palace Examination (the last and the most difficult in a series of civil examinations), a candidate can expect to be appointed to a high office; thus, the metamorphosis, the transformation from an ordinary person to a high official.

Removing the Cotton Garment

> 'Far away
> My darling waits for me.
> I must write to her
> Of my success.

> 'Since I came to the capital I've seen numerous girls
> Flaunting their wealth and beauty behind parted curtains.
> But none
> Can compete with my love.

> 'As soon as I can,
> I'll leave the capital.
> Now I am an official,
> She will be a Lady.

> 'My new girdle is made of rhinoceros horn.
> My cap is of black silk.
> His Majesty has bestowed on me a green robe
> To replace my plain, white gown.

Coda

> 'I'll wait for a commission,
>   then, I'll return to her with befitting pomp.
> My heralds, my guards
> Will no doubt impress my Ying-ying.'

[Prose]

Chang wrote a *shih* poem and sent a servant to deliver it to Ying-ying.

(*Shuang-tiao* mode)

A Visit to the Imperial Capital

> He told
> The servant:
> 'A little over ten miles to the east of P'u-chou,
> You'll find the Temple of Universal Salvation.
> To the west of the Exposition Hall,
> Behind the veranda,
> There's a row of gates;
>   the Ts'ui compound lies behind the third one.

'Tell my fiancée and my future mother-in-law
That I've passed the examination with honors.
I have not changed my mind about marrying Ying-ying,
So let them not change theirs.
Please
Ask them
To look out for my return.'

[Prose]

Chang sealed the poem and gave it to the servant. The servant departed.

Meanwhile, Ying-ying, pining for news from Chang, became ill. On the fifteenth of the third month, as she remembered how on the same day the year before, she had written the poem 'Waiting for the Moon in the Western Chamber', she could not refrain from weeping.

Hung-niang tried to console her: 'Sister, you have been very sickly; it seems that spring is upsetting your natural harmony. Please tell me what ails you so that we can treat it with medicine. Otherwise, you may become gravely ill.'

Ying-ying wept even more bitterly.

(*Tao-kung* mode)

One Who Leans against the Balustrade, ch'an-ling

1   'My beloved
2   Has been gone for months,[133]
3   When will we be together again?
4   I'm distraught beyond measure.
5   I dread the evenings when I lean sadly on the red balustrade;[134]
6   I fear the nights of standing alone by the deserted steps.
7   All around, dark-green moss is covered with fallen flowers.
8   The east wind hurls
9   Catkins against flapping curtains,
10 And dust on the ground exudes a fragrant scent.

11 'How much is my sorrow?
12 It will break a cargo cart pulled by twenty mules![135]

[133] In the Chinese text these two lines read: 'My beloved/Has been gone for almost over a year.' This, of course, is not true as Chang left in the autumn and it is now spring. I have therefore changed the second line.
[134] Leaning on the balustrade and gazing out in the hope of sighting one's friend or lover is a stock stance in *tz'u* poetry. See the discussion in the Introduction.
[135] The Chinese is *'T'ai-p'ing ch'e'* which is a cargo cart pulled by twenty mules.

13	I have such bad luck this year!
14	Never before have I been so unhappy.
15	I've lost all tranquillity;
	my thoughts are confused like tangled hemp.
16	I'm as thin as a rail.
17	My hair hangs in disarray:
	I'm too weary to straighten the hairpins.
18	Listless, depressed,
19	I don't know what to do
20	With myself.

Chuan

21	'My darling, I have cherished you
22	As much as I have cherished life.
23	Yet for this I'm now made to pay.
24	You're in truth a ruthless creditor
25	Exacting payment for a debt.

26	'A debt I must have incurred in a previous life.
27	How strange that I should pay it now.
28	My suffering is predestined.
29	I can do nothing
30	To mitigate my pain.

31	'My reflection in the mirror
32	Distresses me — I look so pale.
33	What's more distressing, though, is that
34	You and I
35	Are separated by this formidable distance;
	You're on the edge of the horizon!

36	'My devotion to you hasn't diminished and
37	You have, I trust, remained loyal to me.
38	We must bear our misery stoically.
39	But alas,
40	Our misery threatens to grow.

Supreme Beauty

41	'I tire of leaning on the balustrade.
42	I'm ashamed to wear any flowers this spring.
43	It's true that I have
44	Brought this suffering on myself.

190

45 But not because
46 My nature is ungenerous or fretful.
47 As petal-tips lose their color,
48 A new gloom darkens my brows.
49 I look toward the capital —
50 Range after range of mountains
        girded by drifting clouds.

51 'Invariably I feel worse at night.
52 My loneliness stabs me then.
53 Tonight I mustn't forget to burn incense
54 To the moon.
55 This time last year,
56 The full moon was radiant; you were here.
57 The moon is the same, but how much have I changed!
58 I strike the balustrade[136]
59 I can write you a letter!
60 But who would deliver it?[137]

Music of the Great Sage

61 'A faded flower, a waning moon,
62 A wilted orchid, damaged jade —
63 I'm losing my beauty.
64 My sadness is unfathomable, ocean deep.
65 Flowers fall by the thousands in
66 Late spring's
67 Subtle wind and
68 Insidious rain.
69 A melancholy sight
70 To deepen my melancholy mood.

71 'Sitting immobile at my dressing table,
72 I push my tongue against my teeth;
73 I close my eyes;
74 Still, my cheeks are wet with tears.
75 When *will* this forlornness
76 End?
77 Surely my hair
78 Will turn grey
79 Before I'm old!

[136] A gesture suggesting that the speaker has had a sudden inspiration.
[137] This is, of course, pure rhetoric, inspired by a convention in *tz'u*. Later in the chapter, Ying-ying easily finds a servant to deliver her letter to Chang.

80 'Hung-niang wonders what ails me.
81 Not a hangover,
82 Nor spring grief,
83 It's your absence, my love.'

[Prose]

Late-spring sights revived Ying-ying's sorrow. She wasted away, pining for Chang.

(*Kao-p'ing-tiao* mode)

Green Jade Tray

> The plight of a lonely woman in an empty boudoir
> Is sad beyond description.
> While a hissing wind blows,
> Ying-ying cowers, alone and cold,
> Beneath one half
> Of a thin quilt.
> Mists of green incense rise languidly in the dark.
> The lamp gutters.
> Ying-ying is consumed with grief.
> Afraid to weep aloud,
> She cries with muffled sobs.

[Prose]

The following morning, jackdaws cawed happily in the sunlight. Ying-ying got up.

(*Hsien-lü-tiao* mode)

Pink is the River

> The ground was covered with fallen flowers.
> Jackdaws flapped their wings in the breeze,
>> delighting in the suddenly fine weather.
> Ying-ying looked haggard.
> She had wept all night, longing for Chang.
> Her handkerchief, her sleeves, her pillow were all stained with tears.

Sleepless at night, she was wont to doze in the day.
Her health deteriorated;
She had become thin.
'My heart is bound round and round by thoughts of him.
There, where he is,
He must be unhappy too.'
Just as she was troubled by such melancholy thoughts,
She heard Hung-niang say that
Someone was at the door.

[Prose Insert]

The gatekeeper announced Chang's servant. Madam Ts'ui and Ying-ying
asked him to usher the servant in. A few moments later, the servant appeared.

He bowed in front of the steps,
Still panting from the trip.
His face was covered with dust.
Madam Ts'ui asked him to approach the curtain,[138]
And inquired herself:
'How's Mr Chang?
Is he waiting for the results of the examination?
When did he take it?
When will the results be known?
Was he pleased with his performance?
Are there messages
Or letters?'
The servant ignored the questions.
He simply congratulated Madam Ts'ui.
Then turning to Ying-ying, he called her: 'Your Ladyship.'

[Prose]

The messenger handed Chang's letter to Madam Ts'ui. Hung-niang snatched
it away and gave it to Ying-ying.
　　Ying-ying opened the letter; it was a *shih* poem with the lines:
A Flower Seeker in the capital
Sends a messenger to P'u-chou town,
To tell his love that he will soon return
Dressed in an embroidered gown.

[138] In traditional China, ladies received male strangers from behind a curtain. They often
avoided speaking directly to male visitors and servants; thus, in the following line,
special note is made of the fact that Madam Ts'ui herself asked the servant questions.
(Cf. n. 141 below.)

Ying-ying interpreted the poem: 'The first line reveals that Brother Chang has passed the examination with the third highest mark, since a Flower Seeker is the sobriquet given to the third most successful candidate. The third and fourth lines mean that he is now waiting for an assignment and will return to us as an official.'

Everyone was delighted with the news.

But after this poem was received, no word came from Chang. Soon it was autumn again. Ying-ying secretly asked a servant to deliver a letter to Chang.[139] With the letter she sent him a few articles of clothing, a zither with jasper mounting, a jade hairpin, and a writing brush with a mottled-bamboo handle.

(*Yüch tiao* mode)

Water Dragon's Chant

> Cold dew, chilly mist;
> > in the courtyard, *wu-t'ung* leaves begin to fall.
> Another autumn draws to an end.
> Sitting in her room,
> Alone,
> Ying-ying feels her bowels tied in a thousand knots.
> Above all, she dreads the coming of evening,
> The melancholy hours, when she sits by the window[140] . . . .
> To the left of the rockeries,
> The last surviving plantain leaves are reflected in the pond.
> From time to time, comes the sound of a fine rain
> > dripping on deserted steps.

> 'Since he has left,
> I spend entire days gazing out from behind the balustrade.
> Sometimes I see dull, dark clouds
> Drifting across an infinite expanse of skies.
> Sometimes I see southborne, migrating geese
> Flying over reeded banks.
> In the twilight, through the din of whining cicadas,
> > mist often rises to obscure ancient trees.
> But always there's the road to Ch'ang-an,
> Passing by a tavern
> On the west side of a rustic bridge.

---

[139] This contradicts the earlier lines in Supreme Beauty (p. 191) where Ying-ying says that she can find no one to deliver her letter.

[140] Another stock stance in *tz'u* poetry; presumably the person who sits by the window is watching out for the arrival of his or her lover.

Returning from Flower-Viewing

'The anguish of separation
Must be the saddest thing in the world.
How I wish
I had a pair of wings and could fly to him.
But he's far away,
Beyond mountains and passes.
In desperation,
I mount the tower
And look out as far as I can: where is he?'

Ying-ying secretly sent for a servant
To convey to Chang her innermost feelings.
She wrapped
A few pieces of clothing in a parcel;
She told the servant to be careful,
Not to delay
Or tarry on the way.
While Hung-niang handed[141]
Him the parcel
Ying-ying said:[142]

Plum Tree in the Snow

'The trousers are made of light, white silk;
They haven't any wrinkles at all.
A singlet and a girdle
Are nothing unusual,
But these are special: I made them myself.

'I hope you won't think the padded socks too thin.
I've spent long hours making them by the lamplight.
Each stitch has been checked two or three times.
It distresses me that I'm not there to mend them
When they're worn.

Uncover a Bowl

'Much work has gone into the blue robe.
It's meticulously cut and measured.
Seated by a bright window,

[141] It was not considered proper for the mistress of a house, particularly a young woman, to hand anything directly to a manservant.
[142] In most of the remaining portion of the suite, Ying-ying is actually speaking to Chang.

I've given great care to every turn of the needle;
I chose the most appropriate threads
To embroider the *lien-li* trees[143]
And the dancing pheasants.[143]

'The fine velvet cord comes from Chiang-chou.
It's ideal for a belt.
The green shirt has an uncommon style.
It should fit you perfectly.
The pendent tassel is made of Wu silk.
Please accept them
And the other things as well.'

Three Stanzas with Reduplicated Words

'The hairpin is small, but it's jade,
I chose this one for its white purity.
Unblemished by even the slightest flaw,
It's like my love for you;
Like my love for you, firm and strong.
Once you treated me like a gem,
Now I'm neglected like dung.

'The brush's mottled handle is unique in the world.
It's made from a bamboo
          which grew at the foot of Chiu-i Mount.[144]
That time, when Lady Hsiang said farewell to Yao Yü,[144]
Her tears were profuse;
Her tears were profuse like the autumn rain.
They touched this bamboo and it became speckled.
Her parting from her lord, I concede,
          could possibly be more sorrowful than my parting from you.

'One night you played on this zither
To woo me.
Now you're like Hsiang-ju after presenting *Shang-lin fu*[145] to the
          throne.
You've become famous in the capital;
In the capital you indulge in countless pleasures.

---

[143] *Lien-li* trees with their intertwining branches and a pair of pheasants engaged in a mating dance are symbols of amatory or conjugal happiness.
[144] Chiu-i Mount is the burial place of Shun (Yao Yü). Cf. n. 125. The bamboo in these lines is supposed to be the one featured in the legend.
[145] Celebrated *fu* by Ssu-ma Hsiang-ju in which he praises exuberantly the marvels of the *Shang-lin* imperial park. Wu-ti was pleased by it and showered favors on Ssu-ma.

196

For days on end you drink;
>you lose your head over *grandes cocottes,*
Forgetting altogether your Wen-chün.

Hsü-sha Coda

'Good messenger, bear the hardships of the trip.
When you see Mr Chang,
Ask him how he has fared
Since we parted.
Show him everything in the parcel.
Urge him to accept.
Watch carefully if he means to decline.
Then, have him read my letter, written while I wept.'

[Prose]

The servant left for the capital.

After Chang passed the examination, he was appointed a scholar in the Han-lin Academy[146] because of his literary talent. However, he fell ill and could not assume his duties. When autumn came he still had not recovered.

(*Hsien-lü-tiao* mode)

Trimming the Silver Lamp

A quiet, sparsely furnished study.
Clear autumn in the courtyard.
Elegant halls and doors are unused.
Within the garden fence, flowers exude intoxicating perfumes.
Chrysanthemums thrive.
The Double Ninth festival is coming,
But Chang is not in a festive mood.
He's laid low with illness, and
No one's around to nurse him back to health.

He grieves over his separation from Ying-ying.
To add to his frustration his illness refuses to mend.
Tears fill his eyes.
His brows are puckered in a knot.
Torn to a thousand shreds are his bowels of nine folds.
Far away,
Beyond ten thousand streams and one thousand hills,
Where exactly is his love?

[146] First founded in the T'ang dynasty, the Han-lin Academy was connected to the Inner Court. Academicians were charged with literary and editorial responsibilities.

Coda

> The phoenix has long parted from his mate.
> Since then, he sees her only in dreams.
> Now, however, he can't even manage to dream.

[Prose]

Chang was pleased by his success in the examination but depressed by his lingering illness. One autumn evening it occurred to him that he had not received any news from Ying-ying; he felt intensely dejected.

(*Cheng-kung* mode)

Liang-chou, tuan-sung

> Outside the bamboo curtains, dried leaves rustle, fall.
> A melancholy time of year.
> Someone plays a mournful tune on the flute.
> Chang looks out
> And sees a mist of fine rain.

> The evening wind sighs.
> On dark clouds are pasted a flock of migrating geese.
> Pressed by the unrelenting wind, they form crooked, broken lines —
> Heng-yang[147] is far away,
> Yet another thousand miles of flight.

Ying-t'ien-ch'ang

> Touched by frost, chrysanthemums begin to wither.
> Chang salvages a few
>   but is too ashamed of his haggardness to wear them.
> His bowels are tied in ten thousand knots.
> He rolls up the curtains
>   and fixes his tear-filled eyes on the horizon.
> Ranges and ranges of mountain, their jagged peaks reach into the skies.
> But where's the road to P'u-chou?
> In vain he strains and gazes:
>   the road is concealed behind evening clouds.

> The large courtyard, the garden pavilion are desolate.
> Coursing by the window,

[147] In Hunan province, where wild geese spend their winter.

A wanton wind threatens to break the bamboos.
Forlorn and downcast,
Chang weeps until blood oozes from his eyes.
From a distance comes the doleful sound of someone washing clothes,
It adds grief to sorrow.[148]

Chuan

Chang lights the lamp.
Lethargically he keeps to his study.
He sighs —
Half of his quilt will again be unused,
And he must endure alone the slow-moving night,
         quite as long as a year.

Seated by the window, wretched with grief,
He tries to read to put himself to sleep.
He leafs through an anthology,
         looking for the chronicles of Ch'in and Chin.[149]
They elude him;
         instead, he finds the story of Wu and Yüeh.[149]
Frustrated, he pinches and rubs his ear-lobe.

Putting away the book, he goes to bed.
But his wicked eyes,
Restive, merciless,
Fill themselves with tears, and refuse to shut.
Chang is despondent.

Such agony, such misery
Will lead to heaven knows what end!
He *wants* to forget his unhappiness,
But involuntary sighs escape his lips, and he feels choked.
He wonders when his suffering will have run its course.

Licorice Root

'I've been stupid.
How I've been stupid!
In my unwavering devotion,
I was blind to her fickleness.

---

[148] The sound of washing and pounding clothes is sad because the clothes are taken to be those of someone soon to depart. The sound therefore evokes the sorrow of separation.
[149] During the Spring and Autumn Era, Ch'in and Chin were friendly states united by marriage ties, but Wu and Yüeh were enemy states.

199

My cursed torturer, wretched love,
Don't you fear heaven's punishment?
We've been parted for a whole year,
Why haven't you sent any news?
I want to tell you I'm worried,
But I'm ill, my hands tremble, and I cannot write.

Removing the Cotton Garment

'Again and again I have tried to forget my sorrow!
I know this suffering is pointless.
After all, I'll eventually see you, my love —
So I say to myself when I'm lucid and rational.'

Liang-chou in Three Stanzas

Leaning on his pillow,
Awake late at night,
Chang listens to the quiet toppling of incense-ashes,
    while waves of perfume inundate the air.
Outside, the rain has stopped, crickets chirp.
Though small,
They make a deafening noise.
Gathered around the deserted steps,
Without a moment's pause they gossip.
Such uncharitable
Insects:
Their din hurts and burns the ear.

Coda

The lamp gutters, Chang weeps on.
Unappreciated are the luminous autumn night,
The clear wind, and brilliant moon.

[Prose]

Chang longed for news as a man thirsts for water. By and by Ying-ying's
servant arrived with the parcel and Chang opened the letter. In brief, it
read:[150] 'The unfortunate Ying-ying lays this letter on the desk of her
talented lover:

[150] The letter is taken, with but minor changes, from Yüan Chen's *Ying-ying chuan*. It is
therefore not appropriate here in *THH*.

200

Ever since last autumn, often for no apparent reason I would feel lost, not knowing what I do or where I am. When I have company, amidst their lively chatter, I force myself to laugh and speak; but whenever I am alone, invariably tears overcome me. At night, time and time again I dream that I am describing to you my deep sorrow and my grief over our separation. Tenderly we make love and for a moment everything is the same as it used to be. But always before we reach the height of our joy, your phantom leaves abruptly and I wake up. Though somehow your half of the pillow feels warm, I know in my mind that you are far away.

Time flies: the old year has vanished since your departure. Ch'ang-an is a mecca for pleasure-seekers; it is easy to be entangled in romantic involvements there. How fortunate I am that you not only remember my love but deign to express yours in an elegant letter. While my limited talent does not permit me to reply in kind, there is one thing I can and will do: I will hold steadfastly to my vow of everlasting devotion and constancy.

You and I are cousins, and it happened that we attended the same banquet. Subsequently you bribed my maid to communicate to me your secret admiration. Being young, I was susceptible, and my aloofness began to weaken. You wooed me with your zither; I did not repulse you with my shuttle.[151] When you offered me your pillow and mat, you revealed the magnitude of your interest and the depth of your affection. Inexperienced and naive, I thought you had meant to make our relationship a permanent one. I thought, in fact, that I had found my lord, on whom I could depend the rest of my life.

But unexpected things do happen. I saw you in private:[152] and then despite myself all the moral principles I have been brought up with failed to restrain my infatuation. I gave myself to you, thus damaging my chance of becoming your wife.[153] Alas, this impetuosity brought me regrets that I will not forget until the day I die; but, what is the point of speaking of that now!

You may be a charitable man, willing to be guided by your emotions. You may indeed decide to make the best of a thorny situation. In that case, you would be giving me a new lease on life just when death stares me in the face. On the other hand, you may be a man of cold intellect, to whom feelings are unimportant. You may disregard insignificant private emotions and focus your attention on broad moral principles. To you, my having offered myself before we are married is a despicable act, and the promise you made, since you felt it was extorted from you, is worthless and retractable. If the

---

151 Allusion to a vignette concerning Hsieh K'un 謝鯤 (280–322) as recorded in his biography in *Chin shu.* 晉書 . 'The daughter of his neighbor Kao was very beautiful. K'un once made advances to her and she threw a shuttle at him, breaking two of his teeth.'
152 I take this to refer to their encounter in the garden. Although Ying-ying reprimands Chang severely on that occasion, secretly she is moved by him. Thus, she goes to his apartment a few nights later.
153 In the moral frame of *Ying-ying chuan*, it is understood that a man will be reluctant to marry the woman with whom he has had a premarital affair even though he is the seducer.

latter case proves to be true, let my bones disintegrate and my body rot away, Yet, even so, my love and loyalty will live on. They will drift with the wind, mingle with the dews, and rest amidst the dust on the ground.

Your decision, then, will either make me live or die; that is all I can say. Bending over this paper, I am shaken with sobs, and I realize I have expressed poorly my love for you. In all events, my dearest, please take care of yourself . . .

With this letter I send you a jade hairpin, a mottled-bamboo brush, and a zither with jasper mountings. In different ways they are emblems of me and my sadness. Jade is firm, smooth to the touch, and stable; the bamboo is stained with tears; the zither strings are like so many strands of sorrow. Please cherish them forever, if only for what they represent.

Our hearts are close but our bodies are far apart. When shall I see you again? Despite the thousand miles that separate us, I feel our spirits often meet, for my thoughts are always on you, my love.

The autumn air is cold and it is easy to catch a chill, so please eat well and keep yourself in good health. Look after yourself in all ways and do not worry about me.'

As Chang read the letter, he could not keep back his tears.

(*Ta-shih-tiao* mode)

Jade-Winged Cicada

> The letter made him weep;
> His shirt was stained with tears.
> 'Ying-ying doesn't know
> I'm ill.
> She thinks I no longer love her.
> How pitiful is this misunderstanding!
> Wrongly accused, I can only fret and sigh;
> Who's here to listen to my grievances?
> Her complaints
> Hurt me deeply.
> Ill as I am, I'll drag my sick body to her side.

> 'I can't put the letter down.
> What an intelligent woman!
> Every phrase
> Is beautifully composed.
> She sends me
> A brush, a zither, a jade hairpin,
> And wrapped in a parcel,

A suit of clothes.
They make me long for her even more.
A letter of just one page
Ties my brows in a knot and
Cut my bowels anew.'

[Prose]

Chang's friend Yang Chü-yüan heard about the letter and presented a *shih* poem to Chang:
Frost chills and leaves fall.
Poring over Hsiao-niang's[154] letter,
P'an An (more beauteous than jade)
Hears spring's provocative call.
Yang urged Chang to marry Ying-ying. Chang began to pack.

Before he could leave however, Cheng Heng, Minister Cheng's son, arrived in P'u-chou. He went directly to the Temple of Universal Salvation to see Madam Ts'ui. When Madam Ts'ui asked him: 'Why have you come?' Cheng Heng replied: 'Father wishes me to congratulate you, Madam, on the completion of your mourning. We can now proceed with my marriage with Ying-ying, whom the late Prime Minister had promised to me.'

Madam said: 'Ying-ying is now betrothed to Chang Kung.'

'The scholar Chang who succeeded in the recent examination?'

'Yes. We have not yet heard what position he has been given.'

'Oh, he has been appointed a scholar in the Han-lin Academy because of his literary talent, and Mr Wei, Chairman of the Board of Civil Offices, has just married his daughter to him,' Cheng Heng said.

(*Nan-lü-kung* mode)

A Sprig of Flowers, ch'an

This evil-hearted beast
Had no principles whatever.
Cunningly, maliciously,
He slandered Chang:
'Chang Kung has recently
Become the son-in-law of a grand personage.
From the beginning, he never intended
To marry Ying-ying.
So seizing the first opportunity, he plied his gallantry elsewhere.'

[154] Conventional term denoting an unspecified woman, like 'a Miss Smith' or 'a Mrs Jones'.

Madam Ts'ui, née Cheng, exclaimed:
'What's this you say?'
Hung-niang stamped her foot in anger.
Ying-ying, listening through the window,
Also heard Cheng Heng.
Through her tender bowels,
Ten-thousand knives twisted and turned.
Hung-niang consoled her:
'Sister, sister, don't pay any attention
To groundless rumors brought from afar.

A Puppet

'I know Mr Chang loves you dearly.
His action makes that clear.
He tried so hard to win you,
Would he casually set you aside?
You can't believe what Cheng Heng says.
He's only trying to win Madam to his side.

'The beast is furious
That you're betrothed to Mr Chang.
Hastily he fabricates this outrageous lie.
Sister, don't break your promise.
You'll know the truth when your messenger returns.
Be patient, he should be back soon.'

Mountains Turning Green

Ying-ying didn't hear a word
Of Hung-niang's counsel.
She was completely lost in a trance.
'I had thought that
We would spend our lives together.
Little did I expect him to break his vows!
Surely heaven and earth will expose the faithless.
Surely they'll expose the faithless.

'If Cheng Heng's words were true,
Why did Chang treat me with such ardor before?
If they were false,
Why haven't I heard from him?
I have suffered
So much for him,

Only to discover his fickleness!
Alas, what a mistake I've made,
What a mistake I've made.

Coda

'When he was poor, I was tolerated as a wife.
Now he's rich, someone else gets the title "Lady".
Still I mustn't be too upset. . . .'
Ying-ying groaned and fell in a faint.

[Prose]

Malicious slander is a vicious thing:
It arouses doubts in the most trusting mind.
Human breath is a vital property:
It stops a moment and a person dies.

Ying-ying's maids all tried to revive her. A long time passed before she
regained her consciousness. Madam Ts'ui wept, murmuring: 'My poor,
unfortunate child!'

Turning aside, she quietly said to Hung-niang: 'If Ying-ying becomes ill,
you will not go unpunished'

Cheng Heng sneaked in to see Madam Ts'ui once more. He said to her:
'Of Chang and I, who is closer to you? Besides, he has now married someone
else and Ying-ying was promised to me long before she became betrothed to
Chang. You must respect the wishes of my uncle, the late Prime Minister.'

Madam Ts'ui was persuaded. Secretly she gave permission to Cheng Heng
to select a date for the wedding. As they were talking. . . .[155]

(*Shuang-tiao* mode)

Wen-ju-chin

How unjust,
Madam Ts'ui sided with Cheng Heng, her relative.
She said to Hung-niang:
'Make sure your sister sees
That fate has ordained
This setback.
Don't let her commit suicide
Or torture herself.

[155] The singer—narrator anticipates here. Logically this phrase should be followed by the
second line in the coda of the ensuing suite.

If anything goes wrong,
I'll hold you responsible.'
And Cheng Heng added insult to injury:
'Tell your sister not to be foolish.
Is my family less illustrious
Or less prosperous
Than Chang's?

'I'm not boasting,
All sorts of families
Hanker after *me* for a son-in-law.
I may not be handsome,
But I've got unusually fine inner spirits.
I look clumsy,
Yet my clothes are impeccably tailored.
Though scabs dot my head,
My scarf is always wrinkle-free.
True, I can't write an essay,
But I *have,* mind you, memorized *A Beginner's Word Book.*
Chang succeeded in the examination,
I'm a Palace Guard by hereditary right.
We're two peas in a pod.
Now he has married someone else,
Why should your sister
Remain faithful to *him?*'

Coda

Before he could finish,
Greetings were heard through the curtain.
Someone cried: 'Now Mr Cheng, you'd better stop this nonsense.
Mr Chang has just arrived!'

[Prose]

Cheng Heng was at a loss, not knowing where to put his hands or feet.

Chang went up to the curtain and paid his obeisance to Madam Ts'ui.

Madam said: 'We are pleased to learn of your recent marriage.'

Chang asked with astonishment: 'Who said I got married?'

Cheng Heng said: 'Someone from the capital; apparently the news was widely known there. Ying-ying is to marry me now.'

Although this disturbed Chang, he gave little credence to Cheng Heng's words.

Then Madam said something which turned Chang ashen with alarm. What did she say?

Rendezvous at the Fragrant Mountain

>Hearing what Madam said,
>Chang fell to the ground with a thump.
>A feeble breath barely stirred around his nostrils.
>His limbs twitched.
>At length he came to and stood up with difficulty.
>He was distraught with regrets for having come too late.
>
>'Who has married?
>Where's the beast who told this lie?
>Call him forward and I'll question him in Madam's presence.'
>Cheng Heng, sitting to one side,
>Nearly toppled from his seat.
>He began to sneeze repeatedly.

[Prose]

Madam Ts'ui said to Chang: 'Please compose yourself, sir. Things have already come to this pass; there is nothing we can do now.'

Chang thought to himself: 'Cheng Heng's father is a virtuous minister and knows me slightly. It would be considered unseemly to squabble with his son over a woman.'

Madam Ts'ui then asked Cheng Heng to salute Chang, saying: 'Pay your respect to Ying-ying's elder brother.'

Chang took a good look at Cheng Heng whose appearance thoroughly disgusted him.

(*Chung-lü-tiao* mode)

The Frontier Pass Where Sheep Graze

>The future son-in-law's greeting
>Casts Chang into greater despair.
>Ugly, gawky,
>Eyes dry and dim.
>Pupils like a sun-gazing cat's.
>A lice-chewing monkey's face.
>He ties his black silk belt around his *chest*.
>A gauze scarf hangs sloppily on the back of his head.
>
>His sideburns are infested with nits.
>Utterly revolting!

His mouth stinks like a latrine.
His voice rasps like a broken jar.
A complete nonentity,
      he's not even either a bully
Or a toady.
Over his torso, massive as a wheat-cracking stoneroller,
Drapes a formless sack, passing for a robe.

Coda

Certainly one can't describe him as:
    'elegant and slender, like a poet'.
In fact his hideousness
Has something of that of Chung K'uei, the ghost-chaser.[156]

[Prose]

Chang said to Madam Ts'ui: 'Though Ying-ying is now betrothed to someone else, she must not neglect to pay me her sisterly respect.'
    Madam sent for Ying-ying, who came out after much delay.

(*Hsien-lü-tiao* mode)

Adorning Crimson Lips, ch'an-ling

The beautiful Ying-ying
Looked at Chang, then lowered her head without a word.
Her handkerchief, even her sleeves were wet with tears.
A frown contracted her leaf-like eyebrows.

Her golden-lotus feet were sore from stamping.
Her scallion-stalk fingers were red and raw.[157]
Chang noticed that
Her face was thinner
Than when he saw her last.

Universal Happiness

She bowed to Chang
    but didn't return his greetings.

---

[156] Chung K'uei 鍾馗 , the hideous-looking ghost chaser in folk tradition, was supposed to be an unsuccessful Palace Examination candidate in the T'ang dynasty.
[157] A result of having wrung her hands continuously in despair.

Her deportment, as always,
Was graceful and appealing.
Yet, she seemed ill at ease.
The gathered tips of her eyebrows
Bespoke infinite sorrow.

'That boorish ignoramus
Doesn't deserve to be her husband!
I've come too late,
      oh, what a terrible mistake!
"You can't unhitch a horse after the cart is loaded."
Likewise, "spilt water can't be retrieved".

Coda

'Ying-ying, a second Miss Willow Strand,[158]
Though supple and attractive as ever,
Is, alas, held in another's hand!'

[Prose]

Ying-ying sat down next to her mother. Chang asked her: 'Have you been well since we parted?'

    Ying-ying gave no reply, but it was clear that she appreciated Chang's concern.

(*Yüeh-tiao* mode)

The Emperor Pacifying the West, ch'an-ling

'A year ago,
I went to Ch'ang-an,
Ying-ying and I were separated
    like clouds blown apart by the wind.

---

[158] Allusion to a T'ang *ch'uan-ch'i* story, *Liu-shih chuan* (*The Story of Miss Willow*) by Hsü Yao-tso 許 堯 佐 (*fl. c.* 806 A.D.) During a period of unrest, Han Hung 韓 翃 loses track of his mistress 'Miss Willow'. Searching, Han inscribes a poem on a white silk purse and has it circulated. Eventually, the purse reaches Miss Willow. The text of the poem is:

    Chang-tai Willow,
    Chang-tai Willow,
    Once brightly green, do you still glow?
    Your long strands may cascade, as of old.
    But are they not held by someone new?
See *T'ang Sung ch'uan-ch'i chi*, pp. 48–9.

Often I recalled how we had shared the farewell cup.
How, while we sighed,
Our tears and blood had rained.
How she had whispered to me
To take care of myself.
And how grief had torn my bowels and made my soul flee.

'On the way, my horse
Galloped forward.
I slept in woodcutters' huts
And fishing villages.
I endured agonizing evenings,
When, facing the bean-size flame of a lamp,
Chilled by stonecold quilt, and
Missing my beloved's company,
I wet the pillow with tears.

Fighting Quails

'I lost weight,
My cheeks sank.
I became haggard,
Ungainly, and gaunt.
After reaching Ch'ang-an,
I gave all I had to my studies.
When I passed the examination,
The Emperor favored me with honor.
But then an illness laid me low.
It lingered on, refusing to mend.

'At long last,
A letter from Ying-ying came.
Immediately I asked for leave and rushed back
To marry her.
Much hardship did I suffer
For the sake of seeing my love again.
Now it rained in torrents;
Now a hurricane raged.
I pushed on,
Without the slightest complaint.

Green Mountain Pass

'How happy I was when finally I arrived!
I saw Madam Ts'ui and the first thing she did was to accuse me

Of having married a grandee's daughter.
Ying-ying, she said, would wed someone else.
I was heartbroken.
The familiar surroundings made me doubly sad.
Her future son-in-law was summoned.
We exchanged greetings.
The way he looked,
The way he moved,
Were clumsy in the extreme
He shuffled like a camel,
Sat like an ape.
A horrid fucking build:
Hunchbacked, his rib cage bulging like a turtle's carapace.
Buckteeth jutted from beneath his harelip.
A *thing*, a monster;
I couldn't help sneering discreetly
At this beloved subject of the King of Hell.

Plum Tree in the Snow

'And the repugnant odor of his mouth!
What luck Ying-ying has!
Ah, the days
When I had shared a quilt with her!
We'd been as close as Ch'in and Chin.

'Soon, an embroidered coverlet will spread over her
        and somebody else.
Who would have expected this!
Furtively I steal a glance at her —
There's no powder or rouge
On her flower-like face.

'Despite a touch of pallor her natural beauty remains intact.
A silk skirt falls from her slender waist.
Merciless,
Utterly merciless,
She doesn't look at me or speak to me at all.

'Her black eyebrows are knit in a frown.
A gold pin dangles from her hair.
How vexing!
How very vexing!

Why is she unresponsive and silent?

Coda

'My tears will not stop.
I'm bursting with unrevealed love.
My cruel darling,
How can you be so calm?
You seem not to notice my despair, as though your eyes were shut.
Do you, at least, remember how much I adored you?
Who will be my Lady
Now that I'm an official?'

[Prose]

Chang and Ying-ying merely exchanged glances. Pain stabbed at their hearts.

(*Chung-lü-tiao* mode)

The Ancient Border Town, Lun-t'ai

'Such unbearable sadness!
Every inch of my bowels is shredded into a thousand ribbons
        by mangling knives.
That scoundrel
Managed to sabotage my marriage to Chang.
Just think, at first I thought
He was telling the truth.
With the most shameless lies,
The vilest schemes,
He deceived us and got his way.
But heaven will open its eyes. . . .
I see, close by, Brother Chang,
Already an Academician at his age!
Exceedingly handsome,
The best writer in the world,
So gentle, so considerate,
Yet I must
Marry this lout.

'Whose actions, appearance, and
Deportment are odious to me!

Totally fatuous,
An ignorant moron,
He has huge, colossal feet; he is a hunchback.
He has bald temples, yellow teeth, and crow's eyes.
I'm safe tonight.
But tomorrow night
I must sleep with him behind embroidered curtains.
Much would I rather sleep alone!
What can be more frustrating than seeing
My darling by my side
But unable to join him!
However confused I may be, I know
I'll never relinquish my love for him.
We fix our eyes on each other,
But the space between us feels like the entire span of the earth.

Coda

' "I know not how to act or what to do".[159]
I can't bring myself to answer
Any of his questions.
"Face to face are my husbands, old and new".'[159]

[159] Allusion to a vignette collected in Meng Chi's *Pen-shih shih* (preface dated 886).
Princess Lo-ch'ang 樂昌公主 of Ch'en 陳 and her husband Hsü Te-yen 徐德言
are separated by invading Sui troops, which capture her and present her to Lord Yang Su 楊素.
Yang showers the Princess with favors. Upon discovering her whereabouts Hsü comes
to call. His visit so upsets the Princess that she cannot eat, and Yang decides to return her
to Hsü. At her departure Princess Lo-ch'ang gives Yang the poem:
       Disconcerting contretemps!
       Face to face are my husbands, old and new.
       I dare not laugh; I dare not weep.
       I know not how to act or what to do.
   There is also a T'ang *ch'uan-ch'i* version of this story, and surviving titles suggest that
the story has been used as stuff-material in popular literature of Sung and Yüan times as
well.

Chapter 8

[Prose]

Uneasy and agitated, Chang got up abruptly. Fa-ts'ung invited him to his quarters. With solicitude he counseled Chang: 'All sorts of desirable matches await your selection; surely there is no need to fret over one woman.'

'True, but unlike you I am not free of worldly sentiments; I cannot help resenting this humiliation.'

Fa-ts'ung shared his couch with Chang that night.

During the night, unable to sleep, Chang rose. Throwing a robe around his shoulders, he took out Ying-ying's letter and gifts. Looking at them he became more dejected.

(*Huang-chung-kung* mode)

A Speckled Woodpecker

> 'The evening has descended;
> > I find myself sequestered in a monastic cell!
> It's now late autumn, the most depressing season of all.
> Outside, bamboos sway;
> > their silhouettes bend this way and that.
> West wind scoops up fallen leaves.
> Cicadas whine anxiously,
> Calling out, each to each.
> If my heart, my bowels were made of iron,
> I might be able to suppress this consuming despair.

Cheng-ch'ien-k'un

> 'Lingering sorrow, nagging rancor,
> How much longer will they plague me?
> On the watchtower,
> A horn wails out the mournful
> Tune of *Plum Blossoms.*
> A guttering, irritating lamp
> Dimly illuminates the decorated walls of the room.
> Its blue flame
> Quivers, yet refuses to die.

214

A Speckled Woodpecker

'I certainly have abominable luck and
A loathsome karma!
We were perfectly happy, my love and I.
Then someone
Drove a wedge between us.
Fate must have ordained this suffering.
Our love-making is now only memory,
Stuff for stories and tales.

Alliterative and Rhyming Binomes

'The clepsydra drips slowly.
The quilt is cold.
Sadly I endure the year-long night.
The precious animal-shaped censer
Sends up curls of smoke
From ambergris and musk.
I close my eyes,
Trying to force myself to sleep.
Not even a miracle
Could bring me repose.
Frustrated, I fidget in bed.

A Speckled Woodpecker

'Recalling past happiness
I'm filled with anger.
I remember how, on a moon-lit night,
        I strolled on the courtyard veranda.
Stroking my beard, I chanted a poem.
Through a half-open red gate
I saw my love walk from the western chamber
Toward the rockeries by the deserted steps.
She leaned against them, as though resting from spring fatigue.

Earth-Scraping Wind

'A spinning fan, white and round, dangled from her hand.
Her beauty was extraordinary.
Her trim waist was as supple as a hank of silk.
Oh, the unmatchable grace of her deportment!
Willow-leaf eyebrows, star-bright eyes.

Apricot jaws, peach cheeks.
A tiny mouth and
Bound feet.
Her dress, her makeup, was impeccable,
My eyes, having espied her,
Couldn't move away.

A Speckled Woodpecker

'Responding to my poem,
She chanted one of her own.
As we stood transfixed in love's first glow,
I saw Hung-niang
Run to her mistress and whisper:
"Madam asks me to fetch you."
Quickly Ying-ying returned to her court,
Leaving behind wisps of provocative scent.

Willow Leaves

'I was dazed for a long time.
Finally, I withdrew to my study.
After that encounter, however I tried,
    I couldn't arrange another meeting.
I decided then to forget her.

A Speckled Woodpecker

'Soldiers in P'u-chou mutinied.
Innocent people were captured and robbed.
The rebels came all the way to this temple
And deployed themselves in the precincts.
Their leader clamored:
"We'll spare you if you give us Ying-ying.
If you delay ever so slightly,
We'll reduce you to a pulp of fat and blood."

Sai-erh Song

'With a bold
And brilliant scheme,
I routed the lawless mob;
I saved the Ts'ui family from disaster.

216

But later, Madam Ts'ui, forgetting my kindness,
    broke her promise.
So my cunning won me only disappointment and grief.

A Speckled Woodpecker

    'At the end, Ying-ying came to me secretly;
    We made love behind silk curtains.
    For months,
    She'd come at night and leave at dawn.
    Our tryst was discovered.
    Madam was persuaded to betroth her to me.
    But the allure of fame and wealth
    Enticed me away from my love.

The Magical Staff

    'I went to the capital,
    To the capital where
    I captured the cassia branch in the moon, and
    My name appeared on the gilt placard.
    I prepared to
    Return and marry my love.
    But alas, I became ill.

A Speckled Woodpecker

    'Then the difficult Madam Ts'ui,
    Her petulant temper unaltered,
    Peevishly changed her mind.
    Disregarding her indebtedness to me,
    Trusting the words of a rascal,
    She decided to call off
    My marriage to Ying-ying.

Ssu-men-tzu

    'I was caught in a terrible muddle.
    What should I do?
    Ying-ying herself
    Also seemed to have forgotten her vows.
    How cruel,
    How foolish,
    The way she treated me when we met earlier today!

How cruel!
How foolish!
You hurt me dreadfully, Sister.

A Speckled Woodpecker

'Thanks to her,
I'm accustomed to suffering.
Clearly she has given her heart to someone else.
She ignored all my questions.
Such ruthless betrayal!
        Doesn't she fear heaven's punishment?
I'm so upset my head feels split a hundred ways.

'All the snow in the world
Can't assuage the burning resentment in my belly.
She wrote
This letter herself —
Lies to mock me —
I tear it in a hundred pieces.

Coda

'The mottled-bamboo brush is now split.
However hard the jade, the hairpin is crushed to bits.
The strings of the zither, now broken, can't be mended.'

[Prose]

Seeing how unhappy Chang looked, Fa-ts'ung got up and admonished him:
'You are an intelligent person, but you allow yourself to be bewitched to
this extent by a woman! I no longer want to be your friend.'
    Chang said: 'I am grieved because, first, it is never easy to find an ideal
mate; then, Ying-ying and I have loved each other for such a long time, yet
malicious slander was sufficient to make her treat me like a stranger!'
    Fa-ts'ung asked him: 'If you are to have Ying-ying, will your suffering
end?'
    'But how can she be mine?'
    'Let me take care of it,' Fa-ts'ung said.

(*Chung-lü-tiao* mode)

Green Peonies

'Stop your sighs.
Have you lost the mettle of a man?

218

People will laugh at you,
And I'd be ashamed to be your friend.
Your behaviour isn't worthy of a scholar,
A scholar of high rank to boot!
Don't worry and
Don't complain;
Set your mind at ease.'

Abruptly Fa-ts'ung got up.
He removed from the wall his three-foot consecrated sword.
'The third watch has just sounded.
Before it ends –
Before this candle is burnt out –
You'll learn what I'll have done.
One thing is certain: there'll be a lawsuit.
But have no fear,
I'll take full responsibility.

Coda

    'I'll chop off the head of the old ingrate.
I'll make mince meat of the trouble-making brute,
And I'll give you back your winsome Ying-ying.'

[Prose]

Before Fa-ts'ung finished talking, laughter was heard from outside the window:
'Planning a murder, are you? Will you not implicate me?'
    Who said that? Who?

(*Ta-shih-tiao* mode)

Jade-Winged Cicada

    Chang moistened the paper window, poked a hole,
And through it he looked out furtively.
Who could've come here
So late at night?
At last, he recognized
The two flower-like women.
One was Ying-ying,

Walking swiftly in the moonlight;
Hung-niang was following behind.

Opening the door,
Chang embraced his darling without a word.
Ying-ying asked:
'Have you been well?'
Too miserable to chat,
They simply wept in front of the lamp.
To make sure he wasn't dreaming,
Chang pinched himself.
The lovers' tears rained
Without pause.
Alas, even at their parting
They hadn't been so sad.

Coda

Each of them had prepared ten thousand things to say
At their reunion
Now face to face, they were completely speechless.

[Prose]

Finally Ying-ying said to Chang: 'Your delay has caused this unfortunate turn
of events. All is lost now.'

(*Chung-lü-tiao* mode)

Young Lord An

She asked quietly:
'How have you been, my love?
After you had left for the capital,
For months
I dreamt of you at night.
My sorrow
Was like the misty summer rain
over the stream and grassy banks.
Fed by longing,
My frustration was as endless as the Yangtze.

'It wasn't until the following spring, in the third month,
That I first heard from you.

I opened your letter hurriedly and read
The enclosed poem.
From it
I learned of your success.
My family and I were delighted;
They called me 'Lady';
And I thought my wish had been fulfilled.

Chuan

'But after that,
No more news came.
So in late autumn,
I despatched a servant
To deliver a letter and some clothes to you.
As emblems of my feelings,
I sent a jade hairpin, a mottled-bamboo brush, and a zither.
Again and again I told the messenger
To urge you to return without delay.

'Unexpectedly, the lout Cheng Heng
Arrived from Ch'ang-an before you.
He volunteered
A curious tale.
He said that in the capital,
Secretary Wei
Recently married his daughter to a dashing scholar,
Aged twenty-six or twenty-seven,
Who was placed third
In the Palace Examination.

Ch'u-shen Song

'A native of Lo-yang,
This scholar had spent some time in P'u-chou.
Currently he edits the Dynastic History. . . .
So, the lout asked, can he by any chance be
        the 'Genius of Lo-yang', Mr Chang Kung?
Mother has always been credulous.
She didn't even bother to verify the rumour.

'Instead, she decided that I should marry my first cousin;
An auspicious hour was chosen for the wedding.

Then you returned.
I saw that
You were still a bachelor.
My heart was pierced by knives.
Ah, why live on
When I'll merely be sneered at by others?'

[Prose insert]

Ying-ying removed her belt and threw it across a beam.

Culu

'My love for you has brought me enough sorrow!
I don't want to suffer any more.
Surely, killing myself now
Is better than dying from unhappiness later.'

[Prose]

Chang said: 'Since we cannot live together, let us die together.

(*Huang-chung-kung* mode)

The Golden Oriole

'Damn it,
Oh, damn it,
Why live on
And be a laughing stock?'
Chang threw his black silk belt across the beam as well.
The two lovers tied nooses around their necks.

Hung-niang, alarmed, seized them.
'Stop this foolishness!
It's fine for you to die.
But what'll happen to your friend, this shaven-headed prick?'

[Prose]

Hung-niang clasped Ying-ying in her arms. Checking Chang, Fa-ts'ung said to him: 'Sir, you are indeed addled. You can easily marry another, why commit suicide?'

'I only want Ying-ying. Now that she is to marry Cheng Heng, life is no longer worth living.'

222

'I have a plan which can make Ying-ying your wife.'

'What is it?'

Fa-ts'ung said: 'I myself cannot help you, but if you visit an old friend of yours, he will put things right.'

(*Pan-she-tiao* mode)

A Whistle Song, ch'an-ling

> Chang tried to hang himself;
> Ying-ying wanted to die;
> Fa-ts'ung saved them just in time.
> 'Your death will land me in court;
> Have you considered that?
> How disgraceful,
> Both of you
> So childishly thoughtless!
> Your foolishness is ludicrous.
> When a person dies, he disappears from the earth
> Like easterly flowing waters.
> No more can he enjoy fame, glory, wealth, and high position.
> His soul drifts in Hades,
>   his body is buried in a deserted mound.
> Once separated,
> The soul can never rejoin the body,
> Not even in ten thousand *kalpa*.[160]

> 'If you don't want to lose each other,
> It's best to seek help from a close friend.
> Without litigation,
> He can give you a hundred years of conjugal happiness.
> Hurry and prepare
> Your carriage, your horses,
> Luggage for you and your servants.
> You must leave instantly.
> No need to go far
> To find this friend —
> He resides in P'u-chou.
> He was a scholar like you and
> Passed the examination in his prime.
> After a few years of distinguished service,
> He's been made a noble lord.

[160] Buddhist term. The duration of the world, from its inception to its final disintegration, is a *kalpa*.

'While he served as a magistrate,
Prisons in the prefecture had no criminals.
Later, he was sent to a frontier pass.
There he exterminated every outlaw and marauder.
As commanding general in battles,
He's always the first to mount his four-horse chariot
  and challenge the enemy to a fight.
Of ten rounds of combat, he usually wins eight or nine.
Stalwarts of the entire world
Tremble before his reputation.
This servant of the throne
Deserves the last coin of his fief.
A pillar of society, he keeps peace in the country.
An excellent scholar, a superb warrior,
History has never seen the likes of him.

A Fast Melody

'He doesn't indulge in whoring or drinking,
He doesn't indulge in archery or shooting,
Neither does he indulge in riding or coursing,
Nor in hunting or trapping.
Last year he beheaded a mutinous general,
For this the Emperor himself presented him with a sword
  which he now wears on his belt.

Coda

'He's none other than the commander of a million troops,
The world-famous
Governor Tu, who may impose capital punishment
  without consulting the Court.'

[Prose]

Chang asked: 'Who is Governor Tu?'
 Fa-ts'ung explained further.

(*Kao-p'ing-tiao* mode)

Epithalamium

'Please tell me
Who this

224

Governor Tu is.
You say he's a close friend of mine?'
Fa-ts'ung said:
'You shouldn't have to ask *me* who he is!
Ah, "People in high positions are forgetful!"
Don't you remember what happened
        when the rebels were at our gate?

'The Governor
Is not
Your relative.
Just an intimate friend.
Madam Ts'ui and
All of us
Are indebted to him.
Who's Governor Tu?
He is last year's White-Horse General!'

[Prose]

'Why was General Tu suddenly made a Governor?' Chang asked.
    'For having subdued the rebellious soldiers and restored peace to P'u-chou.
The Emperor was informed of his service, so a few months ago His Majesty
made General Tu Pacification Commissioner of the Western Region, Gover-
nor of P'u-chou, and Director of Arsenals and Stables of Kuan-yu.'
    Delighted by the news, Chang thanked Fa-ts'ung: 'Without your explana-
tion I would still be in the dark.'
    Chang and Ying-ying hastened to P'u-chou in the middle of the night, at
about the second watch.[161]

(*Ta-shih-tiao* mode)

Song of the Goddess in the Cave

        Collecting together their luggage,
        They set forth on their journey.
        Gradually their frowns relaxed.
        A pale moon, a few stars

---

[161] A minor inconsistency. Earlier when talking to Chang, Fa-ts'ung says: 'The third
watch has just sounded' (p. 219).

Glimmered in the autumn sky.
Soon the eastern horizon brightened.
From the city wall came faint rolls of morning drums.

They passed through the city gate
And went straight to the Governor's yamen.
No time to write out a visiting card,
Chang had the gatekeeper announce him.
The Governor came out.
Before ascertaining the purpose of the visit,
He congratulated Chang on his success in the Examination.
Chang, on his part, asked the Governor
How he'd been since they saw each other last.

[Prose]

The Governor ushered Chang to a side hall. Chang said: 'My wife waits
outside to be presented to you and to our sister-in-law.'

The Governor asked Madam Tu to invite Ying-ying to come in. After
Ying-ying had paid her respects, Madam Tu took her to the ladies' apart-
ments in the rear. Chang and Governor Tu talked over wine. Truly,

One dreams of green hills known in childhood;
One delights in friendship renewed in old age.

(*Yüeh-tiao* mode)

The Emperor Pacifying the West

General Tu,
Chang Chün-jui
Each took the proper seat and
Exchanged news of themselves.
They hadn't seen each other for over a year.
This reunion gave them great pleasure.
Happily they chatted, with
Wide smiles on their faces.

They had always admired each other,
They had always understood each other,
They were intimate friends
Of long standing.
Without further ado, they began to drink with gusto.
The debonair Governor
Filled Chang's gold cup to the brim and toasted him:

'Here's to the new Flower Seeker,
Who has mounted the cloud-reaching ladder.'

Fighting Quails

Chang leaned forward and
Moved to the edge of his seat.[162]
He drained the cup,
Bowed and said:
'Thank you, Brother,
For your kind felicitations.
My talents
Are meager and few.
My success is due entirely
To the merits accumulated by my parents
       through their good deeds.[163]

'It's a privilege and a joy
To see you, my brother.
But please
Forgive me, General,
I've actually come
With a request as well.
As you recall, early last year,[164]
I set out from the eastern capital, Lo-yang,
To travel about and learn from men of discernment.
During my peregrinations, I came to this area.

Returning from Flower-Viewing

'I decided to review my studies
In the Temple of Universal Salvation.
While I was there, unfortunately,
The Marshal of P'u-chou, General Hun, died.
Troops mutinied
And rioted.
First they terrorized the countryside,
Killing innocent people.
Then, mounted on fierce chargers, they crowded into P'u city.

---

[162] A gesture of deference and respect.
[163] A Buddhist concept: one's descendants benefit from one's charitable deeds such as giving alms to mendicant monks, helping to build temples, and providing relief during a famine.
[164] The timing here is correct even though in the reader's mind the time span seems longer.

'Ghosts and spirits wept as inhabitants were massacred.
Wailing and mourning shook the earth.
When the rebels came to Universal Salvation,
The monks were helpless;
They could only close
The temple gate.
The lawless horde used their swords
And hacked at it so ferociously,
That even an iron gate would have been pulverized.

Green Mountain Pass

'The monks hadn't even time to flee.
You see, the rebels came because
        the former Prime Minister's daughter,
Ts'ui Ying-ying by name, lived in the temple.
She was unmarried then.
The bandits clamored for her at the gate:
"Give us Ying-ying and we'll depart!"
Hearing their demand, Madam Ts'ui
Burst out in tears.
At her wits' end
She came to me
For help.
I made Fa-ts'ung
Deliver a letter to you.
Your arrival
Thoroughly petrified Flying Tiger.
His followers laid down their arms and banners.
Your awesome mien alone was sufficient to
Disperse the motley band
And save our lives.

Lake Po Song

'To show her gratitude, Madam Ts'ui
Betrothed Ying-ying to me.
Presently, our gracious Emperor decreed a Civil Examination.
I went to the capital
And was fortunate to seize a cassia branch in the moon.
But after that I was plagued by a serious illness
Which medicine failed to cure.
I was sick for almost a year.

'Unknown to me, Minister Cheng's son,
Ying-ying's cousin,
Willfully ignoring their close kinship,
Attempted with threats to coerce a marriage
    between Ying-ying and himself.

'Intimidated, Madam Ts'ui
Set a wedding date in great haste.
If I hadn't returned in the nick of time,
Ying-ying would've married the brute.

Coda

'Just because he's the son of a powerful minister,
He thinks he can marry his *first cousin*!
He thinks he can force an unnatural union!
I beg you to help me,
My generous friend.
Sort out what's right and what's wrong.
Give me counsel.
If I have your protection,
    the bumptious braggart won't dare to bully me.'

[Prose]

The Governor said: 'Set your mind at ease, my brother. If Cheng Heng
wrangles with you over Ying-ying, I will certainly execute him.'
    After they had chatted a while longer, the Governor excused himself.

(*Ta-shih-tiao* mode)

Music for Returning to the Capital

The middle gate in the yamen opens
To reveal a silent courtyard undisturbed even by cawing rooks.
A flourish of drums,
The Governor takes his seat on the dais.
Soldiers and officials line the steps
In quiet, orderly ranks.
On the table are a mere handful of documents —
People seldom
File suits

When governed with fairness by an honest magistrate.
In the prison, the warders are gentle as lambs,
They know they're answerable to the Governor in everything they do.
True, there are cells and pits;
True, there are pillories and stocks;
True also that there are iron-bound elm-wood canques;
But for almost a year, there's been no occasion
To use them.
Before the prison gate, grass grows lustily,
Untrampled by human feet.

All forms of punishment —
Suspending, flogging, rope-torturing,
Exile, strangulation, and execution —
Have become superfluous.
Clubs and whips are put away: the Governor rules with compassion.
For a thousand miles around,
Law and order prevail.
Even his underlings are not inclined to
Abuse their power or manipulate the statutes.
He's firm but not harsh,
Benevolent yet never cowardly.
The people call him 'Buddha'.
Within his territory, brigands are extinct;
Those who didn't flee were captured by him alive.
His uprightness defies both open investigation
        and covert surveillance.
In fidelity, he matches Chi Cha of Spring and Autumn.[165]
In statecraft, he's the peer of Huang Pa of Ying-ch'uan.[166]
Residents of P'u-chou —
Some six hundred thousand families —
Revere him like a father.

---

[165] Chi Cha 季札 , son of King Shou-meng of Wu 吳王壽夢 (Sixth century B.C.), in whom the virtue of keeping one's promise was thought to have reached its acme. *Shih chi* (*Wu t'ai-po shih-chia* 吳太伯世家) records that Chi Cha is sent to the state of Lu as an emissary. En route, he visits the Prince of Hsü, who admires his sword. Since the sword forms part of his ambassadorial outfit, Chi Cha cannot present it to the Prince. Returning from his mission, Chi Cha once more passes the state of Hsü, only to find that the Prince has died in the meantime. He nevertheless leaves the sword on the Prince's tomb. When questioned by his entourage, he says: 'At our last meeting, in my heart I promised the Prince the sword. Why should I let his death interfere with the fulfillment of my promise?'

[166] Huang Pa 黃霸 , prefect of Ying-ch'uan 穎川 during Han Hsüan-ti's reign. (78–49 B.C.). *Han shu* (*Hsün-li chuan* 循吏傳) characterizes his administration as 'the best in the world' (*Chih wei tien-hsia ti-i*).

Coda

A gold pendant, emblazoned with a tiger,[167] dangles from his waist.
So much awe does he inspire that
Disobedient sons, treasonous ministers tremble before his shadow.

[Prose]

A more scrupulous magistrate than Yang Chen[168] of ancient times.
A more outspoken censor than Pi Kan[169] of yesteryear.
Immediately after the Governor assumes his seat, Cheng Heng rides up,
whipping his horse all the while to a frenzied gallop. Before dismounting, he
knocks without ceremony at the yamen gate.

(*Chung-lü-tiao* mode)

The Ancient Border Town, Lun-t'ai

The Minister's son
Is beside himself with rage.
Pushing aside the guards,
He swaggers
Straight up the audience hall.
Without saluting the White-Horse General,
In a raucous voice,
Accompanied by uncouth, offensive gestures,
He screams out his complaint:
'My uncle, the late Prime Minister,
Promised me Ying-ying
While he was alive.
Our marriage was postponed,
Because of his death.
Recently the mourning was completed,
And I came to wed my betrothed.

'As a bridal gift,
I brought masses of top-grade gold and silver.

---

[167] An emblem of rank given to high-echelon generals.

[168] 楊震 second century A.D., a Han prefect of Tung-lai 東萊 , whose scruples were
much celebrated. According to his biography in *Hou Han shu*, someone once offered him a
bribe at night, saying that no one would know. Yang refused it and retorted: 'Heaven
knows, God knows, both you and I know; what do you mean that no one will know?'

[169] Uncle and Minister of Emperor Chou 紂 of Yin (eleventh century B.C.). Outraged
by Chou's immorality, Pi Kan 比干 censors him in a memorial and refuses to leave the
palace until reform is promised. At the end of the third day, Chou says to him: 'I hear
that sages have seven apertures in their heart.' He has Pi Kan's heart taken out for
inspection. Cf. *Shih chi, Yin pen chi* 殷本記 .

I spent a hundred thousand strings of cash
On brand-new jewelry.
I made her scores of dresses,
Plus embroidered capes and long skirts.
Even the nuptial feast was being prepared:
Delicacies from land and sea,
          dishes upon dishes,
Have been cooked.
And the wedding was to take place today!
Then last night,
Around the fourth watch,
In utmost secrecy,
Ying-ying eloped.
As you can imagine, I'm outraged.
I suspect
It was Chang Kung who engineered this cruel blow to me.

Coda

'How could Ying-ying do this to herself?
Deserting a husband like *me*
To follow someone else!
The poor child has no eyes!'

[Prose]

The Governor says: 'You dare to deceive me? If you are so impudent while
dealing with a magistrate in a court, what will you not do in private?'

(*Shuang-tiao* mode)

Wen-ju-chin

The General,
Infuriated by Cheng Heng's words,
Says scornfully: 'You wretched lout, you deserved to be flogged.
How dare you deceive me with lies?
Now let *me* tell *you* the truth. Some time ago,
Flying Tiger Sun,
Finding himself without a commander,
Ravaged the countryside in search of beautiful women.
He almost kidnapped Ying-ying
From the Temple of Universal Salvation.
The catastrophe was averted

Only because Chang Chün-jui
Wrote me for help.
If you don't believe this,
You can ask the monks in the temple
Or the soldiers in my command.

'To repay Chang's kindness,
  Madam Ts'ui betrothed Ying-ying to him.
Then you tried to sabotage the marriage
By maligning him with fabricated tales.
I know it all, for this morning he has already come
To tell me what had happened,
And to ask me to help him
Marry Ying-ying.
You have influence, he hasn't,
So you think you can take advantage of him.
Just now you even tried to deceive the court
With the most brazen gall.
Look here,
There are laws
Prohibiting unsuitable marriages.
Don't you flout them!
You know it's improper
For first cousins to wed.

Coda

  'Behaving like an abominable ruffian,
    you schemed for another's wife.
It's only out of courtesy to your father at Court
That I'm not having you thrashed
    and sent home with a written censure!'

[Prose]

Cheng Heng admits to the Governor and his entourage that he has acted amiss and that Chang is in the right. He adds: 'I have been wrong; now I am ashamed to face my relatives and friends.'

(*Ta-shih-tiao* mode)

Kun Section of [*the Elaborate Melody*] *I-chou*

  Shamed, mortified, and disappointed as well,
  Cheng Heng feels a knife stabbing him.

'I've acted like a fool,
And my beautiful fiancée
Is to marry someone else.
How can I face
My neighbors, my relatives, and friends
At home?
To be sure, I'm willing to marry another,
But after what I've done, who'd want to marry me?'

Outside the yamen gate, a crowd has gathered to gossip.
They chatter; they sneer.
Mocking and whistling,
They wait
To taunt the Minister's son.
Terrified, Cheng Heng thinks to himself:
'I'll expose myself to humiliation and cruel derision
If I go out.
It's far better
To die in the yamen.'

Coda

Lifting his robe, he jumps down the ten-foot steps.
No one bothers to restrain him.
His head hits the ground; his body makes a loud thump.

[Prose]

In antiquity, a chaste laundress
Weighted herself with stones and drowned.[170]
Today, a lecherous bumpkin
Hurls himself to the ground and dies.
The Governor has Cheng Heng's body dragged away. He withdraws from the
audience hall and orders a banquet.

(*Nan-lü-kung* mode)

Moon above the Jasper Terrace

From time of old,

---

[170] Allusion to the *Wu Yüeh ch'un-ch'iu* (*Kung-tzu kuang chuan* 公 子 光 傳) and *pien-wen* story in which a laundress, after giving food to the fugitive Wu Tzu-hsü 伍 子 胥 (sixth century B.C.), drowns herself. In *pien-wen*, the reason for her suicide is to assure Wu that no one will learn of his whereabouts from her. In *Wu Yüeh*, it is her shame for having had dealings with a male stranger.

The suitable match for a ravishing beauty
Has always been a talented scholar.
Ying-ying is now a Lady,
Her husband being an Academician.
The one, a peerless writer;
The other, an unrivaled charmer.
They're a 'felicity-belt' with entwining strands,
       a *lien-li* tree with interlacing branches.
Thenceforth they'll delight in
       inscribing each other's fans and
       responding to one another's poems.
At long last,
The wishes of Wen-chün and
Hsiang-ju are fulfilled.

General Tu, holding up a goblet brimming with wine,
Urges: 'Let's all get thoroughly drunk today! . . .
       no, I won't let you beg off. . . .'
Chang and Ying-ying are deliriously happy;
Whereas Cheng Heng, the clumsy boor, is dead as a post.
His jaws are tightly locked, his throat stopped up,
His skull is split open,
       and his blood has dirtied the base of the steps.
The corpse is exhibited outside the rear gate
With the sign
Saying:
'A lascivious philanderer
Who died a violent death.'

Coda

Many a rake has been ruined by obsessive love,
But seldom has one, still in his prime,
Killed himself for a beautiful flower.

[Prose]

Chang and Ying-ying, happily reunited, go to the capital.
Cheng Heng, smitten with shame, has jumped from the steps.
First, a scholar shows his kindness.
Then, a beauty expresses her gratitude.
How do I know this romance to be true? Here is the poem inscribed by Liu

Jui[171] of P'eng-lai.

The enchanting romance of P'u-tung is extremely rare.
Its heroine's portrait will leave mirrors unpolished.[172]
Yüan Chen would agree, if he could hear these new tunes,
That the *Ballad's* rivals are just as elegant, just as finished.

[171] Identity unknown, presumably a friend of Master Tung. This eulogy of *THH* appears to have been written after Liu has read the manuscript but before the work is printed, hence the future tense in the second line of the poem (.. ...). The practice of having a friend inscribe praises on one's manuscript and incorporating them as part of the work is akin to a familiar device in T'ang *ch'uan ch'i* stories by which friends of the hero often make comments on the events in the form of a poem and the like. These poems are then either made part of the story or are alluded to (Cf. specifically the quotation of Yüan Chen's *Huei-chen chi,* Yang Chü-yüan's *Ts'ui-niang shih,* and the reference to Li Shen's *Ying-ying ko* in *Ying-ying chuan.*)

The manifest lack of modesty in terminating one's work with a friend's eulogy is, of course, in keeping with the good-humored pride Master Tung takes in his *chantefable* (see Introductory Suites, pp. 2, 4, and 6). Such a show of pride could have been a convention often adopted by *Chu-kung-tiao* writers. It is present in the Introductory Suites of Wang Po-ch'eng's *T'ien-pao i-shih chu-kung-tiao* as well. (See *'T'ien-pao i-shih chu-kung-tiao chi-i'.* 天寶遺事諸宮調輯逸 , ed. Chao Ching-shen 趙景深 , in *Hsüeh-shu* 學術 *Monthly.* no. 3, April 1940, pp. 125–6.)

[172] Ying-ying's beauty will make ladies ashamed to look at themselves in a well-polished mirror. The original line actually says: 'The plates with engravings will leave mirrors unpolished.' Although I like the juxtaposition of a gleamingly new printer's plate and a dull mirror, I cannot find a translation which is both faithful and easily comprehensible.

Bibliography

I. Works used for the translation

Ling Ching-yen 凌景埏 ed. *Tung Chieh-yüan Hsi-hsiang chi* 董解元西廂記, Peking, 1962.
Yeh Ch'ing-ping 葉慶炳 . *Chu-kung-tiao ting-lü* 諸宮調訂律 , unpublished Master's thesis (supervisor: Professor Cheng Ch'ien 鄭騫), National Taiwan University, Taipei, 1961.

II. A partial list of works cited in the Introduction and Notes

Anonymous. *Liu Chih-yüan chu-kung-tiao* 劉知遠諸宮調 , Peking, 1958.
Chao Ching-shen 趙景深 .'*T'ien-pao i-shih chu-kung-tiao chi-i*'天寶遺事諸宮調輯佚 , *Hsüeh-shu Monthly* 學術月刊, no. 3, April 1940.
Ch'en Li-li 陳荔荔 . 'Outer and Inner Forms of *Chu-kung-tiao*, with Reference to *Pien-wen, Tz'u*, and Vernacular Fiction', *Harvard Journal of Asiatic Studies*, 1972.
  '*Pien-wen Chantefable* and *Aucassin et Nicolette*', *Comparative Literature*, vol. 23, no. 3, 1971.
  'Some Background Information on the Development of *Chu-kung-tiao*', *Harvard Journal of Asiatic Studies*, 1973.
  'The Relationship between Oral Presentation and the Literary Devices Used in *Liu Chih-yüan* and *Hsi-hsiang Chu-kung-tiao*', *Literature East and West*, vol. 14, no. 4, 1970.
Ch'ien Nan-yang 錢南揚 . *Sung Yüan nan-hsi pai-i lu* 宋元南戲百一錄, Peking, 1934.
Chou Mi 周密 . *Wu-lin chiu shih* 武林舊事 , in *Tung-ching meng-hua lu wai ssu chung,* Shanghai, 1958.
Chung Ssu-ch'eng 鍾嗣成 . *Lu kuei pu* 錄鬼簿 . Shanghai, 1957.
Doleželova-Velingerová, M. and J. I. Crump. *Ballad of the Hidden Dragon,* Oxford, 1971.
Hanan, Patrick. 'The Early Chinese Short Story: A Critical Theory in Outline', *Harvard Journal of Asiatic Studies,* 1967.
Hightower, J. R. 'Yüan Chen and "The Story of Ying-ying" ', *Harvard Journal of Asiatic Studies,* 1973.
Hsiao Chi-tsung 蕭繼宗 . *Meng Hao-jan shih shuo* 孟浩然詩說 , T'ai-chung, 1961.
Li Ch'ing-chao 李清照 . *Li Ch'ing-chao chi* 李清照集 , Shanghai, 1962.
Li Fang 李昉 et al, ed. *T'ai-p'ing kuang-chi* 太平廣記 , Peking, 1959.

237

Li Shen 李紳. *Ying-ying ko* 鶯鶯歌. In *Ch'üan T'ang shih* 全唐詩, Shanghai, 1887.

Liu I-ch'ing 劉義慶. *Shih-shuo hsin-yü* 世說新語, Shanghai, 1935.

Lu Hsün 魯迅 ed. *T'ang Sung ch'uan-ch'i chi.* 唐宋傳奇集, Peking, 1958.

Lo Yeh 羅燁. *Tsui-weng t'an-lu* 醉翁談錄, Shanghai. 1957.

Meng Chi 孟棨. *Pen-shih shih* 本事詩, Shanghai, 1957.

Meng Yüan-lao 孟元老. *Tung-ching meng-hua lu* 東京夢華錄. In *Tung-ching meng-hua lu wai ssu chung* 東京夢華錄外四種, Shanghai, 1958.

Po Chü-i 白居易. *Po Hsiang-shan chi* 白香山集, Shanghai, 1936.

Su Shih 蘇軾. *Su Tung-po chi* 蘇東坡集, Shanghai, 1933.

T'ao Tsung-i 陶宗儀. *Ch'o-keng lu* 輟耕錄, Shanghai, 1936.

Yüan Chen 元稹. *Ying-ying Chuan* 鶯鶯傳 in *T'ang Sung Ch'uan-ch'i chi* 唐宋傳奇集, Peking, 1958.

An Index of Recurrent Geographic, Historical, and Mythological Names